Memory and Material Culture

We take for granted the survival into the present of artefacts from the past. Indeed, the discipline of archaeology would be impossible without the survival of such artefacts. What is the implication of the durability or ephemerality of past material culture for the reproduction of societies in the past? In this book, Andrew Jones argues that the material world offers a vital framework for the formation of collective memory. He uses the topic of memory to critique the treatment of artefacts as symbols by interpretative archaeologists and artefacts as units of information (or memes) by behavioral archaeologists, instead arguing for a treatment of artefacts as forms of mnemonic trace that have an impact on the senses. Using detailed case studies from prehistoric Europe, he further argues that archaeologists can study the relationship between mnemonic traces in the form of networks of reference in artefactual and architectural forms.

Andrew Jones is a lecturer in archaeology at the University of Southampton. He is the author of *Archaeological Theory and Scientific Practice* and editor of *Coloring the Past*.

TOPICS IN CONTEMPORARY ARCHAEOLOGY

Series Editor
RICHARD BRADLEY *University of Reading*

This series is addressed to students, professional archaeologists, and academics in related disciplines in the social sciences. Concerned with questions of interpretation rather than the exhaustive documentation of archaeological data, the studies in the series take several different forms: a review of the literature in an important field, an outline of a new area of research, or an extended case study. The series is not aligned with any particular school of archaeology. Although there is no set format for the books, all the books in the series are broadly based, well written, and up to date.

Memory and Material Culture

ANDREW JONES

University of Southampton

CAMBRIDGE
UNIVERSITY PRESS

CAMBRIDGE UNIVERSITY PRESS
Cambridge, New York, Melbourne, Madrid, Cape Town, Singapore, São Paulo, Delhi

Cambridge University Press
32 Avenue of the Americas, New York, NY 10013-2473, USA

www.cambridge.org
Information on this title: www.cambridge.org/9780521837088

First published 2007

Printed in the United States of America

A catalog record for this publication is available from the British Library.

Library of Congress Cataloging in Publication Data

Jones, Andrew, 1967–
Memory and material culture: tracing the past in prehistoric Europe / Andrew Jones.
    p.   cm. – (Topics in contemporary archaeology)
Includes bibliographical references and index.
ISBN 978-0-521-83708-8 (hardback) –
ISBN 978-0-521-54551-8 (pbk.)
1. Prehistoric peoples – Europe.   2. Material culture – Europe.   3. Antiquities, Prehistoric –
Europe.   4. Europe – Antiquities.   I. Title.   II. Series.
GN803.J66   2007
936 – dc22   2007006469

ISBN   978-0-521-83708-8 hardback
ISBN   978-0-521-54551-8 paperback

To Hannah and Steph

Contents

Preface

Coincidentally while writing this book I suffered a stroke that affected my memory. Fortunately, it mainly affected my bodily memory, my ability to walk, rather than my cognitive memory. I have therefore had first-hand experience of one of the very subjects I was writing about. It took around three months to recover from the physical effects of this experience, most of which time was spent lying in bed reading detective novels and watching film noir classics. I regard this time spent reading and watching films as probably the most important period of research. This is because it gave me time to think and reflect on the then partially written manuscript. We live in an age of speed. The current value system that most British academics labour under subscribes to a belief in targets and accountability. Coupled with this, academic institutions are overburdened with the British disease of overwork, bureaucracy, and the audit culture (for a useful insight on this, see Madeline Bunting's excellent book *Willing Slaves*, Harper Perennial, 2005). There are times at which we seem to drown under evaluation forms. Research time has become a little like the proverbial candle burnt at both ends and is squeezed into the last remaining moments of the working week (evenings and weekends). As such, research is conducted with no time for pause and reflection.

I regard my illness as a physiological response to the psychological stresses of this value system. As such I have come to believe that we need more time to allow ideas to develop and less for research-for-the-sake-of-fulfilling-targets. I have become a keen advocate of the Slow Movement, which takes time to savour life rather than treating it as a perpetual contest or race to the next staging post. For this reason I am very grateful to the Arts and Humanities Research Council, who partially funded my sabbatical time, which allowed me time for this reflection.

The finished book is therefore a result of this period of reflection, and the book comprises a distillation and reworking of some of the themes and ideas on memory that I have been developing over the past five years or so. Chapters 1, 2, 3, and 4 are all new. Chapter 7 was previously published as 'Drawn from Memory: The Archaeology of Aesthetics and the Aesthetics of Archaeology in Earlier Bronze Age Britain and the Present' in *World Archaeology* 33 (2), pp 334–56, under the editorship of Chris Gosden. It has been reworked for publication here. A fragment of Chapter 8 was published as 'By Way of Illustration: Art, Memory and Materiality in the Irish Sea Region and Beyond', pp 202–13, in the volume edited by Vicki Cummings and Chris Fowler entitled *The Neolithic of the Irish Sea: Materiality and Traditions of Practice*, published by Oxbow Books. A fragment of Chapter 9 comes from the proceedings of a conference to honour the retirement of Professor Barbara Bender held in UCL, in March 2005, and published in the *Journal of Material Culture* 11 (1/2) under the editorship of Chris Tilley. Both of the relevant fragments from these chapters have been substantially reworked for publication here. Chapter 4 comprises a total revision of ideas related to material culture and personhood in the European Neolithic, an earlier version of which was published in the *Journal of Social Archaeology* 5 (2) as 'Lives in Fragments?: Personhood and the European Neolithic.'

A huge number of people contributed help and comments over the occasionally difficult period of writing this book. For helpful comments on the manuscript I thank Barbara Bender, Richard Bradley, and Joshua Pollard. I especially thank Katina Lillios and Alasdair Whittle for their services in correcting my wayward thinking. I am also grateful to Dan Hicks for many stimulating discussions about the subject from a different disciplinary perspective. Chapter 9 was written after hearing a characteristically mind-blowing seminar by Tim Ingold in Bristol on the 12 December 2005. This helped me reorganise my thoughts considerably. For general comments of support during the writing of this book I thank Barbara Bender, Richard Bradley, Thomas Dowson, Davina Freedman, Gavin MacGregor, Colin Richards, Mike Parker-Pearson, Fay Stevens, Aaron Watson, and Howard Williams.

The illustrations were carried out with characteristic professionalism by Aaron Watson. I am grateful to Knut Helskog for providing the illustrations of Norwegian and Russian rock art in Chapter 9. Finally, two people helped to keep me alive during the writing of this book. My wonderful partner, Hannah Sackett, and the best friend and colleague anyone could ask for, Stephanie Moser. This book is dedicated to both of them.

Memory and Material Culture?

Human memory is fragile and finite. We mentally store our experiences as memories. However, memories are easily forgotten, and the retrieval of memories, through the act of remembering, is inexact and faulty. Due to our finite ability to mentally store our memories, human societies have produced a series of devices for storing memory in extrabodily form. These have included notched bone implements, clay and stone tablets, carved stelae, and, at a later stage in history, maps, drawings, photographs, phonographs, and other recording technologies, and, finally, the computer. Each of these offers an increasing capacity for the storage of memory. Each new technology therefore acts as an ever more efficient prop for human memory.

A version of these views can be found in the discourse of a number of disciplines whose purpose it is to debate the development and structure of the human mind – from psychology and cognitive science to philosophy, anthropology, and archaeology. They also represent a kind of 'folk model' of memory, which is broadly representative of the experience of memory for the majority of people raised in Western society. The aim of this book is to question the validity of these views, especially as they pertain to the study of material culture. I argue that such views are predicated on a modernist assumption of the differentiation amongst mind, body, and world. In fact, to assume such a distinction throughout the course of human history is to overlay a series of modernist assumptions upon the distant past. In examining the relationship between memory and material culture, the aim is to propose a more complex and satisfying analysis of the relationship between human memory and material culture.

THE CONTENTS OF THIS BOOK

At this juncture it is useful to define the parameters of the discussion. Those who have opened this book expecting to read about the evolution of the ancient mind (e.g., Mithen 1996) or the cognitive composition of the ancient mind (e.g., Lewis-Williams 2002; Lewis-Williams and Pearce 2005) will be heartily disappointed. Although these approaches have their place, I am less concerned with the composition of the human mind and more concerned with the relationship between people and artefacts and how this relationship produces memory.

With an array of studies from disciplines such as anthropology, history, and sociology, the subject of memory has become a hot topic in academia. The subject is comparatively well served in archaeology, with a series of recent books devoted to the subject (Alcock 2002; Bradley 2002) and a number of edited volumes (Van Dyke and Alcock 2003; Williams 2003). Much of that work has focused on what has come to be known as the 'past in the past' (Bradley and Williams 1998). This is a fruitful strand of research; however, it presents a fairly narrow definition of memory in the past, being concerned mainly with the reinterpretation of ancient sites and monuments in the past over the long term. The subject of memory is vast, and not all aspects of the subject can be tackled in a book of this size. Some topics, such as the cultural biography of artefacts and the issue of monumentality, are comparatively well worn; many other authors have discussed these issues, and to do so again would require at least another volume (or two!). In this volume I touch on these issues only in a tangential manner (biography in Chapter 7; monuments in Chapter 8).

The subject of this book is closer to the set of concerns outlined by Rowlands (1993) in relation to the role of memory in cultural transmission. The intellectual thrust of this book is to explore the implications of Prown's (1996) point that artefacts are the only class of historic event that occurred in the past but survive into the present. As physical materials, artefacts provide an authentic link to the past and as such can be reexperienced. It is through this reexperiencing that the world of the past, the other, is brought into contact with the present. The contents of this book are a meditation on this point. Given the durability of material culture, what are the implications for our understanding of the role that artefacts play in cultural reproduction?

Given this perspective, it is my contention that an investigation of the subject of material culture and memory involves a reconsideration of a number of key archaeological issues. These include the categorisation of artefacts (Chapters 6 and 7), the archaeology of context and the definition of archaeological cultures (Chapters 5 and 6), the relationship between archaeological chronology and prehistoric social change (Chapter 4), and the definition of archaeological landscapes (Chapter 9). I also deal with the relationship amongst history, memory, and identity (Chapters 3 and 4), and the relationship amongst text, history, and prehistory (Chapters 8 and 9). This volume is less concerned, then, with the approach defined as the 'past in the past' but looks instead at how a consideration of practices of remembrance affects how we examine the reproduction and change of prehistoric artefacts.

The book is divided into two sections. In the first, I discuss the treatment of memory in a host of disciplines and look at ways in which memory can be studied archaeologically. The discussion shifts from the study of memory to the analysis of the practices of remembrance and then discusses how the person is framed by collective modes of remembrance. In Chapter 4, I expand upon this theme and discuss the concepts of indexicality and citation in relation to cultural practice, touched upon in earlier chapters. Chapter 5 discusses this issue by comparing practices of remembrance and personhood in the Neolithic of Scotland and continental Europe. Chapter 6 examines the way in which identities are formed through the manipulation of categories of material culture, whereas Chapter 7 discusses the interrelationships and chains of remembrance pertinent to artefacts in assemblages. Chapters 8 and 9 discuss the important role of inscription and remembrance; in Chapter 8 I discuss the way in which inscriptive practices (the production of megalithic art and the decoration of artefacts) reinforce the relationship between place and memory. In Chapter 9, I focus on rock art in two regions of Europe to argue that rock art plays an important role not only in creating place but also in creating cohesive relationships between different kinds of places in landscapes. In each archaeological case study I pursue the way in which indexical fields work in relation to artefacts, artefact assemblages, places, and landscapes.

I argue that while considerable attention has been paid to the relationship between objects and society, insufficient attention has been paid to the way in which material forms come into being and the extent to which things are interstitial to the process of social reproduction. The mediatory and constitutive force of objects on society is a central focus of my discussion. How people act on objects and how objects can be considered to affect social actions are paramount concerns. In order that we understand social reproduction, we need to know how it is that people engage with objects and how, and in what manner, objects are used to mediate for people. An analysis of the role of memory in these processes is therefore key to how we describe society and define what we traditionally term *culture*. I am interested in not only 'how societies remember' but also how things help societies remember.

The societies that I discuss are those of the fifth to the second millennium BC (spanning the Neolithic to the Bronze Age) in Europe. Many of my examples are specifically derived from the Scottish Neolithic and Bronze Age. I make no apologies for discussing this region of the British Isles as a case study because Scotland represents one of the richest, yet one of the least studied, regions of Britain (compared to the prevailing focus on a small region of southern England). I chose Scotland because of familiarity: most of my fieldwork to date has concentrated in this region. However, in what follows, the Scottish material is placed in context alongside materials found in other regions of Europe.

EXTERNAL SYMBOLIC STORAGE

One of the clearest and most provocative discussions of the relationship between material culture and memory comes from the work of Merlin Donald (1991, 1998). Donald takes an explicitly evolutionary approach to the cognitive development of the human mind. He proposes a series of evolutionary phases in the development of hominid (or hominin) cognitive abilities which include the episodic, mimetic, linguistic (or mythic), and theoretic. These phases are cumulative, and each is associated with new systems of memory representation. The final of these phases involves the development of systems of memory storage and retrieval that are external to the person. Earlier phases, such as the linguistic and mimetic phases, are concerned with the information storage capabilities of the human mind and principally pertain to the changing configuration or 'architecture' of the mind. The mimetic phase is related to mainly nonlinguistic representation, which often includes bodily modes of communication, whereas the linguistic or mythic phase is associated with linguistic representation.

For Donald (1991) the Linguistic or Mythic culture is characterised by early *Homo sapiens* and Theoretic culture utilising External Symbolic Storage typified by literacy, urbanization, and the rise of the state in seventh-century BC Greece. Renfrew (1998, 2) has rightly criticised Donald for the abrupt nature of these phases, which jump from the development of language in the Upper Palaeolithic to the earliest writing. To rectify this, he includes the development of symbolic material culture – itself a form of external symbolic storage – during the Neolithic and Bronze Age as an adjunct to Donald's scheme. Renfrew's critique is important because it emphasises the fact that most forms of material culture are mnemonic in character; however, I believe there are more pressing problems with Donald's scheme, which pertain to the core concept of 'external symbolic storage' itself.

On the face of it, the notion of external symbolic storage appears attractive because it seems to capture the sense in which artefacts act to promote human memory and in turn act back on the human subject. It also foregrounds the important point that artefacts act as an external means of knitting societies together. Ultimately, however, there are a series of problems with the notion of externality and with the idea of figuring memory as a form of storage (whether in artefactual form or in the mind). There are also problems with treating the mnemonic role of artefacts as purely symbolic in nature. I address each of these in turn.

■ PROBLEMS WITH THE NOTION OF EXTERNALITY AND STORAGE

Donald's scheme appears to consider the mind as a distinct entity set against the external world. Curiously, despite the discussion of biology in a number of his earlier phases (especially the episodic and mimetic phases and the transition to the linguistic phase) a consideration of the role of the hominid (hominin) body in relation to the mind is also absent from Donald's account. The treatment of the mind as an isolated entity has a series of consequences for our understanding both of memory and of the constitution of the person. Furthermore, it has critically important consequences for understanding our mnemonic relationship to material culture.

Donald's description of the relationship between mind and world relies upon a computational model of the human mind (Lakoff 1987; Thomas 1998, 150). According to such models of the mind, objects existing in the external world are represented to the mind as images. The external world is treated as objective; material things are viewed as ontologically unproblematic – they are simply components of the environment awaiting experience through being sensed by the thinking subject.

This model of the mind emerges with the theories of early modernist thinkers such as Descartes and Locke. Locke, for example, considered memory to be generated by the empirical experience of sense perceptions. Sensations imprint themselves upon the memory. It follows from this that thoughts or ideas are nothing more than actual perceptions in the mind, and the mind has a power to revive perceptions in memory with the additional perception that it had them before (Locke 1997[1690], 147–8). Locke reasoned that after sensation (or perception), the retention of ideas in memory is crucial because it is this that allows us to reflect upon ideas to attain knowledge. Memory is therefore seen as a form of channel, or gateway, which mediates between actual perceptions and the formation of ideas and knowledge. This empirical understanding of how memories are formed has enormous consequences for subsequent understandings of the phenomenon. For example, because memory is figured as an internal mental process, which retains or stores the impression of our perceptions, we tend to treat memory as a kind of object that itself retains the objects of perception. In this sense Locke (1997[1690], 147) refers to memory as the 'storehouse of ideas'.

The metaphor of the 'storehouse' persists in popular accounts of memory:

> I consider that a man's brain originally is like a little empty attic, and you have to stock it with such furniture as you choose. A fool takes in all the lumber of every sort that he comes across, so that the knowledge which might be useful to him gets crowded out, or at best is jumbled up with a lot of other things, so that he has a difficulty in laying hands on it. Now the skilful workman is very careful indeed as to what he takes into his brain-attic. He will have nothing but the tools which may help him in doing his work, but of these he has a large assortment, and all in the most perfect order. It is a mistake to think that that little room has elastic walls and can distend to any extent. Depend upon it there comes a time when for every addition of knowledge you forget something that you knew before. It is of the highest importance, therefore, not to have useless facts elbowing out the useful ones. (Conan Doyle 1981[1887], 19)

So Sherlock Holmes expounds his theory of memory to Dr. Watson upon their taking up rooms at Baker Street, in *A Study in Scarlet*. This idea of the mind as a lumber room or physical space in which thoughts are stored as physical entities has remarkable popular appeal. Precisely the same metaphor is employed by Umberto Eco (possibly conscious of its earlier use by Conan Doyle) in his recent novel *The Mysterious Flame of Queen Loana* (Eco 2005). Upon losing his memory, the protagonist, Yambo, plunders the attic of his family home for the reading matter (comics and books) which influenced his early development. The attic comes to stand for the space of his mind and the books his memories; as cupboards crammed with books overspill, his memories likewise come gushing forth. The metaphor of memory as a storage container both has popular appeal and is treated as a scientific verity (Johnson 1991).

The predominant metaphor of memory as a container in which a finite set of memories can be stored posits that our memories act as repositories of knowledge, as we saw with Holmes's exposition. According to this model, for us to remember, some knowledge must be removed (or forgotten) so that other knowledge can be retained (Johnson 1991). Metaphorically, the form that memory storage takes may vary: memory has variously been conceived as a library, as an encyclopaedia with memories stored on numbered or lettered pages, or as a map with constellations of sites placed around the landscape (Fentress and Wickham 1992; Yates 1966).

An important correlate of the notion of memory as container is the idea that representations are objective and that the authenticity and accuracy of knowledge depends upon the clarity of recall. Such a view of memory relates very closely to a conception of knowledge as a series of semantic categories: objective 'packets' of knowledge retained by the mind. As we shall see, there are problems with this view. As Fentress and Wickham (1992, 31) put it: 'memory entails a degree of interpretation. Our memories no more store little replicas of the outside world made out of mind stuff than do the backs of our televisions'.

The notion of memory as storage container and the emphasis upon authenticity and clarity of recall are two major legacies of early empirical descriptions of memory. Donald's formulation of the mind in relation to body and world would therefore seem to be reliant upon empiricist traditions of thought. It is curious that such a position is adopted, especially when we consider that other strands of contemporary cognitive science explicitly consider the relationship amongst the mind, body, and world. For instance, the analysis of processes of categorisation suggests that it is not helpful to treat the mind as a disembodied entity. Rather, the structure of our cognitive categories indicates that such categories are grounded on what Lakoff (1987, 348) describes as 'conceptual embodiment'. The fact that the body and mind operate as a unified system provides an insight into the formation of our most basic categories, as well as more complex metaphors (Lakoff and Johnson 1980). A clear example is the way in which bodily orientation influences the sense of linguistic metaphors. Because our bodies are upright, to feel 'up' has a positive connotation, whereas to feel 'down' is negative.

In a similar sense, the cognitive scientist Andy Clark (1997) describes a 'classical' view of the mind as one that views mind and world to be discrete entities in which the body serves simply as an input device (see also Lakoff 1987, 338–52). Cognition is centralised and memory is viewed as a simple process of retrieval from a stored symbolic database (Clark 1997, 83). The resemblance between these views and those discussed in the context of Donald and the Enlightenment thought of Locke is evident.

As an alternative, based upon practical experimentation in diverse fields such as computer science, cybernetics, and developmental psychology, Clark notes that we may consider the mind in quite a different light. Instead of treating mind, body, and world as distinct entities, he proposes that we treat them as fields of interaction. The mind is best understood as emergent in its interactions with the world. For example, he discusses how recent advances in robotics have dispensed with producing robots with centralised processing units and instead produce robots able to interact and problem solve within their given environments. Their 'minds' are problem-solving devices produced in and through these interactions. In a similar vein, drawing on studies in child development, he recounts how infants learn to interact with slopes of differing gradients. Depending upon whether they crawl or walk, the slope is negotiated in different ways. Indeed their negotiation of slopes is action specific. Although they may learn to successfully climb a slope as a crawler, this knowledge has to be relearned as a walker (Clark 1997, 36–7). Knowledge is therefore gained through embodied engagement with the world and is dependent upon contingent interactions amongst brain, body, and world. In this alternative view of the mind, cognition is seen as decentralised and distributed amongst brain, body, and world. In Clark's terms, the brain is 'leaky'.

According to this view, memory is treated as a process of pattern re-creation and the environment is considered to be an active resource which, when interacted with, plays an important role in problem solving (Clark 1997, 83–4). Clark's views have important things to say about the relationship between memory and material culture, which we will explore later.

Here it is important to underline the importance of pursuing memory beyond the confines of the brain and to consider its relationship with the body. The role of the body in the production of memory has been widely discussed. The major characteristic of body memory is that it is habitual (Bergson 1991[1908]). It is less consciously articulated than cognitive modes of remembering; nonetheless, it is critically important because it is the basis from which most of our everyday actions are formed. In effect, body memory consists of the memory of the past embodied in our bodily actions. Memory is effectively *sedimented* in the very movement of the body. If this statement seems exaggerated, it is worth speculating on the number of actions undertaken daily, from simple actions, such as brushing one's teeth, to complex actions such as driving cars, to taken-for-granted actions, such as walking, which require a prereflective understanding of how to perform them. Casey (1987, 151) notes that habitual body memory is efficacious and orienting. It is efficacious in that the actions carried out due to a person's bodily memory have an effect upon the world which the individual inhabits. More than this, bodily memory constitutes the ground for individuals to perceive themselves as discrete and continuous entities; it is the continual performance of habitual body memory that provides a sense of constancy. Body memory is orienting because this is one of the ways we gain a sense of our own bodies and their position in relation to the world about us.

It is important to note that this sense of habit is inculcated through cultural practices (Connerton 1989). It is the repetitive *incorporation* of bodily movements that forms habitual body memory, and these movements are culturally prescribed. Connerton (1989, 72–104) describes a whole series of learned behaviours which are concerned with disciplining the body of the child in some way, for example, table manners, the acquisition of 'good handwriting' and speech, deportment, and hand gesture. Bourdieu (1977), too, notes that bodily memory is critical to forming dispositions for cultural action, what he describes as *habitus.* That bodily movement is culturally prescribed is underlined by Mauss's observation that the most mundane of human movements and sequences of action are the domain of culture, from walking down the street to making love (Mauss 1979[1950]). In terms of material culture, it is critical to realise that these 'techniques of the body' not only encompass bodily dispositions and movement but also incorporate the correct usage of extrabodily instruments and objects. For example, the acquisition of 'good handwriting' intimately involves the correct usage of the pen with which to write.

■ MATERIAL CULTURE, MIND, AND SYMBOLISM

We have seen that there are problems with treating the mind as a disembodied entity disengaged from the body. If we are to understand the relationship between memory and material culture it is critical that the body is included in our accounts and that we assume a level of interaction between embodied individuals and the material world. If we return to the notion of external symbolic storage, a number of problems remain. In this formulation, material culture is treated as a repository or product of purely mental activity (Thomas 1998, 149). Ideas that emerge inside a person's mind are then transferred onto material objects (Fig. 1).

Things are therefore treated as initially mute materials, which are made meaningful only once they have received the impress of intentional human minds. In evolutionary terms this is curious because it implies that the material world begins to have meaning only once it

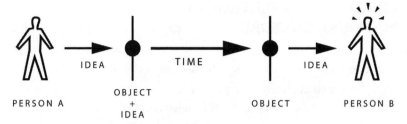

PERSON A — IDEA → OBJECT + IDEA — TIME → OBJECT — IDEA → PERSON B

1. The relationship between objects and people in 'information transfer' theories of remembrance, such as Donald's.

is employed as a means of external symbolic storage. The concept of symbolic storage also encapsulates the idea that the act of inscribing meaning into or onto an object fixes meaning. The meaning captured in this fashion is seen to act back upon the human mind to 'create specific states of knowledge intended by the creator of the external device' (Donald 1993, 747). However, as Thomas (1998, 153) points out, meaning is never fixed by the author; rather, symbols always demand interpretation. In fact, meaning is not simply read out of a signifier, it is read *into* it (Olsen 1990; Thomas 1998, 153.). The act of reading is both creative and situational. The reader is situated within specific cultural contexts; as such, an encultured individual reads on the basis of his or her own life experiences. On this basis, material culture cannot be seen as a storehouse or bank of past experience any more than the human mind can be (Rawson 1998, 107).

However, in this instance we also need to be alert to problems with the metaphor of reading. Although we need to be aware that ideas are not simply inserted into objects to be banked for the future, we also need to critically address the assumption that the material world can be treated as a system of signs to be read. In a sense, the assumption that artefacts might be treated as symbols is in danger of reenacting the distinctions amongst mind, body, and world by treating objects as being made up of two distinct components: a component composed of physical matter and a symbolic component that is 'read'.

▪ READING AND REREADING MATERIAL CULTURE

What do we imply when we say that we are 'reading' material culture? Here I want to critically assess prevailing notions of 'reading' in the study of material culture and ask in what sense the concept of reading is useful to the study of material culture. The idea that material culture might be amenable to the process of reading stems from the conceptualisation of the world of objects as a signification system (system of signs), analogous to language. The theoretical impulse for this treatment of material culture is the structural linguistics of Ferdinand de Saussure. According to de Saussure, a sign consists of two separate components, a signifier (the acoustic image of the spoken word as heard by the recipient of a message) and a signified (the meaning called forth in the mind of recipients resulting from the stimulation of the signifer). The sign is then composed of three elements: the signifier, the signified, and the unity of the two. The unity between signifier and signified is determined by culture. The assignment of the signifier, such as the word *chair* to some signi-fied object, depends upon what a particular community of users understands a chair to mean. The relationship between signifier and signified is not given but is culturally prescribed (Gottdiener 1994, 5–6). This linguistically derived approach to signs has had an enormous impact on the development of Western thought, from structural linguistics to structuralism and poststructuralism, and a similar approach to signs was adopted in archaeology and adapted to the study of material objects (Hodder 1982; Shanks and Tilley 1987; Tilley 1991). It is in this sense that we traditionally speak of 'reading' material culture; excavated artefacts are treated as signs (or vehicles for the expressions of abstract concepts).

The problem with this approach is that – because it is arbitrarily related – the signified (the object or artefact) need have little rela-tion to the signifier (its cultural meaning). If we are to view sign and signifier, idea and thing, to be conjoined only in an arbitrary fashion, the correlate of this is that the mind is again treated as disembodied. It is disengaged from a world of things it can only ever grasp mentally (Gosden 1994, 49). This poses considerable difficulties in archaeology when cultural meaning is the very element we wish to reconstruct. The problems with treating signifiers as adjuncts to the material properties of the artefacts were recognised from the outset. For Hodder (1986, 48) the object was to be viewed as both an object and a sign. This is because objects are always encompassed or framed by language, and the two cannot be separated (Olsen 1990). The arbitrary yet all-encompassing nature of language poses some problems for material culture analysts. Ideally, to archaeologists, the material character of artefacts ought to be of some aid in reconstructing their cultural meaning. Are we to retain a sense that the material character of objects is divorced from their cultural meaning and can be understood only through knowledge of cultural convention?

This poses problems if we want to understand how objects might act as aids to memory. If we conceptualise objects solely as sign-vehicles, we seem to return to Donald's view of objects as simple containers for ideas stored external to the human subject. It may be useful at this juncture to distinguish between a narrow definition of objects as carriers of information (e.g., Schiffer 1999; Shennan 2002) and a wider definition of objects as having the potential for evoking meaning either linguistically or nonlinguistically, in either a codified or a noncodified manner. For example, objects such as the knotted string figures (*Khipu* or *Quipu*) of the Andes (Saloman 2001; Vansina 1973, 37) or the shell-and-stick navigational charts of Micronesia (Gell 1985; Mack 2003) are evidently constructed to convey codified information; however, it seems unrealistic to suggest that all objects convey codified symbolic information. The reading of objects is not a trivial matter of information retrieval. Objects convey meaning in a multiplicity of ways.

The question of how objects convey memory turns on how we consider objects to communicate meaning. Although the act of reading may be more complex than Donald envisaged; as ciphers for the written word, for him objects essentially serve the same function. This again returns us to Lockean empiricism, because if we treat objects as external reservoirs of ideas, then perception and memory serve only as conduits for transferring ideas from the external world to the internal mind. None of these formulations strike me as being satisfactory, mainly because they relegate material culture to a passive role and do not take account of the materiality of objects or their mnemonic role in social practices.

There are other ways in which we might consider 'reading' material culture. To help us consider this let us briefly return to those famous rooms on Baker Street:

> But, tell me, Watson, what do you make of our visitor's stick? Since we have been so unfortunate as to miss him and have no notion of his errand, this accidental souvenir becomes of importance. Let me hear you reconstruct the man by an examination of it.

Needless to say, Watson's reconstruction is vague and erroneous, beyond saying said stick belongs to a country doctor because of the character of the implement and because it is a presentation item (it is inscribed). Moreover, the iron ferrules of the stick are worn, indicating a country doctor who – in the age before motorcars – had occasion to do a lot of walking. Holmes takes the stick and fills in the details:

> I am afraid, my dear Watson, that most of your conclusions were erroneous. When I said that you stimulated me I meant, to be frank, that in noting your fallacies I was occasionally guided towards the truth. Not that you are entirely wrong in this instance. The man is certainly a country practitioner. And he walks a good deal. . . .
>
> . . . . I would suggest for example, that a presentation to a doctor is more likely to come from a hospital than from a hunt, and that when the initials "CC" are placed before that hospital the words "Charing Cross" very naturally suggest themselves . . . I can only think of the obvious

conclusion that the man has practised in town before going to the country.

. . . . Now, you will observe that he could not have been on the staff of the hospital, since only a man well established in a London practice could hold such a position, and such a one would not drift into the country. What was he then? If he was in the hospital yet not on the staff, he could only have been a house-surgeon or a house-physician – little more than a senior student. And he left five years ago – the date is on the stick. So your grave family practitioner vanishes into thin air, my dear Watson, and there emerges a young fellow under thirty, amiable, un-ambitious, absent-minded, and the pos-sessor of a favourite dog, which I should describe as being larger than a terrier and smaller than a mastiff. . . . (Conan Doyle 1981[1902], 9–10)

Holmes later reveals the thinking behind his interpretation: only amiable people are given gifts upon retirement from a job and the person is unambitious because he moved from town to country and absent-minded because he had forgotten his stick! As for the dog, its size and character was estimated from the span of its teeth marks on the stick, a fact confirmed when Dr. James Mortimer returns for his stick followed by a curly-haired spaniel!

Here we encounter a different sense of the phrase 'reading mate-rial culture'. The discourse surrounding the stick which opens his most famous adventure (*The Hound of the Baskervilles*) was based on Holmes's celebrated method of observation. Here the material character of an object is minutely examined for traces of evidence of wider causes. This method of assessment involves quite a differ-ent semiotic procedure from the one traditionally employed when archaeologists talk about 'reading' material culture.

Curiously, around the same time that de Saussure was formu-lating his ideas on linguistics and Conan Doyle was penning his famous detective stories, on the other side of the Atlantic the Ameri-can scholar Charles Sanders Peirce was devising a theory of semiotics in parallel to that of Saussure. His approach to semiotics was far closer to Conan Doyle's than to Saussure's (Eco 1984). Unlike Saussure, Peirce conceived of the sign as a three-part relation: a vehicle that conveys an idea to the mind (which he called the representamen), another idea that interprets the sign (which he called the interpretant), and an object for which the sign stands (see Gottdiener 1994, 9). The crucial difference between the two approaches to semiotics is that Saussure was concerned with language as a mode of communication and he did not consider whether an objective world was essential to language. By contrast, Peirce was not an idealist; he believed that the real world existed because it was the attempt of the sciences to understand reality (as a scientist he worked for the U.S. Coast and Geodetic Survey for more than 30 years; Corrington 1993, 5) and his work sought to establish the necessary conditions for the success of truth claims.

Just as the function of signs was divided into three terms, so the sign itself could be envisaged as having three forms: index, icon, or symbol. The most basic of these is the *index*. The meaning of an index is not a product of social conventions or codes; instead, it is established as a sign through pragmatic understanding of the material world. The association between lightning and thunder is an index; when we see lightning we anticipate the sound of thunder, the meaning of this index is a storm. Holmes's reading of the doctor's stick at the beginning of *The Hound of the Baskervilles* is an example of the way material objects can be read as indexes, or indices, of past events. An *icon* is a sign that conveys an idea by virtue of its close reproduction or resemblance of an actual object or event. A good example of this would be traffic signs, which convey their meaning directly without the aid of language or social convention. They do this on the basis of physical resemblance – the shape of an aeroplane is used to signify an airport. A *symbol* is closer to what Saussure meant by a sign, it is a sign-vehicle that stands for something else which is understood as an idea in the mind of the interpretant; it is conventional and regulated by culture and is a sign by virtue of a law or rule.

The advantage of Peirce's approach is that it acknowledges the existence of the object world, thus avoiding the idealism of Saussure. Similarly his triadic, or threefold, classification of signs avoids simple dichotomies and allows for the analysis of all systems of signification, including natural signs and cultural signs. For these reasons I believe Peircean semiotics is especially appropriate for the analysis of material culture (see also Bauer and Preucel 2001; Gardin 1992; Gottdiener 1994) because it allows of the fact that – at a fundamental level – the significance of artefacts might be effected by their material properties. The basic tenets of Peirce's approach determine both lower-order and higher-order archaeological interpretations. Consider a fundamental or lower-order interpretation of material culture: if I were to analyse the profile of a sherd of pottery I would look for colour changes as an indication of the atmospheric environment of the fire or kiln. Such a procedure involves indexical analysis because the colour is treated as an index of the oxidising or reducing atmosphere in the fire/kiln. The atmosphere has a direct effect on the colour of the clay and leaves a trace to be read by the archaeologist. Higher-order interpretations also involve indexical analysis: for example, Bauer and Preucel (2001, 91) note that a jadeite axe deposited in a burial context in the Eurasian steppes indexes trade or interaction with Central Asia (the geographical origin of jadeite). Approaches to material culture which focus upon indexical analysis therefore permit a wide range of interpretations of past behaviour.

AN ARCHAEOLOGY OF TRACES

I argue that we can no longer simply treat objects purely as symbolic media; rather the materiality of objects is best seen as impinging on people sensually and physically at a fundamental level. What I develop herein is an understanding of the way objects can act as physical traces of past events which are amenable to the process of reading. It is this aspect of material culture which helps us consider how artefacts act as aids to remembrance.

The notion of objects as physical traces of memory originates with Freud's discussion of the 'Mystic Writing Pad'; the pad preserved an image of what was written on its surface and for Freud provided a technological metaphor for the workings of consciousness (Leslie 2003, 172–3). Drawing on Freud, Walter Benjamin also employs a series of technological metaphors – including cinematic film and photography – for the notion of the memory trace (Leslie 2003, 176–84). The concept of artefacts as forms of memory trace is pursued later. Jacques Derrida employs the concept of the trace to reconsider the significance of the philosophy of presence. For Derrida the notion of trace evokes the absence of full and present meaning; meaning is differential, a matter of constant referral onwards from term to term, each of which has meaning only from its necessary difference from other signifiers. Meaning is therefore constituted by a network of traces. We will pursue this line of thought further in Chapter 4; here I want to highlight the way in which artefacts embody traces of the past.

Alfred Gell (1998, 233–42) provides a useful basis for our discussion. Gell is concerned with the temporal position of artworks in networks of causal relations. He draws on Husserl's model of time-consciousness as a means of examining how objects are positioned in time. For Husserl, time moves forward as a series of temporal events, but each of these events encapsulates elements of past events (retentions) and embodies components of future events (protentions). Gell employs this concept to analyse the artistic *oeuvre* of both individuals and collective groups. Artworks are positioned in time as a series of 'events' embodied in material form by the artwork itself. By drawing on preexisting artworks the artist embodies, in the new artwork, elements of what has gone before. By materialising the artwork in physical form, the artist projects his or her intentions forward in time in the form of the artwork. What Gell is concerned to relate here is the extent to which artworks can be treated as indexes of human agency and how, as indexes, artworks subsequently affect human action. I will elaborate upon Gell's analysis at a number of points in subsequent chapters because it has much to say about the temporality of material culture. Gell is especially concerned to describe material objects as indexes of human agency and intentionality. The material attributes of the object index, refer to, or focus attention on, the intentions and skill of the artist. A link is established between the object and the artist; such a link is made possible due to the visually attractive and cognitively powerful nature of artworks. This example is especially pertinent because it provides a good example of the dual and interconnected role of objects and people. The ability of the artist is manifested through the artwork; whereas the material properties of the artwork provide the artist with the ability to act. Without producing artworks the artist cannot be truly thought to exist as an agent, as an artist. We will explore this aspect of materiality further in the next chapter.

What I particularly want to emphasise at this juncture is the point that artworks index events that happened in the past, the event of their production by an artist. This provides one example of the way in which material culture might be considered to index past actions; objects are physical *traces* of past action. Through their very reference to previous works, once they are produced, artworks physically embody memory. As Gell (1998, 233) puts it, without repetition art would 'lose its memory'.

It is not only through production that memory is embodied but also through use and alteration. The history of an object is read in its wear. The shell valuables circulated amongst the group of Melanesian islands known as the Kula Ring are good examples of this. The value of each shell is read from its patina as, over time, the shell passes through the hands of the many men involved in its exchange. The passage of time is reflected in the way the shell changes colour from white to pink or red (Munn 1986). The shell in effect indexes the events of past exchanges and is imbued with value because of this.

Buildings and monuments also index the past. Marshall (1998) describes the way in which the traditional Nuu-chah-nulth (Nootka) house, of the northwest coast of America, underwent curation, cycles of repair and refurbishment, based on the expansion of the residence unit. The history of the kin group was read in the history of the house, and its very fabric remembered these changes and alterations.

Monuments also embody cycles of past events as they are built of components of previous monuments and altered over the course of their use and their eventual abandonment. A classic example of this is the incorporation of decorated stones in the Neolithic passage graves of Brittany at sites such Le Petit Mont (Bradley 1998b; Lecornec 1994; Scarre 2002), La Table des Marchand, and Gavrinis (Bradley 2002; Le Roux 1984; Whittle 2000). The sequence of monument construction at these and other megalithic sites also encapsulates past events. The passage grave at Barnenez, North Finistère, provides an excellent example of this. The cairn is a long mound containing 11 passage graves. The history of the site is complex, with passage graves F to J the earliest component of the monument. These passages were lengthened and further passage graves added during later episodes of construction (Scarre 2002, 36–9). The whole was eventually encapsulated in an immense long mound. Memory is embodied in the material *traces* of cycles of architectural alteration and repair.

ARTEFACTS AS INDICES OF THE PAST

I use the term *memory* in relation to objects, buildings, and such as a way of re-addressing the relationship between people and objects in the activity we call remembering. If we take on board the point that people and objects are conjoined through practice and that causation (the seat of action) is distributed between people and objects (I will discuss this point in more detail in the next chapter), then both people *and* objects are engaged in the process of remembering. This is not to say that objects *experience, contain,* or *store* memory; it is simply that objects provide the ground for humans to experience memory. Let us consider this point and the wider problem of how we characterise memory by returning to Gell's discussion of the *oeuvre* of the artist.

Artworks provide a means of materialising the agency of the artist; artists are remembered by their works. However, if we can consider memory to be embodied in artworks then the subsequent reception or 'retrieval' of memory is not a simple matter of storage-access-retrieval in the sense described by Donald's notion of external symbolic storage. Rather the 'memory' of the agency of the artist embodied in artworks is a version of the artist transubstantiated in the form of paint, canvas, or whatever medium. The artwork is an index or sign of the artist's past agency. The reception of this sign is felt bodily and through the senses and is not simply an uncomplicated feedback loop of information storage and retrieval. But what is an index and how can thinking about indices help us consider the process of remembering with things?

I want to consider the term *index* and the related term *abduction* in a little more detail. I find the notion of the index especially useful in the context of discussions of memory because it captures a sense of the way in which material traces or natural phenomena are perceived as signs of past events. By focussing on causation, the directive force of events, it also implies a sense of conjunction. Smoke equals fire because it is a product of fire. Hoofprints refer to the horse because they resemble the shape of its hooves. When dealing with material culture, this seems more useful than an approach to signification which treats meaning as arbitrary to the signifier. However, while there is contiguity, the sign is not identical to that to which it refers, smoke is not physically the same as fire and hoofprints do not look like horses. To use an example referred to earlier, the patina on Kula shells refers to the passing of time and the touch of many hands; it does not represent time or hands directly.

How are such relationships inferred? To consider this question we need to introduce a further term: *abduction*, also derived from the philosophy of Peirce. Abduction is a form of inferential reasoning which links perception and experience with semiotics. Essentially, abduction is a process which involves inference from a given case to a hypothesised general rule (Peirce in Corrington 1993, 60); this is the form of reasoning Holmes conducted when reading James Mortimer's stick (see Eco 1984).

Abduction as a reasoning process relies on the unconscious perceptual judgement that comes with the habitual experience of the world. Abductive inferences are often made from indexical signs. For example, whilst out taking a walk we may understand that a paw-print in soft sand refers to the passage of a dog in the recent past. The print is therefore an index of the dog, and if we were to see the print we would abductively infer at an unconscious level that a dog had been in the vicinity. Such an inference would be confirmed were we to see a dog on our walk. Without the actual physical presence of the dog we cannot be absolutely certain that dog and print are linked, but in common experience the two are associated. The process of abduction describes the unconscious level at which we make these kinds of immediate and general hypotheses.

Gell (1998) uses both of these terms to describe the way in which artworks act as an index for the agency of the artist and how that agency is inferred. I want to adopt these concepts more broadly to think about the role of material culture in the process of remembering. The artwork acts as an index of the artist precisely because it is distanced from the artist spatially or temporally. It is this sense of temporal distance that is crucial here. In the examples I referred to earlier, artworks and buildings physically indexed past events. They do not simply represent past events directly; rather, past activities of production, construction, and wear are transformed in physical form – they simply refer to the past. But how are these past events recalled? Not through a process of information retrieval but through a process of sensory experience, by inferring the presence of past events through the senses. The key point here is that due to the physicality or *perdurance* (physical persistence) of material culture, things act as a means of presencing past events to the senses. If we treat objects as indices of past action, then we come to realise that objects do not so much preserve distinct memories in fidelity; rather,

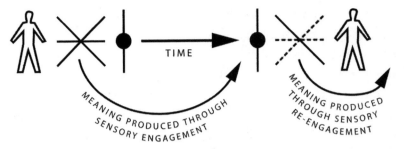

2. The sensory relationship between people and objects.

they *evoke* remembrance (Kwint 1999). Material culture therefore actively precipitates remembrance (see Fig. 2).

At a basic level, Casey (1987) suggests we experience a distinction between primary and secondary remembering. Primary remembering relates as much to the experience of time and describes the way in which instances of experience are retained in the mind before they disappear from present consciousness. Without this basic form of remembering we would have no time consciousness (for a similar argument, see Gell 1992) and would effectively live in a series of unconnected present moments.

Secondary remembering is a twofold process, beginning with the retrieval of past experience and then the revival of that experience. As Casey notes, this is not so much a simple case of retrieving past experience but of reexperiencing past objects and events. By conceptualising objects as indices of past events we can begin to see how objects act as a means of underpinning the phenomenal world for people; they provide one means by which people are able to reexperience past activities. In Chapter 3, I expand upon this point to consider the significance that the tempo and periodicity of interaction between people and things has for the process of remembrance.

I suggest that this conceptualisation of the relationship between people and objects alters our traditional views of remembrance. Rather than treating recall as a process of abstract contemplation and reflection that occurs in the mind we can instead conceptualise remembrance as a dialogic encounter between the experiencing person and the artefact. The dialogic encounter between person and artefact of course assumes a less distinct division between the internal subject and the external objective world, a dialogue in which objects impress themselves perceptually and sensually upon humans as much as humans impress themselves upon objects (Pels 1998). Remembrance is not a process internal to the human mind; rather, it is a process that occurs in the bodily encounter between people and things, as people do not remember in isolation, nor do objects. As material indices objects have the capacity to elicit remembrance. Remembrance is a process distributed between people and objects, and the process of evocation indexed by objects allows people to remember.

If we are to consider remembrance as a dialogue, we need to think differently about the role played by the senses. The senses are obviously crucial to the apprehension of the material world, and ordinarily we assume that the senses act as a vehicle for the conveyance of knowledge about that world. However, I believe we need to take on board Tim Ingold's (2000a, 243–89) argument that our emphasis needs to shift away from thinking of the body as a conduit for sensations (which are then ordered by the mind) to thinking of the body as the subject of sensations. Sensations change as the experiencing person moves within his or her lifeworld. Thomas (1996a, 19) puts the point neatly: 'the body is not a container we *live in*, it is an aspect of the self we live *through*' (original emphasis).

To reiterate, the central argument of this chapter is that remembrance is a process made apparent to the experiencing subject by the continual and dynamic encounter between the subject and the material world he or she inhabits rather than an abstract and dispassionate transaction between the external world and the mind. This opens up the possibility of thinking about memory differently. Rather than treating memory as a function of the internal processes of the human mind, we might consider memory to be produced through the encounter between people and the material world. In this sense it is useful to think of objects as indexes, or reminders, of the past. We take up these important points in the next chapter.

From Memory to Commemoration

I n Chapter 1, I suggested that the idea of external symbolic storage was not helpful when considering the relationship between objects and memory. As an alternative I suggested that memory emerges from the mutual engagement between person and world. Yet the idea of memory as a storehouse is powerful. One of the prevailing models of the way memory is stored in the mind adopts the metaphor of depth to explain the way in which memories lie buried beneath strata of experience. This 'poetics of depth' (Wallace 2004) has attracted thinkers in a diversity of disciplines to adopt an archaeological metaphor for memory and the mind; we see discussion of layers of memories analogous to layers of soil or strata, to the excavation of artefacts as akin to the retrieval of memory, or, in Walter Benjamin's case: 'genuine memory must therefore yield an image of the person who remembers, in the same way a good archaeological report not only informs us about the strata from which its findings originate but also gives an account of the strata which first had to be broken through' (Benjamin 1999a, 576).

As Thomas (2004) has recently pointed out, one of the principal themes of modernist thought is to construct a sense of human interiority. Benjamin's characterisation, along with Freud's before it, provides a good example of just such a strand of modernist thought. The construction of human interiority produces a human being whose 'truth' had to be sought in the depths of their body and their psyche. Along with this development comes a search for deeper structures, manifested in structuralism, hermeneutics, and, ultimately, psychoanalysis (see Thomas 2004 for a useful overview).

Modernity produces a new model of the person. Such a person was seen as being composed of chains of memory and responsibility. This person is described by the Enlightenment thinker John Locke as a 'forensic' person; a person defined by law. This novel figure emerges not only from the field of jurisprudence but also from the Enlightenment ideals of commerce and property (Douglas 1992; Hacking 1995).

A change in perspective can perhaps be traced to Locke, whose empirical methods were concerned to establish the fundamentals of knowledge. Despite this early empirical outlook, Hacking (1995, 203) suggests that knowledge about memory, or the uncovering of facts concerning human memory, was a development, which came much later towards the end of the nineteenth century. He places the development of the study of recall with the psychological research of Hermann Ebbinghaus in 1879, the study of neurology with the first systematic investigation of the brain by Paul Broca in 1861, and the study of psychodynamics in 1879 with the lectures on diseases of memory delivered by Théodule Ribot in Paris. He argues that these developments were an attempt to provide a surrogate method for the exploration of the composition of the self, an area that had previously been the concern of metaphysics. Via the study of memory, these early developments in the emerging discipline of psychology were concerned with the scientific documentation and study of one of the last enclaves of the spirit; they were effectively engaged in mapping the human soul.

As Thomas (2004, 169) remarks, 'the modern emphasis on the distinction between depth and surface . . . is ultimately attributable to changing concept of the person, and a growing concern with human interiority in the post-Reformation era'. It is important that we recognise the metaphorical character of these formulations and their link to a historically specific notion of the person. There is no necessary physiological reason why memories should be allied with depth – they could equally be conceived as being spatially distant rather than buried; indeed with connectionist views of the mind such a metaphor may be more appropriate. Depth simply seems to capture a sense of the temporal distance of memory as it fades from experience, making it readily conflated with the modernist view of the interior self. Once we realise this, how do we proceed?

One path forward is offered by reconsidering the nature of the individual, the self, or person. The universal character of the Western model of the individual – Locke's 'forensic' person – has been questioned by anthropological research (Thomas 2002, 31). For example, the anthropological literature on Melanesia offers a fully realised critique of the Western individual as the paradigm of the person (Strathern 1988; Wagner 2001). Melanesian conceptions of the person stand in marked contrast to those of the West. The Melanesian person is constituted from the totality of their social relations. Because this is the case, the boundaries around the human body do not define the boundaries of the person. The intentionality and agency of persons is therefore extended, often through the medium of material culture (Battaglia 1991; Gell 1998) to the extent that objects may be considered to be external components of the person (e.g. Gell 1998; Munn 1986). These 'relational' models of the person – although highlighted by the Melanesian literature – are also a feature of the pre-Colombian Americas (Allen 1998; Monaghan 1998), southern India (Busby 1997), and traditional Greek society (Seremetakis 1994).

In effect the Melanesian person is rather like a Western individual turned 'inside out' (Wagner 2001), in which case we might expect memory to be less an internalised capacity hidden deep within the individual than as something participated in externally. The crucial aspect of this enquiry into the character of Melanesian personhood is that it promotes a framework of analysis in which there is less focus on the relationships between concrete objects and people and more on an analysis of how things and people are composed of the relationships between them (Weiner 1995, xiv; Gell 1999).

The character of objects is quite different in this alternative vision of the relationship between people and things. Gosden (2004a, 37) usefully draws a distinction between the terms in which objects are treated in these two alternate systems of relations. He describes these as a distinction between 'things of quality' and 'quantifiable things'. 'Things of quality' are produced where objects are embedded in local sets of social and sacred relations, such as we observe in the case of Melanesia. However, 'quantifiable things' are disembedded from immediate social relations and can operate in a broader universe of valuation, as we observe in the capitalist economics of the modern West.

In drawing these distinctions it is important that we do not draw a hard and fast line between 'the West and the rest' (Fabian 1983; Latour 1993), moreover, as I have argued elsewhere, it is equally important that we do not figure all prehistoric societies as relational (Jones 2004, 2005a). I introduce the concept of relational personhood simply to highlight the historical specificity of the modern Western individual and concomitant theories of memory and the mind. Edward LiPuma (1998) usefully discusses the distinction between the Western individual and Melanesian person. He notes that all societies will promote aspects of individuality and relationality. Individuality of course arises from the autonomous physiology of the human body and provides the ground for the individual person and their individuality. At the same time, relational aspects of personhood exist in all societies simply because the construction of identity is a component of social relationships.

I consider these issues here simply because they help us question long-held assumptions about the character of memory in relation to historically specific (but presumed universal) aspects of personhood. In what follows I want to chart a shift away from the characterisation of memory as an internalised cognitive function to consider not only the wider role of human communities in the practice of remembering but also the participatory role of material culture in the process of remembrance.

MEMORY AND REMEMBERING

The problems we have so far encountered with memory partly stem from the distinction between 'memory' and 'remembering.' Memory (as we saw in Chapter 1) is often conceptualised as a representation to be stored cognitively. When we speak of material culture as surrogate or carrier of memory then we treat objects as a form of representation; this is precisely what is intended by the notion of external symbolic storage. Remembering, however, is the process of recall, which is produced less at a contemplative distance and more in the current of quotidian activities. As shown in Chapter 1, remembrance is a bodily activity as much as a cognitive one. However, we also saw that 'mind' is emergent and that cognition develops through interaction with the environs. What is the status of material culture in the activity of remembering and forgetting? If we solely conceptualise objects as carriers of information or representational knowledge, then they simply act as channels or conduits for recall. If instead we consider the interaction between people and things to occur at the sensual and physical level and we assume that things enable efficacious action, how then do things aid remembrance?

This question is especially pertinent in the context of the previous chapter's discussion of the semiotic role of material culture as physical traces (or indexes) of past events. Such a proposal shifts our view of the meaning content of material culture. In the traditional Saussurean-inflected view, meaning is arbitrarily imposed on objects by cultural convention. The approach adopted here is that meaning is derived from physical engagement. This view, developed by Peirce under the philosophical heading of 'Pragmatism', suggests that meaning is a function of the physical or perceptual effects things have on the person. The conception of these effects is the whole of our conception of the object (Peirce 1958[1904], 181).

For example, we do not understand electricity in the abstract – we understand it by its effects on us. If we turn on an electric light or if we touch an electric fence, each of these things is a physical and perceptual aid to understanding the concrete meaning of 'electricity'. We therefore need to pay close attention to the physical engagement between people and things if we are to understand more fully how objects help instigate the act of remembrance. To put this in more familiar terms we need to understand the role of objects in social practices to understand the meaning associated with objects. How objects can be considered to act on the person is the subject we will turn to now.

▪ FETISHISM AND MATERIALITY

On the Gold Coast of Africa in the sixteenth and seventeenth centuries, a curious figure emerged: the fetish. The word *feitiço* (and the later derivation *fettiso*) was coined by Portuguese and Dutch merchant-adventurers to describe both a class of objects and an attitude towards them (Pietz 1985, 1987). What are fetishes? They are generally freestanding wooden figurines or wooden or metal amulets worn around the neck. The point is not what physical form fetishes take – in fact, almost anything could pass as a fetish object:

trees, rocks, bones, animals – but that fetishism was an idea: an idea imposed on West Africans by Europeans to describe their spiritual relationship with the inanimate world. The concept was produced out of colonial encounters and for Europeans was felt to describe a confusion of the religious and the economic, a denial of the proper boundaries between things, between animate subjects and inanimate objects (Spyer 1998, 2). In this sense the fetish, and fetishism (the belief in the fetish), were treated in a derogatory fashion. How is it reasonable, or even possible, to treat material objects as social actors in the same sense as people?

The notion of fetishism has often been associated with the work of Marx. Marx employed the concept to describe the relations between people and things in capitalist economics. It occurs in his description of commodities; a commodity becomes a commodity not as a material thing but as an abstract value of exchange. Any given material thing works as a commodity because it has as an equivalence as an abstract exchange value. For Marx, to fetishize the commodity was to fetishize the abstract exchange value. As Stallybrass (1998, 184) points out, for Marx *fetishism* is not an intellectual or categorical problem, it is the fetishism of *commodities* that is the problem. What capitalism does is to make a fetish of the invisible and *immaterial.* This stands in contradistinction to colonial definitions of the fetish, which signified the apparently arbitrary attachment of West Africans to *material* objects. It is the material correlates of fetishism that I want to discuss here.

For Pels (1998, 91) the fetish 'foregrounds materiality because it is the most aggressive expression of the social life of things. Fetishism is animism with a vengeance. Its matter strikes back.' It can both subjugate and dominate persons. Pels (1998, 94) is quite clear in distinguishing fetishism from animism; whereas animist belief proposes that spirit resides *in* matter, fetishism posits an assumption of the spirit *of* matter: objects have spirit and are able to act of their own volition to attract or repel people. These distinctions are important because they help us clarify and reposition our perception of the object world. The key point here is that fetishes concentrate or localise human experience and belief in the power of objects. As Pietz states:

> The fetish is always a meaningful fixation of a singular event; it is above all a "historical" object, the enduring form and force of a singular event. This object is "territorialized" in material space (an earthly matrix), whether in the form of a geographical locality, a marked site on the surface of the human body, or a medium of inscription or configuration defined by some portable or wearable thing. (Pietz 1985, 12)

I discuss the notion of the fetish here precisely because it highlights some fundamental problems we have when dealing with objects. We operate in a conceptual universe where objects have no independent life; if they are made to act or are imputed with meaning, then this is through human intentionality. Things have no meaning unless meaning is endowed upon them by human agency. The issue turns on where we imagine control to rest. Are we detached from objects in which case we act upon them in a disinterested fashion as and when we choose, or are objects attached to us and as such are they components of what makes us act? These are especially pertinent questions if we want to consider how objects help us to remember.

Latour (1999a) discusses this problem in some detail. He addresses the distinction that is made between facts and fetishes. Facts are seen as rational and self-evident entities, a component of a modernist world in which things and people are discrete and separable entities. However, in European eyes, fetishes are denounced as irrational entities that crop up when non-Westerners confuse things with people. Latour uses the hybrid term *factish* to force us to rethink the way subjects and objects are routinely conjoined. He argues that people and things are *always* conjoined in action; he claims that causation or action is distributed between people and things. Rather than thinking in oppositional terms of freedom or detachment from things (as in modernism) and bondage or attachment to things (as with fetishism), we should shift our attention to consider *how* people are attached to things.

To take an example from the Neolithic we might question the proposition that stone axes are indicative of forest clearance prior to agriculture. It is not the axe by itself that chops down trees but rather the axe in its wooden haft acting in concert with a person to achieve the end of woodland clearance. Taking a materialist stance we might say that axes chop down trees, but taking a sociological stance we might equally counter that axes don't chop down trees, people chop down trees. Both views have their problems; obviously axes alone don't chop down trees, but to say that people chop down trees ignores the role of the axe. Doesn't the axe play any part in the chopping? Wouldn't a person equipped with a fine stone axe feel tempted to chop down a tree to prove the worth of their new acquisition? My point is that things and people working together achieve action, not one or the other isolated. But to say that things mediate action is relatively simplistic; we need to look in more detail at the relationship. Stone axes did not spring from nowhere at the onset of the Neolithic. In a number of regions of Europe their use can be traced back to the late Mesolithic. Moreover the form and materials of axes are the result of a considerable network of social relations. As many studies have shown both in Britain and the Continent the acquisition of raw materials is the result of complex systems of resource procurement and gift exchange (Bradley and Edmonds 1993; de Grooth 1998; Pétrequin et al. 1998). Indeed the situation is even more complex when we take into account the *chaînes operatoires* (sequence of actions) associated with the manufacture of the axe (Pétrequin et al. 1998).

So, even the humble stone axe is situated in an extensive web of activities along which action and causation are distributed. The social relations bound up in the acquisition and exchange of the axe are, if you like, 'folded' into the fabric of the axe. It is this as much as anything which enables the axe to achieve the action of chopping. Pels (1998, 98) underlines this point by noting that materiality should be treated as a quality of *relationships* rather than a quality of things. It is how people use things and how things enable them to act that is the focus of discussion here.

Attempts to overcome the problematic ties between people and things might be sought by viewing the relationship as mutually constitutive. For example, Miller (1987) describes the mutual constitution of people and things as a process of 'objectification' in which people construe their own capabilities and labour in material form. Things therefore act as concrete vehicles for social and individual expressions of power and energy. In turn the objectified material world acts back upon human subjects (Miller describes this process as sublation). Human capabilities are therefore personified through the production of things, and material things are subjectified in people (Gosden 1994, 71). This kind of approach is taken by Julia Hendon (2000) in her analysis of the role of storage in the Trobriand Islands, Mesoamerica, and Neolithic Europe. She examines the occurrence of storage pits in a series of house sites and argues that the social practice of storage, and the material fact of stored produce, is a form of what she calls 'mutual knowledge'. She relates the production of stored materials to the acquisition and reproduction of social power. People act on the world to produce stored goods, and the stored goods then serve to produce social power for generations to come.

What is critically important here is the movement or flow of relations between people and the material world; people and things are engaged in a process of mutual making. Moreover, this process is relational; it is the relationship between each that gives things and people their character (Gell 1999; Gosden 1994; Strathern 1988, 1998). Importantly, this process of mutual creation is a continuous historical process. However, rather than treating this as an abstract engagement between people and 'nature', Gosden (1994, 77) analyses the mutual constitution of humanity and world by considering the act of making itself. He points out that the world created by past social groups becomes the platform for the socialisation of future groups. The world is thus not just something they *know* but something they *are* and is a component of their social creative powers. Thus construed the world enters into human history as an ever-changing and active force; it is both transformed (by past social groups) and transforming (of future ones). To return to the example of storage offered by Julia Hendon, she also offers an alternative perspective on the relationship between people and things when noting that 'by creating and modifying a landscape of natural and built forms, groups construct a setting that gives concrete, permanent expression to relationships and identities (Hendon 2000, 50). She goes on to say that 'storage, whether utilitarian or ritual raises issues of secrecy, memory, prestige and knowledge that help construct the moral system within which people live' (Hendon 2000, 50). Stored goods form a kind of moral substrate or network, which allow people to conduct themselves appropriately. Here she emphasises the view of causation as simultaneously determining and determined.

Latour (1999a) echoes this point using the example of language. We could say that a subject or person speaks a language; equally we could say that the language speaks the subject (it gives them words with which to articulate their thoughts). However, the key to understanding the relationship lies in the analysis of practice or action. In speaking a language we use words and concepts that exist prior to us, but in speaking words we give them life and the language endures.

This offers a different perspective to that of Miller and Gosden. We are not simply saying that people make things and in turn are made by them, in which action shifts from one place to another; in the first instance people act on things, and in the second instance things act on people, and so on, in a cyclical manner. Instead, action or practice is interstitial to people and things; each is held together in and through action. Things provide people with the capacity to act and through action things and people endure. Things make people exist, and people make things exist. As I have said elsewhere social action occurs as the result of a company of actors – composed of both people and things – working in tandem (Jones 2002a; see also Olsen 2003 for a forceful reiteration of this point). Rowlands (2005,

197) usefully defines the shift in perspective discussed above as an analytic contrast between materialism (the stance taken by Miller and Gosden) and materiality (the stance taken by Latour) underpinned by a contrast between modernist and premodernist explanations for the source of social power.

The mutual engagement between person and world is also stressed in the cognitive analysis of mind. Andy Clark (1997) usefully describes this process as 'scaffolding'. Scaffolding signals a process in which the environment provides the support for action. Rather than adopting the classical view of the mind as a device for cognising representations of the world, Clark makes the point that 'the world is its own best representation' (Clark 1997, 46). Drawing on the analysis of neural networks, he suggests that the brain should not be seen as the locus for inner descriptions of external states. Rather, it should be seen as a locus for inner structures that act as operators upon the world via their role in determining action (Clark 1997, 47). Representations are therefore action oriented; they both describe the world and prescribe action in it. It is the manipulation of objects in the world by embodied minds that describe the process of cognition. It is that which provides directives for future action. Therefore, the engagement of the embodied mind with objects is fundamental to how we think.

This perspective suggests that perception and action are not distinct. Perceptions are not neutral descriptions of the world so much as context-specific and activity-related specifications of potential modes of intervention in the environment. Such an approach to perception closely resembles Gibson's notion of affordances (Gibson 1979). As Clark notes, Gibson's approach was to advocate that perception was direct and action centred. For Gibson, perception was not mediated by inner states of representation. Clark insists that there are indeed inner forms of representation but that these are action centred, thus overcoming some of the major criticism of Gibson's ideas. The key point, however, is that in perceiving the world as a potential for action, objects in the world are treated as *affording* action. Gibson stresses mutuality between organisms and their environment, different aspects of the environment will afford different things for organisms of variable kinds. This is why the perception of the environment is so important, because perception allows organisms to decide how to act and using what materials.

The approaches to materiality adopted above fundamentally shifts our perspective on the object world. The concept of the fetish teaches us that things do not reflect human intention but instead concentrate human experience and belief. Things are essential and interstitial for efficacious human action. The idea of affordances helps us to realise that not all objects are treated in the same way; some are abstracted from the background of the environment and are accorded special attention because of their capacities for affording action.

ARTEFACTS AND THE PRACTICES OF REMEMBERING AND FORGETTING

As Forty notes, 'it has generally been taken for granted that memories, formed in the mind, can be transferred to solid material objects, which can come to stand for memories' (1999, 2). The durability of objects is then taken to indicate the preservation and endurance of memory – a process of remembering. Concomitantly, the iconoclastic act of destroying objects has been taken to be the opposite of this process – an act of deliberate forgetting. Yet the relationship between memory and objects in this theory is too simple and is not borne out by experience. Forty cites three reasons for rejecting this theory (1999, 4–7). The first is Freud's point that all memories are retained and that forgetting is an active process. The second is that many societies produce artefacts deliberately contrived to decay; indeed, it is the absence of once present physical objects that ensures remembrance. Thirdly, as the experience of the Holocaust has shown, the problem is not so much forgetting – as many survivors attempted to do – but of remembering. If the experience was consigned to oblivion, it risked being repeated. But this posed the difficulty of how to produce monuments to survivors' memories. To produce memorials that simply preserved survivors' memories would be impossible. Instead a series of antimemorials have been produced (Young 1996) which attempt to capture the fleeting relationship between objects and memory.

As we saw in the previous chapter, it is difficult to assert that memory is simply attached, imprinted upon, or otherwise fixed to objects. Artefacts cannot be taken as simple agents of memory and their ability to extend or preserve memory cannot be relied upon.

At one level Forty's conclusion is pessimistic, especially if we are interested in the relationship between material culture and memory. However, I would argue this difficulty is somewhat alleviated if we treat objects as traces or indices of the past. A constructive position on this subject is taken by Buchli and Lucas (2001, 81), who note that rather than viewing remembering and forgetting as polarities, they should instead be thought of as in a state of tension. The material correlates of this tension may be either constituted or remain unconstituted, materialised, or materially 'left unsaid'. They argue that, on the one hand, although the simple construction or destruction of artefacts can create or destroy memory, on the other hand, making an artefact or monument can leave out memories, there are gaps in remembrance. Similarly, the destruction of an artefact or monument leaves residue, carrying with it memories of past events. This perspective is encouraging because it addresses the wider problem of how we investigate the relationship between material culture and memory. Rather than simply noting that the relationship between the two is fugitive or problematic, it is important to stress that the specific mnemonic character of material culture is promoted by the involvement of objects in social practices. As Emma Blake makes plain: 'memory and tradition alone do not preserve an object's identity, it is the ongoing incorporation of that object into routinized practices that generates meaning' (Blake 1998, 68). We may be best thinking of memory emerging from the use of artefacts or monuments in social and cultural practices; the acts of remembering and forgetting are performed by material practices, not imprinted in material objects. We can understand the role of artefacts in the dual processes of remembering and forgetting only if we foreground practice.

REMEMBERING THINGS TOGETHER

Memory can no longer be thought to reside solely in the mind but emerges through intersubjective experience with the material world. People typically share memories of events and objects. This statement points up the fact that people inhabit worlds that extend beyond themselves. Memories are not simply shared but are actively created or constructed through collective remembering. As Middleton and Edwards (1997, 7) point out, in the 'contest between varying accounts of shared experiences, people reinterpret and discover features of the past that become the context and content for what they will jointly recall and commemorate on future occasions'. Just as individual memories undergo a process of updating and reworking, so, too, does social memory.

Middleton and Edwards (1997) outline a series of aspects of the process of social remembrance that they describe as 'remembering together': firstly, they note that social memory provides a foundation and context for individual memory. Secondly, they note that processes of remembering and forgetting occur in rhetorically organised forms; some versions of the past are sanctioned, whereas others are excluded and it is the process of telling the right kind of story at the right time that forms the framework for so much remembrance.

Ultimately, they note that the continuity of social life, as a component of certain forms of social practices, and in terms of our identities as individuals, is dependant on the continuation and preservation of practices of remembering and forgetting. These practices are objectified in the social environment; they are 'externalised' to the extent that the world we inhabit both embodies and is shaped by the past. These series of statements have important implications for our understanding of the relationship between individuals and society. As Halbwachs (1993[1950]) noted long ago, there is a reflexive and mutual relationship between individual and social modes of remembering. We need to realise that the context and practices of remembering provide a framework for the generation of individual memories but, equally, individual memories are imbricated or woven into the fabric of the context and practices of remembering.

Echoing this, Middleton and Edwards (1997, 10–11) claim that the coherence and integrity of an individual's mentality is closely related to their participation in an environment which owes its shape to social and cultural practices. If we take this as a reasonable proposition then we begin to see that it makes little sense to compare individual memory against social memory or to ask what part of memory is internally or externally located.

▪ TECHNOLOGIES OF REMEMBRANCE

In the previous chapter I rejected the view of the meaning of artefacts being based solely upon a linguistic model in favour of meaning being erected from the sensual and physical experience of artefacts. Over the course of this chapter we have shifted away from a view of artefacts as repositories of memory to discussing the role of artefacts in intersubjective practices of remembrance. At this juncture it is important to reintroduce the issue of language. When discussing the intersubjective nature of practices of remembrance it is important to state that meaning is not simply formed from individualised sensual experience but is also created through discourse. It is in this case that we return to the third of Peirce's category of signs: the symbol. Symbols are designated by cultural rules or norms, and it is because of their commonly recognised currency that they provide a framework for intersubjective understanding. Rather than discussing artefacts strictly as symbols, I prefer to consider how they act as metaphors.

As Lambek and Antze (1996, xi–xii) remark, to come closer to an understanding of the experience of memory we erect a series of metaphors. Metaphors are used in this context to transform a transient temporal phenomenon into a concrete spatial phenomenon, making it easier to comprehend. In a similar sense Tilley (1999) discusses the way in which material culture acts as a form of concrete metaphor. It is the physical immediacy of material culture that is significant: 'material metaphors have a quality of density in that every aspect of an artefact contributes continuously to its meanings and is interdependently significant' (Tilley 1999, 264). It is due to this physical immediacy that material culture provides such potent metaphors for the experience of memory.

Indeed it is precisely because of the physical immediacy of material culture that artefacts provide the perfect intersubjective medium for modelling the experience of memory; artefacts are a medium available to all which simultaneously allow people to speak of both personal and collective experiences of memory (Radley 1997). The ability of objects to provide a medium for recall and remembrance is amply documented by Janet Hoskins (1998) in her account of the role of what she calls 'biographical objects' as prompts for the narration of life histories in Sumba, Indonesia.

The relationship amongst objects, metaphor, and memory is historically important because we see a consistent relationship maintained between physical objects and memory. This began with the Classical 'arts of memory' or architectural mnemonics described by Yates (1966). Descriptions of memory alter during the modern age, with rapid changes in material products. As Draaisma (2000) shows, machines such as the phonograph and camera acted as metaphors of memory, whereas in a contemporary setting the computer provides us with the supreme mnemonic metaphor. It is not necessarily true that descriptions of memory irrevocably change with the utilisation of fresh technologies, rather, new technological products provide us with fresh metaphorical perspectives on memory.

The metaphors used to describe memory need say little about the biological structure of memory (though they may provide insights; Rose 2003); rather, they tell us a great deal about how the experience of memory is treated *socially*. It is for this reason that I believe closer attention needs to be paid to such 'technologies of remembrance'. This approach is informative because the analysis of such technologies provides an insight into the close relationship between the way in which memory is experienced as a personal and social phenomenon.

■ COMMEMORATION, MATERIAL CULTURE, AND COLLECTIVE REMEMBRANCE

This is especially true if we consider commemorative practices, because commemoration highlights the way in which individual and collective memory and material culture are seamlessly interwoven. In considering commemorative activities as a form of remembrance we have shifted our perspective from remembering as a state of mind to an activity which encompasses not only individual minds and bodies but also the minds and bodies of others. Michael Stewart (2004) underlines this point in writing of the European Roma (or Gypsies). The Roma were victims of the Holocaust and are often portrayed as a people who forget, rather than remember, history. Stewart argues that Romany communities, on the contrary, 'remember' their past through they may not commemorate it. They do this because as a community in interaction with non-Roma their implicit memories are embedded in their dealings with others. The wider non-Roma communities help the Roma to remember. Memory is therefore socially distributed between and within communities.

This case highlights an example in which remembering is not a formalised activity. It is important to note that commemoration is often highly formalised and is rarely a fugitive or random form of remembering (Connerton 1989, 61). For Casey (1987) commemorative practices are characterised by a series of features including memorialisation and recurrence. Memorialisation is, of course, the act of remembering in an appropriate way and through an appropriate medium. Recurrence is perhaps the most important component of commemoration. Recurrence is here used to indicate the process of 'changing while staying the same'; the rituals enacted as part of commemorations are meant to produce the continuation or endurance of tradition, though, of course, because they are enacted periodically their content subtly alters through performance. Although variable in their actual performance, rituals are meant to appear invariant.

This feature of rituals is familiar to prehistorians who regularly study sites with extensive histories of ritual activity. An excellent example of this is Stonehenge, Wiltshire, which was used and altered over a period of 1,500 years but remains an important ceremonial and ritual focus. I discuss this example in more detail in Chapter 4.

The features of commemoration discussed above underline the overarching fact that commemorations are performative in nature (Connerton 1989, 58–9). Performance relates partly to the evocation and utterance of key components of ritual texts or narratives but also relates to bodily movement. One of the primary ways in which commemorations are enacted is through a set series of postures, gestures, and movements. Actions are prescribed according to the formulation and formality of the commemorative performance.

Again this component of commemorative practice is well known to prehistorians who have examined the way in which the architecture of early Neolithic megalithic tombs (Barrett 1994; Richards 1992; Thomas 1992) or Late Neolithic henges prescribe movement in and around their spaces (Barrett 1994; Pollard 1992; Thomas 1993). This 'monumental choreography' (Richards 1993) is echoed in the formalised use of the liturgical spaces of the Medieval period, such as the English parish church (Graves 1989), monastery, or nunnery (Gilchrist 1999).

Commemorative performances primarily concern participation, whether bodily participation or engagement with specific places, objects, or a coherent narrative or text. Either way each person involved in a commemorative practice is participating through an external medium. Casey (1987, 247) points out that primary participation is with a *commemorandum* – the commemorated object, person, or event. This commemoration takes place through the medium of *commemorabilia*, objects or places which index or presence the past objects, persons, or events to be remembered. Such commemorablia might be witnessed in the often extraordinary movement of materials used to make up sites of commemoration. The Stonehenge bluestones, or the granodiorite and quartz incorporated into Irish Megalithic tombs, discussed in Chapter 8, are both good examples of this phenomenon. Likewise, the objects often deposited at sites of commemoration, such as the huge numbers of ceramic vessels deposited around megalithic tombs in southern Scandinavia. Casey (1987, 219) remarks that it is almost as if the function of *commemorabilia* is to offer a translucent or direct access to the past to those participating in commemorations.

Commemoration is of great importance for my argument as a whole. This is because commemoration is paradigmatic of the kind of connective practices which tie together people and things. Precisely because of participation and immersion both with other people and with external objects, places, and texts, commemoration is ultimately a connective process. It is this very connectivity that is important, because we can think of commemoration as a framework for remembering itself.

Commemorative practices provide a key tool for thinking about the relationship between material culture and memory. Perhaps the most important point to be drawn from the discussion of commemoration is the way in which material culture provides a participatory framework for action. As an index of past action, material culture is ultimately connective, it connects people to the physical world, to temporal processes, and through its physicality directs them to future action. In this sense, like commemoration, there is a sense of recurrence. Material culture likewise provides the ground for connecting individual and collective remembrance. In short, material culture is critical to the maintenance and performance of tradition.

3

People, Time, and Remembrance

How do people and societies situate themselves in time? One way in which time is stabilised and measured is through the use of material culture. In what way are artefacts used as mnemonic devices to present and measure temporal spans? The way in which the material world is drawn upon as a means of situating a person or a society in time is complex and multilayered. To explore these ideas, this chapter begins by looking at an example of the relationship between memory and material culture from Mesoamerica.

People inhabiting the Classic Maya world of Mesoamerica between 500 and 1000 AD would have lived in ordered spaces replete with signs of social commemoration. Free-standing sculptures, such as stelae and altars, surrounded monumental plazas. The walls, lintels, and stairs of these monumental buildings were carved with inscriptions and friezes. Inscriptions of this kind were used to convey the biography or history of the elite. As Joyce (2003, 105) puts it: 'their primary message is one of remembering a monumental past and linking it to the future'. Because the carved image of a persons head or face on standing stones or stelae was perceived to be a literal embodiment of the essence of that person (their *Bah*), the provision of carved and inscribed stelae was also a device for physically presencing absent elites. Through representation Classic Maya rulers were able to perform the extraordinary trick of being in two places at once, thereby transcending space and time (Houston and Stuart; 1998, 90).

Social memory was therefore physically impressed upon the inhabitants of these spaces in the form of elaborately carved and immense stone sculptural forms. But remembrance was performed in other ways, too. Daily activity in settlements was shaped by the performances that a person witnessed whilst growing up in certain spatial settings, spatial settings that were designed to produce specific hierarchical conceptualisations of the person (Houston and Stuart 1998). The performance of activities in these settings implicitly provided precedents for later reiterations and the evaluation of later actions as successfully performed (Joyce 2003, 109). Memory is also precipitated through more intimate forms of material culture, such as costume ornaments. Joyce (2003) discusses a number of ornaments, such as obsidian ear spools, carved pins, and bead pendants, that are inscribed with texts which would have been invisible (and illegible) to the wearer. Such texts provide a way of cueing memory, and, like inscriptions in monumental formats, they provide a sense of genealogical relationships and political succession. In relation to ear spools, Joyce notes that the widening of the ears is a Mayan bodily practice used to transform children into adults. Inscribing ear spools with texts was a means of cueing and reiterating genealogical relationships, relating one generation to the other during ceremonies surrounding life cycle rituals. These provided one context for declaring genealogical ties; the other was the deposition of such ornaments with burials in tombs, an arena for recalling and contesting kinship relations.

This Classic Mayan example perfectly illustrates the multiple and layered way in which material worlds promote and precipitate different orders of remembrance. Immense sculptured stones set in monumental structures provided the means of impressing or cementing a sense of social or collective memory; the structure and spatiality of buildings provided the means of generating a sense of the past and offered a setting for the performance of daily events. Set against this scale, but linked to it through inscription, were the series of practices associated with dressing the body, with the performance of life cycle rituals, and with the declaration of kinship ties in the mortuary context. These were associated with small decorative ornaments of obsidian and bone.

There are a series of points I want to draw from this example. As I noted in Chapter 1, if we wish to understand the role of material culture in producing collective remembrance and promoting cultural transmission, we need to attend to a series of factors. The material properties and qualities of material culture, the scale, endurance/transience, and malleability of objects, are all key to how and why they are used to promote remembrance. However, it is insufficient to focus solely upon material properties; it is also essential to understand how material culture is enrolled in the performance of remembrance. Remembrance must be practised. How objects act to promote remembrance or forgetting depends upon the performative capacities of materials: are they highly coloured or decorated, are they dull or worn, are they easily fragmented, broken, or burnt, or do they resist destruction and decay? Finally, the temporality or periodicity of performance is critical to how material culture shapes remembrance: are objects glimpsed briefly or are they placed in prominent public positions? The materiality of objects and the performance of remembrance are closely interwoven; both operate in concert to facilitate acts of remembrance or forgetting.

■ MATERIALISING TIME

All important is the way in which – as media for the performance of remembrance – material culture provides individuals and societies with ontological security. Material culture helps to situate people in a temporal order – helps them to cognise – and organises that temporal order. It also provides a means of marking their own temporal spans within wider temporal trajectories and of extending their agency beyond that temporal span. The use of artefacts in the performance of remembrance is therefore a means by which we give form to, and come to an understanding of, ourselves and others (Miller 1994, 397). Through the practice of remembrance using artefacts people are produced and identities are formed.

Miller (1994, 409–15) draws out the significant connections among people, identity, and the materiality of artefacts. He suggests that our engagements with the material world are ordered and understood with reference to the duration of our own temporal spans. He characterises three major modalities of engagement: longevity, temporal equivalence, and transience. The first (longevity) is related to the experience and positioning of the person in historically extensive schemes. As Miller (1994, 410) notes: 'all people initially experience the world as something given by history rather than something they create'. In this temporal register, artefacts are the vehicles by which persons attempt to transcend their own temporal limits. In the second (equivalence) there is a temporal equivalence between people and artefacts: artefacts may be used to comment upon the life history of the person. In the third instance (transience) artefacts are treated as ephemera by comparison with persons; here the focus is on how people express themselves temporally alongside the ever-changing character of things.

The significant point to be gained from this perspective on the relationship between people and things is the tempo of the relationship, the way in which people and things 'resonate' relative to each other. Rather than treating longevity, equivalence, and impermanence as strict modalities, I want to use Miller's insight to suggest

that these are components of a continuum; properties of the relationship between people and things which are produced relationally.
A starting point for my argument is the important point that ideas of
durability and impermanence are positioned in relation to the temporal spans of human beings. Similarly, the perception of longevity
or ephemerality is partly the product of the relative life histories and
material qualities of different substances. Things are perceived as
durable or ephemeral relative only to the uses to which they are put
and the practices they are enrolled in.

A couple of examples may be useful here to clarify these points.
Amongst the Zafimaniry of Madagascar, the social and kinship ties
that come with marriage are successively materialised in houses made
of bamboo. After a number of years the success of the marriage is
then formalised in the shape of the central post of the house, made
of hardwood. On death, the tombs of men or women are made of
stone and are often modelled upon the wooden posts of the house or
the hearthstones (in the case of women). The use of stone to make
tombs is important because relative to hardwood it is even more
permanent; it is a medium for permanently placing the dead in the
landscape (Bloch 1995b). Materials index time by reference to each
other and by their use in social practices; there is a continuum of
materiality in which hardwood is perceived as less permanent than
stone and as such is used to build houses rather than tombs.

In other regions trees themselves are seen to define or 'ground'
images of timelessness. For example, amongst the Foi of Papua, New
Guinea, long-growing Sago Palms, cultivated by the Foi, are used to
describe intergenerational time (Weiner 1991). Likewise, amongst
the aLuund of southwestern Congo, Africa *muyoomb* trees offer the
very image of rootedness and permanence and provide the means
for anchoring notions of place (De Boeck 1998). I use these examples simply to emphasise the point that notions of permanence and
impermanence are contingent and relational (Helms 2004). They
depend upon the local perception of substances and their deploy-
ment in social practices. The perceived temporal stability of things
depends upon their relationship with other materials used in other

kinds of social practices. For example, Helms (2004) observes that the qualities of durability recognised in a variety of material forms, including rocks and minerals, metals, shells, seeds, bones, and teeth, lead societies to develop an understanding of those cosmological issues associated with ontology or eschatology, as well as temporal stability and duration. She quotes one mourner at a Wayapi funeral questioning his position in the cosmological scheme by referring to the durability of different elements of the natural world: 'Why do we die? Stone doesn't die. Earth doesn't die. Trees do die but only after a long, long time. Why do we die?' (Campbell 1989, quoted in Helms 2005).

What I want to develop here is the notion that time, history, and memory are produced by societies with relation to the human life span. Barbara Adams (1990) points out that multiple levels of temporality are connected together by the fact of being human. We have a relationship to time, we experience it, and we reckon time. We also create time as a resource. All of these ways of treating time are bound together by different aspects of being human. She relates how once we create time as a resource it fundamentally alters and structures our existence. Using the example of clock time:

> Once this created time is related as a resource to be used, allocated, controlled, spent or sold it affects our relationship to death, the timing of our activities, our institutions, our technology, our understanding of reality, and our practices of work, leisure, and even sleep. Our environment, too, and even our bodies, are different because of it. (Adams 1990, 161)

The objectification of time recursively structures both our material environment and our bodily experience. I want to retain the notion that times are connected to being human to consider the relationships amongst time, memory, history, and materiality. Firstly, let us consider the relationship between memory and history. These are not hard and fast categories, but we might begin by thinking of memory as the practical subjectification of the past and history as the discursive and disciplinary objectification of the past (Lambek 2003, 208). Equally, we might think of these in terms of incorporative practices and inscriptive practices in the sense described by Connerton (1989), in which the past is incorporated into bodily practices, on the one hand, or represented in an objectified form, on the other. Importantly, the ground from which these different perspectives are calculated is the human body. A useful starting point for teasing out the differences and similarities in the relationship between an objectified and subjective past is to examine the relationship between material culture and social practice.

Material culture represents an objectification of the past, yet it is also experienced subjectively. If we consider material culture in this way the distinctions between history and memory blur substantially. Instead, we might think of material culture occurring in different presentational forms and speaking to differing temporal registers. In this sense history is simply social memory objectified in certain material formats, whether books, maps, statue stelae, or monumental inscriptions. History is also a species of social memory with a narrative structure that spans lengthy time scales (Fentress and Wickham 1992).

To consider in more detail how social practices employ material culture to mediate temporality I focus on the work of Chris Gosden. Gosden (1994, 15–17) notes that practical actions involving material culture are situated in what he describes as a 'structure of reference.' Activities are not isolated; rather, each act is directed towards the past and oriented towards the future. Each activity is implicitly linked to past actions and towards future ones. Activities therefore embody retentions from the past and protentions to the future. One way in which such activities might be linked is through the perdurance (or physical persistence) of material culture; because material culture endures, it offers a means of linking different times. For Gosden (1994, 124) material practices create spatial and temporal structure. Activities reference other places, but as they are performed in sequence they reference other times. In a sense, material practices are embedded in networks of causality; each action refers to past or future action, this place or another. A useful way of thinking about these networks of causality is in terms of the notion of the index introduced in Chapter 1.

In Chapter 1, I noted that – as indices – artefacts offered a means for people to remember through the perception of the flow of time. The physical presence of the artefact and the visible traces of wear or reconstruction indexed a sense of the past. I now want to utilise this insight by considering not only how isolated artefacts index the past but also how artefacts are used by societies to index a sense of the past in different ways. It is my contention that this process is relational: each mode of indexing the past relates to the other as a system of differences. The use of differing substances/materials in different social practices is likewise relational and indexical. As we saw in the examples given earlier, stone represented absolute permanence for the Zafimaniry because it is harder than the hardwood used to indicate strong marriage in the household context. However, for the aLuund, *muyoomb* trees are the epitome of strength and permanence. Finally, I want to suggest that such a perception of memory and history as indexed by material practices is generative. That is, as a system of differences it is produced and maintained by social practices motivated towards its reproduction.

The use of certain substances in social practices is a means of producing or materialising memory and, in turn, history. The relative durability of artefacts helps to articulate a sense of different qualities of temporal existence and experience. Time tends to be objectified as history in the form of durable artefacts, although it is treated subjectively in the form of ephemeral objects. As Helms shows, certain durable substances are often associated with a cosmological sense of history.

Again it is worth underlining that these perceptions of history and memory are relative, and their major reference point is the human life span. Notions of history and memory need to be treated as a continuum. Monuments, for example, can be considered as timeless and enduring only if they are treated as such relative to other forms of material culture. To consider how the two are articulated in relation to each other we need to consider the tempo of social practices. Here we need to consider not only the substances from which material culture is composed but also the routine and periodicity of social practices in which they are enrolled.

To foreground the rhythm and performance of material practices I want to introduce the concept of citation. The notion of 'citation' captures the sense that for a word or thing to make sense it must reiterate components of previous sentences or objects. The performance of a citation both encapsulates previous ideas or things while also re-articulating them afresh to create or define novel categories. The concept of citation may be used to describe verbal and textual (Derrida 1982) or material performances (Butler 1993). In some senses citations can be treated like indices as they also reference previous performances. However, unlike an index, they do not simply refer to past action, but through the act of citation they reiterate that action. Citations are more clearly understood and interpreted if they are continually reiterated, just as a commonly used word is better known and understood than an archaic word. The repetition of practices therefore creates stronger referential links between practices.

To explain the relational and performative framework I am proposing here I want to return to the example from Mesoamerica. In her analysis of Classic Maya modes of remembrance, Joyce (2003) indicated that the form and character of remembrance differed according to how memory was materialised. In the case of long-term collective or social memory, it was produced in the form of inscriptions on immense blocks of stone incorporated in monumental structures. These signal a sense of permanence and timelessness. As inscribed public monuments they speak to a sense of narrative history. The performance of daily practices was also conducted with reference to the architecture of these structures. The localised, intimate, and periodic enactment of remembrance at the tomb or at life cycle rituals was related to the use of small-scale artefacts whose use referred back to the modes of commemoration found in monumental public settings. The scale of the artefacts and their periodic use in social practices signalled their impermanence. Importantly, through the use of textual reference, each of these modes of remembrance indexed the other; the system of differences was produced as a totality and through practice the system was reproduced. Although the system of differences was held together by textual citations which were themselves performed as recitations or declarations, it was also produced and maintained by the differences in the quality of substances used in differing social practices.

The upshot of this is that we cannot consider remembrance as an isolated act. 'Remembering with things' is always embedded in a relational structure of reference. A key point to emerge from my analysis is that precisely because material practices are situated in a relational framework we cannot simply single out individual acts of remembrance against collective modes of remembrance. Rather, individual remembrance is grounded in collective remembrance and the relationship between the two is likewise relational; indeed, the two are partly framed by the kinds of materials and the forms of practices used to express individual or collective modes of remembrance.

EVOCATION AND REMEMBRANCE

Having considered the relational framework or space within which mnemonic practices are performed I now want to consider how it is that objects precipitate remembrance. How are objects able to embody retentions from the past and how do they speak to future actions or events?

Artefacts connect past actions and events because they physically endure. It is the fact of this endurance that I pursue now in considering the nature of evocation. How does material culture evoke memory? I noted in Chapter 1 that objects evoke remembrance precisely because they offer a means of sensually presencing past events. Evocation, in the words of Kwint (1999, 3), 'implies an open dialogue between the object, the maker and the consumer in constructing meaning'. It is this dialogic aspect of evocation I discuss.

I argued above that the human temporal span offers a perspective from which to view the temporality of material culture. Notions of time and history, and their articulation using material culture, are calculated with respect to the human life span. Rather than treating the human life span as a datum, I now consider how the temporal span of people and the temporal span of objects operate relative to each other.

My argument turns on the way in which people and material culture 'resonate' temporally in relation to each other. People and things 'resonate' in two major ways: either material culture remains the same as people move in time or both objects and people change over time.

In the first instance, because material culture endures while people change, objects have the power to affect us as a kind of material 'echo' from the past. Objects do this because people sensually experience material culture and move in time. Some time later the identical sensual experience of material culture offers a way of evoking and reexperiencing the past (Fig. 3).

In the second instance, if objects alter as time goes on they also offer a means of evoking remembrance. In this instance the person perceives the changes in material culture from the point of view of the ontological constancy of the person. The changing character of objects offers a means of perceiving change and thereby evokes or foregrounds the change undergone by the person (Fig. 4). The presence of material objects and their sensual difference to similar objects experienced in the past offer a way of perceiving difference.

A few examples will help to illustrate the first case in which material culture endures while people change. The consumption of food is one means by which memories are sedimented in the body. The oft-quoted example of this is – as described by Walter Benjamin (1999b, 200) – Proust 'dunking a cookie in his tea'. As Sutton (2001) shows, the involuntary memory evoked by Proust's madeleine dipped in lime-blossom tisane is a component of a wider phenomenon. The involuntary memory evoked by a sensation tasted, felt, or heard has been a staple literary trope since Proust. A recent example is used by the Japanese novelist Haruki Murakami, whose protagonist evokes the entire felt experience of 1960s Tokyo after hearing the Beatles' 'Norwegian Wood' drifting over the public address system in a German airport.

David Sutton (2001) discusses in detail the relationship between food and involuntary memory. Sutton (2001) indicates, with reference to the experience of food on the Greek island of Kalymnos, that both the everyday and ritual consumption of food are important. Due to the seasonal availability of foodstuffs the same foods are not consumed continuously; rather, their consumption is punctuated by the seasons. Food is therefore experienced and then a year later reexperienced. It is this reexperiencing of seasonal food that sensually evokes memory. A similar example is discussed by Seremetakis (1994), who notes how specific varieties of peaches grown locally in Greece had the power to evoke the past. It was the absence of such peaches due to periods spent abroad by the author and their consumption upon her return that evoked memory.

Another key example relates to place. Places impress themselves upon people through habitual experience. As Bachelard (1964) shows, the habitation of our houses provides an early framework for the child to orientate themselves, an image of stability. The past is held in place. Once habitually experienced in this way the re-experiencing of places also has the power to evoke memory. It is the familiarity and sustaining character of place (Casey 1987, 191–8), the fact that place has been impressed upon us physically in the past and does so again once reexperienced, that is important here. Because of the familiar and bodily habitation of place the past of places is nearly always remembered by reference to the body. The body's position in relation to place is a means of anchoring, of staying put in relation to the scene remembered (Casey 1987, 196).

Places need not be reexperienced by physically visiting them. They can also be evoked at a distance because of the presence of the

PERSON STAYS THE SAME, OBJECT CHANGES

3. Remembrance produced when person remains the same and object changes.

PERSON CHANGES, OBJECT STAYS THE SAME

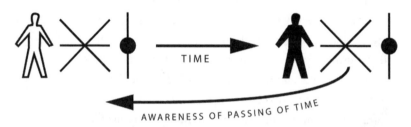

4. Remembrance produced when person changes and object remains the same.

things associated with place. As Casey indicates, 'things are *of* place as well as *in* place' (original emphasis). Things are pivotal points in places; they constellate place by their presence (Casey 1987, 205). Like places, objects also have the power to evoke memories of place.

We have discussed the recursive way in which material culture, once experienced, acts to evoke memory. Let us now consider some examples of the way in which the changing state of material culture also offers a means of evoking remembrance.

Food, again, provides a good example of the way in which changes in material culture promote remembrance. Seremetakis (1994, 1–2) notes that the absence of the peach known as the 'breast of Aphrodite' from Greek markets (forced to compete with cheaper imported fruits) evoked recollection. The superior taste of this peach is compared against the tastelessness of more recent varieties. Difference is made visible or sensible by change. The absence of the peach was important. As Seremetakis (1994, 2) says: 'in the presence of all those "peaches," the absent peach became narrative. . . . My naming of its absence resurrected observations, commentaries, stories, some of which encapsulated whole epochs marked by their own sensibilities'.

Places, too, offer a way of perceiving change. Precisely because of the familiarity and apparently unchanging nature of places, change in place offers a stark way of experiencing the passing of time and evoking memory of the past. We have all experienced the unsettling sense of witnessing the same-but-different quality of houses and places we are familiar with, such as the houses we first grew up in our old hometowns. Because of the close-grained way in which we inhabit places, it is possible for places to seem familiar (their overall structural appearance and position in place is the same), yet the features within them have perceptually altered. We noted the significant relationship between things and places above, and the changing character of places is partly dependent on the constellation of things. We might think of things and places existing in a figure–ground relationship. Because things help people to orientate themselves within place, the alteration of things in place alters the character of place. It is as much the changing configuration of things in place as the changing physical character of place which emphasises difference. The differing character of places is then read through the presence and absence of both architectural forms and things.

We have seen, then, that the temporal relationship between material culture and people is critical to the evocation of memory. Memory is experienced precisely because of the temporal disjuncture between people and things. In the first instance memory is made apparent because of time lapsing between the primary experience of the object and the secondary experience of the same (or similar object). Here there is a temporal disjuncture between the initial experience of the object by the person and their reexperience of that object. The person has altered while the object remains the same. In the second instance the disjuncture between the primary physical character of the object and the secondary character of the object is subtly different and makes apparent the passing of time. In both cases the ability of material culture to evoke remembrance depends upon the physical endurance of the object and the temporal duration it occupies with respect to the duration of the human life span. It is precisely because the material world impinges upon the person in a physical and sensual way and occupies a different time span relative to the person that material culture offers a way of perceiving or cognising the passing of time. It is because of the physical ability of objects to presence the past, and because their physical change indexes the past, that the passing of time is made apparent and it is through the sensual and physical medium of material culture that times past are reexperienced. It is because of, and through the medium of, the temporal framework offered by material culture that memory is produced and made apparent.

PERFORMING REMEMBRANCE

Material culture evokes the past because of the way in which its physical and sensual character impinges upon and interacts with the person. Sensually, objects index past bodily experience. Such experience is not embodied or retained in objects in any empirical sense; rather, it is the dialogic relationship between person and thing that evokes recall. Sensual experience is sedimented in the body through repetition. This may occur at the level of the quotidian or may occur at cyclical, seasonal, or periodic intervals. We can think of this sensual exchange between person and thing as a form of citation. Objects index past experience and act as a form of 'material citation'; the past is simultaneously referenced and reiterated. Citations may then occur on a daily level through the repetition of daily activities, or they may occur over more extensive periods. The important point here is that objects reference the past precisely because of their sensual qualities. By reiterating past experience sensually, material citations not only refer to the past but are also directed towards future experience.

This is illustrated by an example from Frederik Barth's analysis of the initiation ceremonies of the Mountain Ok of Papua New Guinea and West Papua (Irian Jaya):

> The initiation makes up a many-day, complex ritual sequence with considerable dramatic nerve. Now the cult master is supposed to make its secrets of the ancestors suddenly and powerfully manifest, shaping the messages in the visual idioms to make them compelling so that they will do their work to induce fertility and inform and transform the novices. This is emphatically not an occasion for personal invention, which would compromise the messages' validity as the visions of the ancestors. Yet a mere mechanical repetition of the ritual of many years ago may not be adequate, even if the cult master were capable of the rote memory needed: it has to be a re-creation of revelation, with the force to compel the audience of both novices and more advanced knowers. In such a situation, one would expect the cult master, in an honest effort to reproduce the mystery, to be very concerned to secure a maximally effective performance. (Barth 2002, 5)

As we can see from this account, performance, drama, and revelation are all emphasised as being critically important to the successful completion of ritual. Accompanying this dramatic performance was the use of 'animal species, ancestral bones, natural substances, fire, water and colours' along with 'taboos, deception, pain, and fear, sacrifice, spells, prayers and songs' (Barth 2002, 4). Remembrance is reinforced and precipitated by the use of sensually charged substances whose significance is literally impressed upon the bodies of initiates through bodily pain as well as the repetitious nature of spells and songs.

Remembrance is in part produced by the nature and drama of action. Here material culture acts as a means of embodying the past and presenting the future. As material citations, these practices are doubly effective: they serve to reiterate past practices, and they do so because of the sensually and dramatically spectacular nature of the ritual. However, these ritual actions are also directed towards future moments of remembrance. The effectiveness of the performance will be judged on how well it is remembered by both initiates and audience alike. To ensure that this is the case, sensually spectacular objects are employed in a dramatic and repetitious sequence of activities.

We established above that memories are evoked by the sensual reiteration of interactions between people and things. Clearly the sensual attributes of material culture are of signal importance here, but the way in which objects are enrolled in the performance of activities of remembrance is also crucial. The significance of performance is highlighted in Judith Butler's analysis of the performativity of speech (Butler 1997). It is not only *what* is spoken but *how* it is spoken that is critical to how speech may injure or affect the person. She invokes Austin's distinction between illocutionary speech and perlocutionary speech to distinguish how speech impresses itself upon the body. Illocutionary speech acts are those that in saying do what they say and do it in the moment of saying. Perlocutionary speech acts produce a certain effect as their consequence. The distinction between these two forms of speech turns on when they produce effects, with illocutionary speech the effect is immediate – by saying something you are simultaneously doing – Butler (1997, 17) uses as an example a judge saying, 'I sentence you'. By uttering perlocutionary speech, by contrast, the consequences produced are temporally distinct.

I find this discussion of linguistic performance helpful for thinking about material performances and how they relate to the production of memory. A critical point we need to adopt from this discussion is the point that the character of performance is crucial to understanding the effect of that performance. When discussing the character of material performances we need to be mindful of both the material properties of the objects and how these properties are deployed in activities.

A key difference between speech acts and material performances lies in the presentational character of material culture. As Susanne Langer (1942, 79–102) observes, objects do not work grammatically in the same way that words in a sentence do. Words are sequential and to perform their work they must be heard in sequence as language unfolds. Artefacts, by contrast, present themselves with all their aspects at one time (Tilley 1999, 260–73). Unlike speech, it is difficult to treat material culture as producing either illocutionary or perlocutionary effects. Language unfolds, as Langer says, and in this sequential unfolding we can define either a primary or secondary effect. Material culture endures and its performative effect is *both* immediate and enduring.

We are best considering the mnemonic aspects of material culture as performative in both an illocutionary and perlocutionary sense. Performances utilising material culture are simultaneously illocutionary and perlocutionary. For example, habitual actions are repetitive and therefore illocutionary in their effect. But such habitual activities also have a perlocutionary dimension because – as actions have been sensually sedimented in the body – they can be evoked by sensual experience at a later stage. The effects of habitual actions endure. By contrast, dramatic performances like those of the initiation rituals of the Mountain Ok are perlocutionary in their overall effect – they are meant to impress the memory of events on the body through use of powerful substances and dramatic actions (Whitehouse 1996). However, their performance is also illocutionary because the performance of such actions produces the ritual.

The relationship between the illocutionary and perlocutionary effect of material performances depends upon a relationship between the tempo of activities and the material culture used in these activities. How does material culture produce mnemonic or sensual effects? To consider this let us return to Gell's analysis of artworks. Gell (1998) describes the way in which artworks captivate the viewer. They do so because of the technical expertise displayed in their manufacture and the visual complexity of design. Visual captivation is a component of a wider process by which people are attached visually, emotionally, and physically to material culture. The mnemonic capacity of artfully designed objects is not emphasised by Gell but is surely a critical component of captivation. More memorable and visually spectacular objects will come to mind more easily and therefore will be closer objects of attachment. I want to widen the discussion of captivation and the attachment between people and things by considering the wider sensory effects produced by material culture. If we wish to consider how objects affect people both physically and mnemonically, we need to widen our net. It is not only complex design that has visual effect but also aspects such as colour, brightness, and contrast that will have a visual and mnemonic effect. Similarly, size and scale will also determine visual impact and memorability.

The emotive effect of material culture is critical to its ability to produce memorable experience. The emotive effect of material culture is bound up with an objects sensory impact and evaluation. When speaking about the emotive force of material culture it is important that we distance ourselves from the possibility that specific objects embody certain emotions, rather their sensual appreciation and use in specific social performances, produces emotion. Returning to my earlier discussion of the impact of performance, emotions are produced in and through the act of performance. Emotions are shaped by performance.

Gosden (2004b) has recently discussed the relationship between emotion and material culture. He makes the point that the sensual appeal of objects is grounded in a relational system of aesthetic appreciation. Further, he points out that the multisensorial nature of our engagement with the material world takes on the complexity of emotional experience. Actions of the body and the material settings this takes place are vital to the valence and intensity of the performance (Gosden 2004b, 36).

The potential of an object to be remembered will partly depend upon its emotive force. The capacity for an object to produce an emotive reaction will depend upon its sensual qualities. These qualities are valued in a relational framework as a system of differences. Finally, the ability of objects to produce a memorable experience depends upon its role in social performance. The lengthy duration and long-term effects of memories associated with traumatic social actions is well known (Cappelletto 2003; Lambek and Antze 1996; Whitehouse 1996). Cappelletto (2003, 251–2) discusses the significance of visual images for the retention of memories of massacre and trauma during the German occupation of two Tuscan villages during the Second World War. She describes images as an 'emotional experience in visual form' and highlights the significance of sensual (and especially visual) experience for the formation of memories.

As noted above the use of spectacular objects in dramatic performances is likely to produce long-term mnemonic effects. In terms of dramatic force visually or sensually spectacular events need little reiteration to be remembered; the visual and sensual dimension of artefacts and the drama of performance carries perlocutionary force. By contrast, mundane objects require numerous citational events (in habitual actions) to be remembered. Each of these will produce short-term effects although – through repetition – these serve to also produce long-term memories. The texture and duration of memories is therefore relational and depends upon differences in the regularity and tempo of practice, their dramatic force, and the sensual quality of the substances used in social practices.

PERFORMANCE AND PERSON

In considering the role of material culture in performances and the mnemonic effects objects produce on people, I return to the discussion with which I began this chapter. Although consideration of the relationship between memory and history is important, we also need to consider how the two relate to practice. Moreover, it is critical that we also acknowledge the role of performance in the constitution of persons.

I began by outlining the point that the temporality of things is best understood in relation to the person. I argued this is key to understanding how time is culturally apprehended. History and collective memory tends to be visualised or materialised in concrete and permanent form, whereas personal memories tend to be visualised or materialised in ephemeral material forms. By focussing on the relational structure of mnemonic practice, the division between collective and individual remembering blurs; each is viewed through the lens of the other. We have also considered the way in which, as embodiments of past activity, objects sensually affect people at both the collective and individual levels. Objects and people are therefore recursively related and it is through this interaction that time is cognised and memory produced.

The relationship between the temporality of the person and the variable durability of material objects is central to my analysis. I emphasise the point that notions of history and memory are produced by people's aesthetic and temporal comprehension/evaluation of the material world. However, we also need to consider the point that history is not just created by people but is also something that creates persons (Bloch 1998, 69). Bloch (1998, 70–1) discusses the major contrasts between Plato and Aristotle's view of memory and the person. For Plato, originary humans knew everything of significance from the outset. Unfortunately, due to the vicissitudes of time, they forgot. People therefore need to learn afresh, but learning here is a process of remembering what they already knew. When learning something new, people are simply recalling original and unchanging truth.

Conversely, Aristole thought that people were created by what they learnt; their minds were shaped by new knowledge, which shaped it as they remembered it and used what they remembered. For Aristole, to remember is to search for the imprint of past information or events, which are overlain by more recent memories. This model of memory closely resembles the view of memory we saw manifested by Locke and cognitive scientists like Donald in Chapter 1.

These views of memory are linked to two distinctive views of history. Platonists sees the person as aloof from history, whereas for Aristotle the person is in a dialectic relationship with history. As Bloch (1998, 71) points out, these two views of history and memory are inseparably linked to differing concepts of the person. Bloch uses this discussion as a means of drawing out the differences in notions of personhood in three societies: the Sadah of northern Yemen, the Bicolano of the central Philippines, and the Merina of Madagascar. The Sadah, as descendants of the Prophet Mohammed, are privileged vessels of divine and legal knowledge by the fact of their ancestry. As Bloch shows, such a conception carries with it a contradiction: some descendants may be holy and wise; however, others may be lazy and ignorant. Equally, nondescendants of the prophet may be wiser and more holy. The contradiction is transcended by determining that descendants of the Prophet, because of their original contact with God, have something in their inherited potential which makes them develop more holiness and wisdom than lesser people. The Sadah person is therefore unchanged by history, and the living of life and attainment of knowledge is simply a perpetuation of past knowledge and a projection of this unchanging knowledge into the future.

As poor peasants the Bicolano, by contrast, represent themselves as people who have nothing. They describe themselves as people who are at the mercy of more powerful others – rich landowners, government officials, and colonial powers like Spain and America. The Bicolanos feel themselves to have been shaped by history, albeit the external forces of colonial change. The value of becoming and metamorphosis is important to them.

The Merina conception of person and history sits betwixt and between these two views. The Merina are likewise open to change and the external forces of history. However, as members of descent groups they are also tied to static conceptions of history. Thus while many Merina are flexible to the forces of history, to the extent that they live most of their lives in France, on death their corpses are flown back to Madagascar at great expense to be permanently placed in the stone tombs of their ancestors. People are therefore both motile and static.

Interestingly, Bloch notes that these conceptions of the person determine how mnemonic objects are treated. For the Sadah, the Quran is a means of accessing eternal truth; for the Bicolano the wooden statues of saints were not so much conserved as thought to have grown and decayed, having a mutable life cycle like that of a person. Finally, for the Merina, the tomb represented a fixed point in a mobile and changing world. The conception of time and memory is critical to the formation of the person and to the sense in which material culture is utilised as a mnemonic. The practices in which material culture is employed simultaneously produce a conception of the person and a mode of remembrance. Memory and the person are thereby imbricated or enfolded in practice.

4

Improvising Culture

What links together purposive human acts is not the
presence of the environment as a continuous adver-
sary, but the network of expectations and retained
memories which provides the context for the projecting forward of human agency. (Thomas 1996a,
37)

In Chapter 3, I examined the way in which societies situate
themselves in time using material culture. I showed how
the materiality of objects is employed to signify qualitative
temporal differences. I suggested that these systems of differences are produced and reproduced by the performance of
activities which engender an active process of remembrance.
I described this process as something akin to literary citation

in which the citation of a work both refers to and revitalises its significance. In this chapter, I examine this concept further. I argue that if we accept citation as a useful device for thinking about the relationship between past and present activities, then the concept forces us to rethink how we conceptualise cultural practice more generally. In Chapter 3, I considered the nature of systems of differences synchronically over a single unitary historical period; in this chapter I discuss how the notion of citation helps us think diachronically about the nature of social change. In Julian Thomas's terms, I aim to examine the network of expectations and retained memories which produce the projection forward of human agency.

▪ CULTURE: AN OPEN-AND SHUT CASE?

The world which people inhabit is complex and multilayered and at any one time people may be occupying territory containing objects from multiple periods of history (Bergson (1991[1908]). As discussed, materials with different degrees of permanence or ephemerality will impinge on human societies in different ways and will be accounted for depending upon how they relate to the time span of the human life cycle. At different points in history certain aspects of the past will be emphasised while others are placed in the background. Consider, for example, the way in which the classical world formed an important template for people in Renaissance Italy or the way in which the art of earlier pre-Colombian cultures was revived by the Aztecs (Umberger 1987). In both of these cases the past was not copied slavishly but was interpreted afresh and helped to revitalise later epochs of history. The idiosyncratic nature of these periods of revivalism or antiquarianism jars with the traditionally ordered accounts of cultural succession favoured by archaeologists (Olivier 2001).

Such a realisation alters the way in which archaeologists deal with time. Gavin Lucas (Lucas 2004, 24–31) argues that a linear approach to time is unsatisfactory for dealing with the complexities of the material record of the past. He draws on the philosopher Edmund Husserl to suggest that at any one moment in time a succession of other moments impinge upon the present and mediate and shape the experience of the present. As a result, Lucas proposes that we adopt a nonlinear approach to chronology (Lucas 2004, 59). However, he has less to say about what a nonlinear chronology might look like in practice (though see Holtorf 2002) and how this might determine our approach to social change. The purpose of the present chapter is to explore the implications of Lucas's argument in this direction.

In what follows I provide a brief overview of changing approaches to the concept of culture. Throughout I characterise the way in which archaeologists have dealt with cultural change as either 'closed' or 'open'. I suggest that of the two approaches those which deal with culture as 'open' is more helpful to us in accounting for the multilayered nature of the way the past is drawn on to produce cultural change. Alongside this distinction we also observe a major difference between those who treat culture as a substantive entity and those who treat culture as an analytic category. The differing views of culture broadly define themselves along the faultlines seen below:

Culture as analytic category: culture as substantive entity
Culture viewed as 'open':   culture viewed as 'closed'

As we will see, views of culture as 'closed' or 'open' are concomitant upon descriptions of culture as either a substantive entity or analytic category.

Substantive Approaches to Culture

Is culture a substantive material entity which we can grasp in the external world? As archaeologists, we often beguile ourselves into thinking as such. This occurs because we believe that we can classify culture concretely through the occurrence of distinct forms of artefacts. The assumption that culture is materially expressed in the distinctive form of certain artefacts and the documentation of such artefacts across areas of geographical space or units of time are a hallmark of culture-history (e.g., Childe 1981[1950]). As Thomas (1996a, 20–5) shows, culture-history is founded upon the notion of holism. Thomas traces the holistic thinking of V. Gordon Childe – one of the prime European exponents of culture-history – to his influence by Western Marxist philosophy. Holism proposes that the parts of any social totality are comprehensible only through an appreciation of the whole. Such thinking requires that cultures be seen as real and substantive entities around which can be drawn conceptual boundaries. Cultures are therefore viewed as functioning wholes set apart from other cultures. Thus the definition of a single culture requires that it be abstracted from other cultures. According to this model of culture, change rarely occurs to cultures from within but happens mainly through external contact. As Thomas notes, 'as a Marxist Childe might have been expected to emphasise social conflict and contradiction, we could suggest that his adherence to the Hegelian notion of the expressive totality had the implication that culture was related to norms and values held in common by all members of society' (Thomas 1996a, 25). Social change was therefore something that occurred somewhere at a distance and had an external influence upon a given culture.

How did conceptualisations of culture differ for New or processual archaeologists? As Siân Jones (1997, 26–9) shows, although the adoption of New or processual archaeology was largely founded upon a critique of the normative conception of culture in culture-history (in which culture is treated as a set of norms or values held in common by all members of society), the reconceptualisation of culture as a system often involved the retention of normative views of culture. As an alternative to traditional accounts of archaeological cultures, New archaeologists argued that societies constituted integrated systems, made up of different functioning subsystems. Here the role of culture is primarily functional, as it facilitates the process of adaptation and human evolution (Binford 1972, 107). For New or processual archaeologists, archaeological remains were to be regarded as the product of past cultural processes rather than the reflection of cultural norms.

The description of material evidence shifted from the definition of cultural groups to the definition of societies of varying size and functional complexity: bands, tribes, chiefdoms, or states (e.g., Earle 1991). In fact this method of classifying societies was evident in earlier accounts. For example, Childe uses a broadly similar division of societies in his analysis of prehistoric Europe (Childe 1981[1950]).

For New or processual archaeologists, social change could now be conceptualised as occurring from within, as stasis and change depended upon the smooth functioning – or homeostasis – of competing subsystems within the culture as a whole. It was less cultural change than social change that became the object of study. The transformation or evolution from smaller societies to those of greater size and complexity – or the interaction between social groups of similar size (peer polity interaction; Renfrew and Cherry 1986) became important focusses of analysis (Earle and Ericson 1977).

It is easy to see that again the view of cultures as integrated systems made up of differentially functioning subsystems is another example of holism. Such a view requires a prior definition of precisely which subsystems comprise a culture before explaining the processes by which such subsystems might operate to sustain a given culture.

A further research strand in this tradition deals explicitly with the evolution and transmission of culture (Shennan 2002). Drawing upon the neo-Darwinist thinking of Richard Dawkins, cultural ideas are modelled as 'memes', or units, of cultural information. Just like their genetic predecessors (genes), memes are seen to pass on cultural information by inheritance. Artefacts are viewed as extended cultural phenotypes whose change over time is affected by the environment of humans within which they find themselves.

Curiously, although cultural transmission theory stands in contradistinction to interpretative or postprocessual approaches to the past (we will discuss these in more detail below), the notion of artefacts as cultural phenotypes is equally idealist. As shown in Chapter 1, the idea that artefacts might be signs or vehicles for the expression of abstract concepts tends to overlook the materiality of artefacts. The notion of artefacts as cultural phenotypes seems to enact the same error because artefacts are treated simply as carriers of information. The idea that artefacts-as-memes can be viewed as extended phenotypes returns us to the problems with the notion of external symbolic storage with which I began this volume: artefacts are conceptualised as mere storehouses or banks for information, their material properties play little part in the transmission and evocation of knowledge or memory.

The concept of memes constitutes, par excellence, an example of the reification and objectification of culture; culture is here literally viewed as a substantive entity which acts of its own volition. In practice, the discussion of artefacts as cultural phenotypes returns us to the *modus operandi* of culture-history as artefacts are now mapped as units of information extending over time and space. However, unlike culture-history, material culture is no longer the expression of commonly held ideas and beliefs; rather, 'the key to tracing traditions and understanding how they are maintained and why they change is to put the artefact (or other) tradition at the centre of our investigation, *not* people' (Shennan 2002, 266, original emphasis). This proposition seems to do damage to the people of the past because their social relations are absent from our analyses; equally, it damages the role of the artefact, because, as I've argued, the material properties of the artefact are also absent from analyses as artefacts become mere vehicles for the transmission of information.

Rather like geneticists who have no interest or understanding of animal physiology or behaviour and only a passing interest in the mechanisms of animal reproduction, any theory which separates out the process of cultural transmission from an understanding of the material properties of artefacts and the way those material properties are employed in practice to reproduce or transmit cultural ideas is unsustainable. One is left wondering what culture is for: why is it worth transmitting? Why is it even worthy of study?

Analytic Approaches to Culture

For those who view cultural transmission as a simple matter of information transfer, the form of the artefact is everything. It is only the fidelity or similarity of form which allows the archaeologist to determine that information has been successfully transferred (see Shennan 2002, 78–83). Such a view is predicated upon the notion that culture is a substantive entity which inheres in the form of the artefact. Such a view ignores the role of context.

Anthropological examples abound which foreground the significance of context. For example, Nicholas Thomas (1990) discusses the importation of guns to the islands of the Marquesas in the Pacific. Guns were understood and utilised in the context of indigenous values and according to the system of indigenous warfare; they did not affect a wholesale adoption of European values as if by a form of cultural osmosis. Cultural context matters; the mere transference of artefacts or techniques from one context to another is an insufficient motivator of cultural change and cannot be taken as an indication of such.

My appeal for the consideration of context shifts us from substantive approaches to culture to analytic approaches. Strathern (1996) makes the important point that culture is not a thing. It can neither be grasped nor is it an autonomous entity that we can group, classify, and define. She observes that we cannot, for example, define a population as possessing half a culture or one-and-a-half cultures. It is not divisible precisely because it is an abstraction, a tool for thinking with.

How then do we observe culture, if it is abstract? Cultural practices reveal themselves to us, precisely because they are practised. One way in which we can consider cultural practice is through the analysis of the production of cultural meanings. Ian Hodder (1986) argues that a major aim of archaeological analysis is to

> make abstractions from the symbolic functions of the
> objects . . . [excavated by archaeologists] . . . in order to
> identify the meaning content behind them, and this

involve[s] explaining how the ideas denoted by material symbols themselves play a part in structuring society. (Hodder
1986, 124–5)

This quote very clearly signals that we are now dealing with
culture as the realm of ideas.

In Ian Hodder's contextual approach, the analysis of past cultural
meanings is achieved by treating the archaeological record as a text
in which the meaning of any symbol (an artefact, for example) is
derived from the associations and differences established between it
and other symbols (other artefacts). Repeated patterns of association
or exclusion constitute the archaeological text.

Such a view provides a nuanced understanding of cultural meaning. Culture is no longer viewed simply as a device for adaptation or
as a unit of cultural information; culture is not expressed in the form
of the artefact but in the arrangement of artefacts. The way in which
artefacts are patterned or arranged expresses cultural differences. As
Siân Jones notes, if we are to understand cultural differences (such as
ethnicity) archaeologically it is essential that we shift our focus from
artefacts as the embodiment of culture to the use of artefacts in cultural *practices* (Jones 1997, 119–27). The advantage of this approach
to culture is that it promotes a view of culture as *open-ended and fluid*;
cultural difference is signalled by the changing use of artefacts.

However, in practice, the contextual approach often involves
artificially circumscribing a cultural group in order that we interpret
the associations and differences between material culture groupings.
Indeed, the ability of symbolic approaches to provide a holistic cultural analysis is discussed by Hodder (1995, 24–7). Often this results
in interpreting cultural meaning at a meta-level of abstraction. A
good example of this is Hodder's (1990) discussion of the European
Neolithic as the playing out of a series of symbolic principles. Such an
analysis involves conceptually circumscribing the area of study ('The
European Neolithic') and tends to divorce the analysis of cultural
meaning from the historical conditions that helped to create them
(Barrrett 1987, 471). Is the meaning evoked by Hodder part of an

idealised cultural system in the European Neolithic? Was it available to all or maintained by the practices of particular groups? Are those people who built monuments in the third and fourth millennia BC in Britain aware that they are drawing on symbolic schemes produced in central Europe in the fifth millennium BC, or indeed in Anatolia in the sixth or seventh millennium BC? As Barrett (1987, 471) notes, questions such as those above expose a fundamental problem: meaning appears to have emerged outside any specified social context. Through a process of abstraction contextual archaeology performs a process of decontextualisation in which meaning is apparent only to those in a position to read the culture from the outside; in effect cultural groups again emerge as closed systems or entities.

Beyond Context: Rethinking Contextual Archaeology

There are other problems with the concept of contextual archaeology. One of these emerges from the analysis of the cultural biography of artefacts. As is well known, the concept of artefact biographies proposes that the use-life of an artefact may be considered analogous to the human life course, encapsulating the events of birth, growth, maturation, and, eventually, death. There is an extensive literature on this subject, which has been reviewed elsewhere (Gosden and Marshall 1999; Jones 2002a; Meskell 2004; Tilley 1996). I want to consider how cultural biographies are constructed. As Tilley (1996) indicates, in the absence of ethnographic observation or written records, cultural biographies are idealised; they encompass the life course of classes of artefacts rather than individual artefacts. This involves linking the various contexts within which specific artefacts are deposited to map their life course. A biographical route is charted in the imagination as the object is presumed to move from one context to another. For example, in my own work on Late Neolithic Grooved Ware pottery in Orkney I examined certain categories of pots from production in the settlement to their eventual deposition in henges and passage tombs (Jones 2000, 2002a). Although thin-section petrology was used as a means of tracing specific pots from context to context, the career of certain categories of pots was nevertheless idealised. What interests me here is how the notion of context functions when we reconstruct artefact biographies. Context does not so much frame the meaning of the artefact; rather, meaning bleeds or flows beyond the context: it is carried with the artefact. By producing cultural biographies of this kind we are presuming that meaning flows from context to context as the artefact is moved from one context to another; we are no longer treating the archaeological text as a set of signs whose patterns of association and differences enable us to establish an abstracted cultural code.

In many ways this mode of analysis circumvents some of the problems with contextual archaeology raised above, because by tracing the movement of artefacts from one context to another we can conceptualise how meaning may shift through practical action. But all is not well. Where does this leave the concept of context? How do we define or tie down meaning if meaning flows beyond context? These questions lead us to consider the critique of Saussurean linguistics made by Jacques Derrida, which is of special relevance to our understanding of contextual archaeology. Derrida questioned the simple link made by Saussure between signifier and signified, assumed to be performed by the listener upon hearing words in a sentence (signifiers) and linking them to concrete objects (signifieds). Such an assumption – for Derrida – further assumed the existence of a 'transcendental signified', which is able to circumscribe the meaning of any signifier. The only way for such a signifier to be understood is through the medium of another signifier; such a concept of course leads to an infinite regress of signifiers. Meaning is always deferred along chains of signification.

Hodder (1986) employs Derrida's notion of the deferral of meaning to propose a relational contextual framework for meaning, although I would argue that in practice much contextual analysis has leaned heavily upon the approaches of structuralism, rather than the poststructuralist position offered by Derrida. Hodder employs Derrida to argue for a contextual approach to meaning in material culture in which meaning is deferred along chains of signification. Here I do not so much want to critique the concept of contextual archaeology as recast it for another purpose.

To do this I want to return to a discussion of traces. As shown in Chapter 1, Derrida's use of the term *trace* expresses the absence of full and present meaning: meaning is differential; it is continually referred onwards from one term to another – each linguistic term has meaning only due to its difference from the next. Meaning leaves traces as it shifts from one term to another. Rather than tying down meaning I believe a more fruitful task is to examine the trace of meaning along various pathways of signification. I believe this is a helpful perspective to take if we are interested in how objects act as mnemonic traces; how are they related to past and future objects? To determine the connections between objects in these pathways of signification we need to focus on difference. How does object X differ from objects Y and Z? By determining difference and similarity we are thus able to examine the influence one artefact has upon the production of the next. My interest is less in determining the meaning of material culture and more in analysing the connections between artefacts, embodied by physical or material traces. In fact, if we take on board Peirce's view that meaning derives from engagement, discussed at the beginning of Chapter 2, then we need to look at the connections amongst meanings if we are to understand the full meaning of an object. The deferral of meaning along chains of signification is therefore an essential means by which we understand the *totality* of an object's meaning.

To help us think about this I want to reintroduce two key concepts, which emerged in previous chapters: the notion of the *index* and the idea of *citation*. The first concept (the index) is derived from the philosophy of Charles Sanders Peirce, the second concept ultimately arises from the work of Jacques Derrida (Derrida 2001[1978]), via the work of Judith Butler (1993). I want to employ these two concepts fairly loosely, because I believe they ultimately describe the same processes, in particular, the ways in which signs are related to each other. In using the terms *index* or *citation* I want to emphasise the way in which – as cultural performances – artefacts are situated in networks of referentiality; the way in which the 'event' of artefact production or use refers to both past and future events (see Fig. 5). I conceptualise such networks in the same way that Gell (1998, 232–58) describes artworks as components of wider *oeuvres*. For Gell the *oeuvre* consists of objects extended in space and time, each related to their neighbour due to the possession of traces in common. Each object therefore possesses traces that embody retentions from previous objects or protentions to a future object. Objects therefore exist as nodes in networks in which each object relates to others strung out through time and space. Such a condition exists because each object is the instansiation (or actualisation) of the social relations of either a single person or a group of people.

I want to introduce the term *indexical field* to describe such a network because it captures the way in which artefacts act as nodes in a web or network of relations; each artefact is an index of past artefacts (retentions) and of future artefacts (protentions). The alternative term *citational field* similarly relates to the way in which artefacts are components of a field or network of relationships. The concept of citation differs from the index because it also captures the way in which, as novel cultural performances, the production of artefacts draws on past artefacts and in doing so both reiterates and transforms them. It is helpful to consider citations as activities which both reiterate past events and through the creative juxtaposition of differing elements of past events, also recombine to create fresh cultural performances.

This process of remaking in performance is nicely captured by the artist Barbara Bolt in her analysis of art practice. Here she uses dance and drawing as examples of cultural performance which slip between the net of symbolic (or representationalist) approaches:

> The mutability and multiplicity...of so many different traces referring back to other traces...is analogous to improvisations in dance. A dance improvisation begins by referring back, to other dances, to other steps and

movements. In the movement back, in the recall, the dancers move forward and the dance breaks open and divides and multiplies. It becomes a production, both a presence and a representation. Drawing could be similarly described. One begins by referring back: to the pedagogy of one's training, to the motif, to the imagination or whatever it is. However in the movement back and forward, from looking up and down and looking back, recalling and doing, there emerges a multiplicity where many traces or marks refer back to other traces and the traces of others. In the process of doing, we find we are no longer in the grip of representation. (Bolt 2004, 35)

By considering cultural performances (or artefacts as the products of performance) to operate in this way – as components of fields of referentiality – how do we understand context to function? Rather than treating context as framing meaning we are perhaps better thinking of context participating in the recombination or reproduction of meaning; contexts are 'frozen moments' along chains of reference and as such contexts are important participants in the process of meaning production and re-production. As Hodder (1995, 15) notes, 'there is a dialectical relationship between object and context . . . the context both gives meaning to and gains meaning from an object'.

The advantage of thinking of the relationships or connections between artefacts in terms of a network is that such a model does not rely on linear notions of time. There are two major ways in which we can think about artefacts connecting networks together depending upon whether artefacts physically endure or are ephemeral. The first would occur where material culture physically endures over time. Here we can think of artefacts projecting their influence over time and acting as indexes or objects worthy of citation over considerable periods of time; they physically *extend through* networks over time (see Fig. 5, following). A good example of this is Richard Hingley's (1996) analysis of the influence of Neolithic material culture on Iron

TRADITION DEVELOPED FROM PAST MATERIAL CULTURE

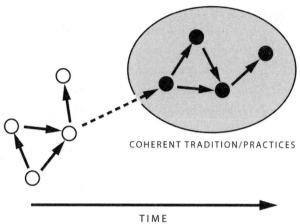

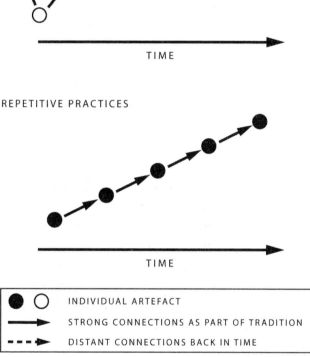

COHERENT TRADITION/PRACTICES

TIME

5. The position of artefacts in networks of referentiality. In the upper diagram a network of traditions refers back to an earlier artefact. In the lower diagram networks of traditions are created through repetitive practices.

REPETITIVE PRACTICES

TIME

● ○   INDIVIDUAL ARTEFACT

⟶   STRONG CONNECTIONS AS PART OF TRADITION

⤑   DISTANT CONNECTIONS BACK IN TIME

Age populations in Scotland. For example, the Neolithic chambered tomb at the Calf of Eday, Orkney was reopened during the Iron Age, and the designs on Early Neolithic pottery was cited in the decorative schemes of Iron Age pottery. Although the production of Neolithic pottery and Iron Age pottery is separated by over 1,000 years, due to the endurance of Neolithic pottery, it served as an object for citation by Iron Age potters.

Alternatively, if artefacts are ephemeral, then they will extend through networks to a much lesser degree; in order that ephemeral artefacts influence the future they must be bound up with repetitive practices. So we can imagine a series of short connections between artefacts in networks and the use of ephemeral artefacts in a continuous process of citation (see Fig 5). A good example of this comes from Richard Bradley's analysis of depositional practices during the European Neolithic and Early Bronze Age (Bradley 1990). Axes of stone, and eventually of bronze, continued to be deposited as votive offerings over a period of millennia. Physically the objects were not ephemeral, although the practice in which they were involved rendered them so as they were taken out of circulation. The practice of deposition involves a process of repetitive citation in which past practices and the artefacts associated with them were continually drawn on in order that they were understood.

The approach I am advocating alters the way in which we understand change. Rather than viewing time as units which move forward in a linear fashion, and treating artefacts as bound up with specific units of time (e.g., Neolithic polished stone axes and Bronze Age metalwork), we adopt what I believe to be a more realistic position in which artefacts extend over time to different degrees (depending upon their physical endurance or the practices in which they are involved) and have the ability to influence events in the future. The extent to which artefacts influence the future is determined by the practices that connect artefacts. This approach therefore offers a truly open conceptualisation of culture. Cultural practices are components of networks of referentiality, and as such change can occur by drawing on any other component of the network. Such an approach offers us a situated view of context (Barrett 1987) because at any one point in a network it allows us to understand the myriad threads of influence which shape cultural practices.

Networks can both constrain and enable change depending upon the components that are drawn on at any one time. I now want to explore this idea by turning to the discussion of open and closed works in music.

OPEN AND CLOSED VIEWS OF CULTURE: THE EXAMPLE OF MUSICAL PRACTICE

At this juncture I want to develop the notion of 'open' and 'closed' views of culture. Music has more than once provided an analogy for culture (Barthes 1977; Levi-Strauss 1969), and here I focus on the musical practices of composition and improvisation to help us think more broadly about different approaches to cultural practice. Over the course of the twentieth century classical music underwent a series of radical shifts. Some commentators believe this shift marks a boundary between two technological eras: the age of print and the age of recording (Cutler 2004). Broadly speaking we can think of this in terms of two different treatments of the musical score (Cox and Warner 2004). The conventional musical score represents a 'closed' work which determines pitch, rhythm, meter, instrumentation, and formal shape, offering only minor latitude for interpretation by individual performers. By contrast, during the 1950s and 1960s, a series of composers began to produce 'open' works that gave huge freedom to performers. Often two faithful productions of such compositions could produce radically different musical experiences.

Umberto Eco (2004) discusses some examples of 'openess' in terms of musical composition and performance. For example, in *Klavierstück XI* by Karlheinz Stockhausen, the composer presents the performer with a single large sheet of music paper with a series of note groupings. The task of the performer is then to choose amongst these groupings, first the one to start the piece and, next, for the successive units in the order which they elect to weld them together. Another example comes from Luciano Berio's *Sequenza for Solo Flute* in which the composer presents the performer with a text which predetermines the sequence and intensity of the sounds to be played. However, the performer is left to choose how long to hold a note within the framework provided.

Eco goes on to relate the concept of the 'open' work (which emerged in the midtwentieth century) with the comparable findings of contemporary physics. In particular, he invokes Heisenberg's principle of complementarity, which rules that it is not possible to indicate the different behaviour patterns of an elementary particle simultaneously. Eco relates the indeterminacy of particle physics and the indeterminacy of works of art or music to the discard of a static view of order and a corresponding shift of intellectual authority to personal decision, choice, and social context (Eco 2004, 170). He goes on to develop the concept of openness to describe works as 'works in movement', which are characterized by the invitation to make the work together with the author and suggests that on a wider level works exist that, although organically complete, are open to a continuous generation of internal relations which the addressee must uncover and select in his or her act of perceiving the totality of incoming stimuli (Eco 2004, 173).

TRADITION AND INVENTION

I find these ideas stimulating for thinking about cultural practice more generally. I have already described cultural practices as performances composed of networks of referentiality in which artefacts act as indexes of the past and may be drawn on or 'cited'. The process of citation, as I described, draws on, reaffirms, and transforms cultural practice. Here I want to combine this view with the view of cultural practices as open works to be improvised by subsequent cultural practitioners. The notion that authorial works are open to later interpretation by the reader is encapsulated in the concept of the 'death of the author' (Barthes 1977) and has had considerable influence upon postprocessual or interpretative archaeology (see Hodder 1986; Tilley 1991). Here I am not especially interested in the concept of reading and interpretation; instead, I want to emphasise the generative aspect of the concept of 'works in movement'. The way in which compositions enable free movement and choice; compositions act as constraints or mediums for action which simultaneously allow for creativity. A series of commentators discussing the notion of creativity in the material record observe that it is the interplay between constraint and openness which acts as a prompt for creativity (Bradley 1998a; Hodder 1998b). The kind of interplay between the citation of traditional practices and the opening up of fresh approaches is well illustrated by Geismar's discussion of the production of contemporary art in Vanuatu. Vanuatu is a nation comprising over 70 islands in the Pacific southwest. Geismar (2004) discusses an exhibition held on the island of Erromango in which a painting by the artist Moses Jobo depicts a scene from the colonial history of the islands in which a missionary was butchered by Erromangans. The painting adopts a realistic style to reference an earlier picture of the event drawn but adds a bolt of divine light reaching from the sky to empashise missionary hagiography. Moses Jobo's painting is framed by painted barkcloth, referencing Erromangan tradition. As Geismar relates 'the exact appropriation of the image of the troublesome murders is used as a material method by which to overcome a series of divides: between Christians and non-Christians, and Erromangans and missionaries' (Geismar 2004, 52). The image is a citation of the past, which in the act of citation transforms past events in the context of the present; it acts as a node in a network of referentiality.

Given the openness and flexibility of 'tradition' I believe we need to rethink Hobsbawm's famous discussion relating to the invention of tradition (Hobsbawm 1983). While traditions are undoubtedly invented afresh, inventiveness is not confined to the creation of novel traditions. We also need to consider the *tradition of invention*. Tradition is both invented afresh out of the components of the past, while at the same time the components that make up a tradition are subject to a continuous process of revision and alteration. This process was discussed in Chapter 2. Whilst discussing commemoration I highlighted the importance of *recurrence*, the process of changing while staying the same. This is also a key aspect of tradition. In effect, cultural practice involves a continuous process of improvisation within the constraints imposed by the material residues of past peoples; a continuous process of creative production.

Stonehenge offers an excellent example of this kind of process:

The site was used for practically 1,500 years, yet elements
of every successive phase of construction and reconstruction are still visible to us today. They would have been even
more obvious in the past, when each of these features carried
a significance that is now lost. The surviving monument
encapsulates an extraordinary history, but its layout also
maintains a striking continuity from its earliest use to its
final phases. Throughout that time it was defined by the
same circular earthwork, with just two entrances control-
ling access from outside. After its construction, the bank
and ditch were respected but no longer maintained, yet in
virtually every phase the central area was occupied by circular settings of uprights, of stone and quite possibly of
timber. In more than one period the same parts of the monument provided a focus for intentional deposits of artefacts
and bones, while the landscape visible from the centre of
the site was abandoned, the remains of the first Stonehenge
could still be identified: the bank and ditch survived intact,
and shallow hollows containing offerings of human bone
and other material could still be recognised on the surface.
The monument remained the pivotal point of a landscape
in which the distribution of human activity was constantly
changing. (Bradley 1998b, 91–2)

Richard Bradley's account of Stonehenge captures the sense in which
traditions are subject to recurrent practices. Stonehenge provides a
constant or pivot within the landscape, yet activity is constantly
changing. Stonehenge remains, yet architecturally it is never the
same. At each stage of reconstruction features from the past either
provide platforms for change (they are mediums for citation) or
they remain unaltered. They cannot be ignored due to their physical presence. Improvisation occurs within the framework provided

by the physical settings of the past. Stonehenge is then a 'work in movement'.

ARTEFACTS AS NETWORKS

The discussion of the relationship between material culture and tradition returns us to an important point raised in Chapter 2: people and things are interstitial to each other. Things are the agents which enable people to act. Each is a component of a network which is reliant on the other. This is especially the case when we realise that things encapsulate, enfold, or 'black box', social relations. Black boxing is a term derived from the sociology of science which defines the way in which scientific and technical work is made invisible by its own success. If a machine works smoothly, the technical decisions embodied in its manufacture are not examined; rather, the input and output are the main focusses of attention (Latour 1999b, 304). The intentions of past people are therefore encapsulated in material form, and these material forms will act on people in the present. Callon (1991, 136) suggests we can think of technical objects as programs of action coordinating networks of roles. Objects act as nodes then that entrain other people in their production and use. For Callon (1991, 136), technical objects 'act, communicate, issue orders, interrupt one another and follow protocols'. This is easy to understand when dealing with a complex technical tool such as a computer. We are all familiar with computers interrupting the smooth flow of activity ('why won't the bloody thing print this document!'); this is because it has been designed to follow a strict set of instructions. Is this true of simpler technical objects? If we take a polished stone axe, for example, then it, too, has a precise set of protocols determined by its manufacture; its shape and form means that it affords a particular type of activity rather than another: chopping wood rather than grinding grain. As we saw in Chapter 2, the stone axe also enfolds social relations as the materials used in its manufacture, along with its movement from source and its exchange are all the result of complex social decisions.

In terms of the reproduction of cultural practices we can then see that the physical endurance of things is critical to the process of remaking, or, to put it in another way, 'technology is society made durable' (Latour 1991). Things not only act as indexes of past events, and not only serve as prompts for the reiteration of past activities, they also act as nodes that both encapsulate and coordinate activity. Artefacts thus more or less explicitly define and distribute roles to people and other artefacts. They serve to link together entities in networks. The way in which artefacts do this is the subject of the case studies in the next section of the book.

5

Continuous Houses, Perpetual Places

Commemoration and the Lives of Neolithic Houses

In the last series of chapters we have seen that the material properties of objects are crucial to their use in commemorative practices, that these properties are drawn on in commemorative performances, and that the temporal relationship between material culture and the person is significant to how objects are utilised. I want to reprise each of these points by discussing the example of houses in two regions of Neolithic Europe.

As archaeologists we are faced with a challenge when attempting to consider the long-term durability of social practices against the short-term nature of social change. Ian Hodder (1998a) deals with the relationship between structure and contingency by proposing the long-term durability of a symbolic scheme centred on the house which is played out over the course of the European Neolithic. In earlier works he proposes that the concept of the home – the *domus* – provides a metaphor for the domestication of society (Hodder 1990, 41). I have always felt uncomfortable with this interpretation because I found it difficult to see how the concept worked in practice. Clearly Hodder also had the same reservations because in a later revision of his ideas he offers a more concrete proposal (Hodder 1998a). Rather than treating the house as a metaphor for domestication, he notes that the very durability of the house is the means of its reproduction as a concept. He invokes the work of Bruno Latour to argue that the house itself acts as a seamless web linking the material and cultural. The house acts as a node in a network of relationships. In this sense the house is both a metaphor and a mechanism.

I find this idea useful because it encapsulates the way the concept of the house is expressed in and through its architecture; the house binds together social groups and creates a frame within which people were bound by ritual ties and historical associations (Hodder 1998a, 89). If we are to focus on the materiality of the house as a mechanism of social reproduction we need to consider not only how the durability of the house frames social practices but also how social practices provide a medium for change and continuity. We need to shift from considering the house as concept to considering the house as *process*.

Although I am persuaded by Hodder's argument, I believe that a sole focus on the durable nature of the house is predicated on a passive model of memory transmission, which tacitly assumes that the physical presence of material objects act as mnemonic prompts. The problems with this view were discussed in Chapters 1 and 2. If we are to focus on the transmission of the concept of the house we need to focus on a range of social practices and we need to be aware that differing social practices may engender quite different modes of cultural transmission, different concepts of memory, and, in turn, different conceptualisations of the person.

To examine how houses act as nodes for knitting together social relations I examine Neolithic house architecture and related activities in central Europe and compare these with Neolithic architectural constructions on the rim of Europe – in Scotland.

HOUSES AND SETTLEMENTS OF THE LINEAR POTTERY CULTURE

The houses and settlements of the Linear Pottery Culture of central Europe offer an excellent example of houses as both concept and process. The Linear Pottery Culture has tended to be discussed as a unity, although recent reassessments are beginning to stress the variability in the Linear Pottery Culture (Coudart 1998; Gronenborn 1999; Modderman 1988; Sommer 2001; Whittle 2003), using phrases like 'diversity in uniformity' (Modderman 1988) or 'variation on a basic theme' (Gronenborn 1999). Although we are increasingly recognising the variability in Linear Pottery Culture architecture, material culture, and burial across Europe it is also important not to lose sight of the similarities that have been drawn between sites across central Europe. In what follows I want to ask why we see such a degree of uniformity, but I also want to examine the Linear Pottery Culture as an illustration of culture as a form of network (Whittle 2003, 135), in which cultural practices are related as components of indexical or citational fields (see Chapters 3 and 4 for discussion of this concept). I will argue that if we are to understand Linear Pottery Culture houses as both concept and process our accounts need to take on board the recurrent 'same-but-different' quality of the Linear Pottery Culture. I focus principally on the character of the houses, settlements, and burials of the Linear Pottery Culture.

The Linear Pottery Culture (Linear Pottery Culture or LBK) is normally considered to span the period from around 5500 BC to 5000 BC, although some commentators suggest it could go back as early as 5700 BC (e.g., Price et al. 2001, 594; Sommer 2001, 250). The early history of this cultural group is uncertain, although Gronenborn (1999, 146–9) suggests it emerges from the social transformation from the Starcevo-Körös-Cris complex to the early Vinca on the Great Hungarian Plain. Kaczanowska and Kozlowski (2003, 232) note that in terms of lithic technology, raw material procurement, morphology, and function of stone tool assemblages there is a smooth evolutionary trend from the Körös-Starcevo to Linear Pottery Culture on the Great Hungarian Plain.

In the earliest phases of the Linear Pottery Culture in the east, two types of buildings were constructed. Small rectangular buildings, which are likely to have originated from the Körös house, were constructed without internal posts, the walls being strengthened by timber beams. In the same territory larger, post-constructed buildings were also built; these were more akin to the longhouses found in the west of Europe (Kaczanowska and Kozlowski 2003, 233). In this earliest phase we note variability, with houses of different dimensions and construction overlapping territorially.

It is likely that the classic components of the Linear Pottery Culture did not simultaneously come into being (Whittle 2003, 135); Gronenborn (1999) notes that we observe a degree of hybridity between elements of the Vinca culture and the AVK (Alföld Linear Pottery Culture, the local variant of the LBK on the Great Hungarian Plain). Elements of LBK pottery form and decoration are found in both culture groups; longhouse architecture is found in later AVK contexts.

Traditionally the Linear Pottery Culture is seen as a classic example of prehistoric migration with an apparent expansion in the earliest phases from northern Hungary to the Czech Republic, Slovakia, and eastern and northern Austria as far as the middle Rhine occurring between 5600 and 5200 BC (Gronenborn 1999). This is followed by a second phase of expansion eastwards as far as Poland and westwards as far as the Meuse; the middle phase sees a stabilisation, followed by a further phase of expansion west into the Hainaut region of southern Belgium and the Paris Basin (Coudart 1998, 17). After Price et al. (2001), the chronology can be divided into three phases in the east, early Ia 5700–5500 BC, early Ib 5500–5300 BC, and early Ic 5300–5200 BC, whereas the phases of expansion in the west are as follows: early I 5500–5300 BC, middle (Flomborn) 5300–5250 BC, and Late 5250–5000 BC.

Whether the process of settlement expansion occurs through colonisation or the acculturation of indigenous hunter-gatherer groups is a matter of some debate (Gronenborn 1999; Sommer 2001; Whittle 1996). I do not want to rehearse this issue here; instead, I want to examine the similarities and differences in settlement architecture across the region occupied by the Linear Pottery Culture. Homogeneity seems to characterise many elements of the Linear Pottery Culture, including pottery form and decoration, house architecture, and burial rites. I will discuss the last two of these as a means of charting processes of cultural change, stasis, and transmission.

The Linear Pottery Culture is exemplified by the architectural form of the post-built longhouse (Fig. 6). Longhouses are enormous structures – typically of five rows of posts, with the internal rows as roof supports and the external rows as wall supports. Walls were lined externally with daub, most likely derived from the borrow pits which run parallel to house wall exteriors. Houses varied in length from around 10 m to 30 m. Apart from the uniformity in house plan, a degree of uniformity occurs in the orientation of houses within individual settlements (Fig. 7). Contemporary houses in settlements were usually situated around 10 m apart and were often oriented in the same direction; in central Europe they are often oriented N-S, while in the west they are often oriented NW and W. The uniformity in orientation has traditionally been explained in practical terms whereby longhouses are oriented in the direction of prevailing winds (Coudart 1998; Marshall 1981). Coudart's analysis of orientation against the direction of prevailing winds across Europe suggest little correlation (Coudart 1998, 88–9), although she does raise an alternative possibility that houses – especially those in western Europe – are oriented towards the coast. Although this is possible, the practicality of orienting the back of the houses to a coastline up to 600 km distant makes this an unlikely explanation.

An alternative solution to the issue of orientation is offered by Bradley (2002, 26–8), who suggests that the doorways of longhouses are oriented towards the previous area of settlement. This is supported by the dating evidence for the expansion of the Linear Pottery Culture through Europe; there is a consistent relationship between the chronology of expansion and the orientation of doorways to the previous region of settlement (Bradley 2002, 29). The orientation of the longhouse is partly a cosmological decision rather than a wholly practical one.

Another aspect of the uniformity in settlement relates to settlement location; settlements are consistently located in the same kind of places in the landscape. In western Europe, they are consistently situated on the fertile soil known as loess; in fact the distribution of settlement conforms to the northern limits of the loess soils (Whittle 1996, 146). They are also typically situated near water on valley sides or low-lying situations (Whittle 1996, 149). The uniformity in houseplan and settlement location has often been taken as read. I think that rather than taking this uniformity at face value, we should consider some of the possible reasons for the uniform reproduction of houseplan and settlement location. Typically the uniformity in settlement location is treated as a functional decision. The location of settlement in areas with rich soils and close to water suggests that cereal cultivation may have been an important consideration (Modderman 1988).

Although this may be so, given the cosmological decisions involved in the orientation of doorways it may be that other aspects of settlement are also the result of cosmological considerations. The migration of the Linear Pottery Culture through Europe is not in dispute, coupled with the apparent uniformity in settlement location and the orientation of houses it could be said that an idealised image of settlement was being consistently reproduced. This is striking, especially when we consider the view of settlement taken by shifting hunter-gatherer groups. In a recent discussion of Evenk forest hunters in the Siberian Arctic, Grøn and Kuznetsov (2004, 217) note that when faced with the evidence of shifting seasonal

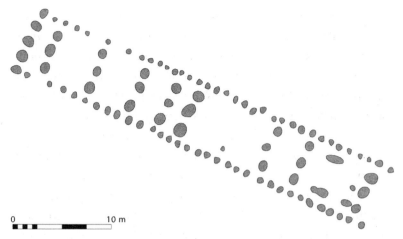

0   10 m

6. Groundplan of a Linear Pottery Culture house from Larzicourt, Marne, France (after Modderman 1988, 100).

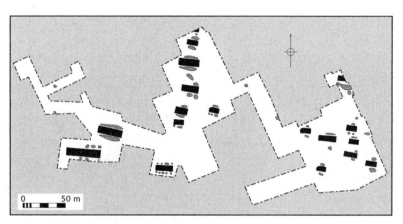

0 50 m

7. The layout and orientation of the Linear Pottery Culture settlement at Cuiry-les-Chaudardes, Aisne, France (after Modderman 1988, 101).

settlement the Evenk stated that they had not moved, rather *the world had moved around them.* This 'egocentric' attitude (commonplace amongst hunter-gatherers; Grøn and Kuznetsov 2004, 217) was taken precisely because of the consistency in the organisation of house and settlement; wherever they live their settlements are organised in the same way. Given the uniformity of Linear Pottery

Culture settlements it seems possible that similar attitudes may have prevailed. This is not to suggest that the people of the Linear Pottery Culture were hunter-gatherers (although the possibility remains that the Linear Pottery Culture is partly the result of an indigenous transformation; see Whittle 1996, 150–1), it is simply that this attitude to settlement is a strategy adopted by people on the move to create stability in an ever-changing world by locating themselves in a place that always remains the same. The similarity in settlement architecture and location is a good example of *recurrence*, the process of changing whilst staying the same. Although the settlement has physically moved the organisation of the settlement remains the same; 'place' remains cosmologically unaltered. The orientation of longhouses and their location in the landscape therefore index past forms of settlement.

So far we have focused upon uniformity in settlement. I now want to look at variation in Linear Pottery Culture settlements. Modderman (1988) stresses the variability in houses with a typology of houses, noting the differences in house size from the largest longhouses: his type 1 or *grossbau*, which is divided into three distinct sections and which has foundation trenches running longitudinally; his type 2 or *bau*, which may or may not have the front porch section of the house and may be with or without foundation trenches; and, finally, his type 3 or *kleinbau*, which is without foundation trenches and is generally composed of the central section of the house without the presence of the front porch or back section.

Gronenborn (1999, 161) observes that much of the earliest LBK houses are type 2 or 3, with only the occasional example of the larger type 1 building. Coudart has analysed the differences in building architecture across Europe through detailed multivariate analysis. She divides the Linear Pottery Culture into four geographic regions (Fig. 8): an eastern zone, central zone, western zone, and marginal southwestern zone (Coudart 1998, 16). The results of her analysis indicate that the central European zone has the greatest degree of variability, whereas the western and marginal southwestern zones exhibit minimal variability (Coudart 1998, 95).

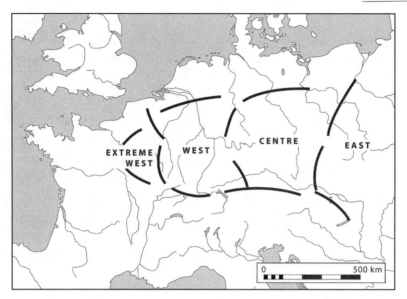

8. The distribution of the Linear Pottery Culture and its division into zones (after Coudart 1998, 15).

A more detailed analysis compares variability in regions with a high density of settlement sites against with those with a low density of settlement sites. Taken region by region, those regions with a high density of sites indicated the greatest degree of variance, while those with a low density indicated minimal variation (Coudart 1998, 96). This result suggests that in regions with a high density of sites, close social contact is critical to the expression of variability and difference in house architecture (Coudart 1998, 101); this may be the result of differences in the functional use of houses in high-density settlements with a variance of architectural constructions. Because of this Coudart (1998, 101) suggests that isolated villages such as Hienheim, Cuiry-lès-Chaudardes, Missy-sur-Aisne, and Miskovice are of secondary importance (ibid.). Whatever their importance, it is worth noting that these isolated examples are also indexing the cosmological ideal produced in those regions with denser settlement.

We have seen that settlement architecture and organisation is commemorative, because the very construction of the house and its location in specific landscape locales indexes past practices. Cosmology and tradition provided a way of coping with new environments; through common traditions people were both able to move forward in the present while remaining attached to the past.

Although distant places are indexed in the form and orientation of longhouses, they are also made tangible through the long-distance exchange of raw materials and artefacts. Lithic materials were exchanged on the western edge of the Linear Pottery Culture distribution. Maas valley sources – from places such as Rijckholt and Vetschaue/Lousberg – were exploited and exchanged over considerable distances (de Grooth 1998). This was an exchange network whose roots lay in the Late Palaeolithic, but it was during the earliest Linear Pottery Culture that exchange was intensified (Gronenborn 1999, 168). During the early phases at Bruchenbrücken flint was obtained from the Maas Valley, situated 200 km to the west (Gronenborn 1990). Many of the sites on the Aldenhoven Plateau obtained flint from the same sources, some 30 km distant. Chert from Wittlingen on the Swabian Alb – a source first utilised in the Late Mesolithic – was exchanged into the Upper Neckar and the Rhine. On the eastern edge of the Linear Pottery Culture distribution, the Szentgál source of radiolarite continued to be of importance (Gronenborn 1999, 168–9). In the region between the Tisza and the Danube the exchange of small quantities of radiolarite and obsidian between the eastern and western groups of the Linear Pottery Culture provides evidence for bilateral contacts between the two groups in the earliest phases of settlement expansion (Biró 1991).

Along with the commemorative practices involved in house construction and the exchange of material culture it is also important to consider the commemorative aspects of Linear Pottery Culture burial rites.

Linear Pottery Culture burials are curious because we find so few of them in the earliest phases of settlement. Formal, organised cemeteries are a feature of the middle (Flomborn) period of the Linear Pottery Culture and later. The paucity of cemeteries in relation to settlements suggests they may serve as a focal place for a number

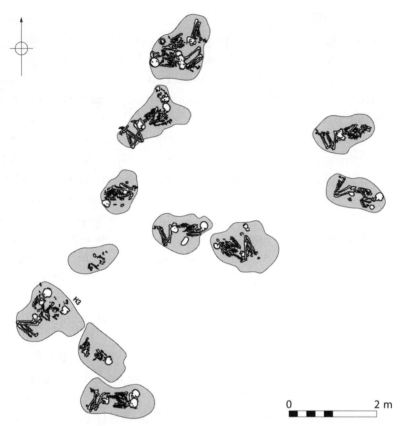

9. The Linear Pottery Culture cemetery at Sondershausen. Eight graves are oriented east or northeast, while four graves are oriented west (after Jeunesse 1997, 46).

of communities, as the Niedermerz cemetery appears to do for the Merzbachtal group (Lüning and Stehli 1989) – although van de Velde (1997) suggests that large cemeteries such as Niedermerz in the Merzbach region of the Aldenhover Plateau of Germany and the Elsloo cemetery in the Graetheide region of the Netherlands are related to large, well-established settlements; Nidermerz being related to the settlement at Langweiler 8, whereas the Elsloo cemetery is related to the Elsloo settlement (van de Velde 1997, 86).

The dead are usually inhumed or cremated (Fig. 9), and there are generally equal numbers of men and women (Jeunesse 1997).

Detailed analysis of grave goods at Niedermerz and Elsloo by van de Velde (1996, 1997) suggests paired groups of men and women. However, due to the relatively small size of cemeteries it is likely that only some people were formally buried in this way (Nieszery 1995). Gender and age differences are expressed through the deposition of differing artefacts, with men often being buried with stone adzes or flint arrowheads and women with pottery; although at Elsloo adzes and arrowheads were associated with males, while red ochre and rubbing stones were deposited in female graves and artefacts such as pottery or lithic blades could be associated with either male or female (van de Velde 1997, table 1). The position of the corpse in burials is remarkably consistent; flexed inhumations with the body placed on the left-hand side are common throughout the Linear Pottery Culture world. In the cemeteries of Bavaria, 95% of burials were positioned this way, while 5% are laid out as full inhumations (Nieszery 1995). Flexed inhumations are a particular feature of the larger cemeteries.

Like the orientation of settlements, it is typical for burials in cemeteries to occupy a common or dominant orientation, usually E-W, with the head placed at the E. However, there are a number of cemeteries with orientations to the NE or SE (Jeunesse 1997). Like settlements, the dominant orientation may alter regionally. For example in the Haute-Alsace dominant orientations are NE, while in Bavaria the majority of burials are in the axis of the E-NE and E. In the large cemeteries of the Neckar valley, meanwhile, the dominant orientation is SE. It is likely that the axis of orientation is a cosmological decision like that of contemporary settlements. Bradley (2002, 28) concludes that, in those regions such as the Paris Basin where the orientation of burials can be correlated with settlements, the 'corpse may be buried on the same alignment as the house, so that the head corresponds to the position of the door'. Where the body is laid out on a different axis to the house, the head is often oriented so that it is facing in the same direction as the building (Bradley ibid.).

Cemeteries are not the only contexts in which burials are found. Many burials occur in association with the settlement (Hodder 1990, 107; Veit 1993). Burials may occur in pits, the trenches of the enclosures which occasionally encircle Linear Pottery Culture settlements, or the borrow trenches alongside the external walls of longhouses. Occasionally burials are found in the interior of houses. Notably, child burials predominate in these contexts (Veit 1993, 121). Intramural burials within settlements seem to increase in number from east to west (Veit 1993, fig. 2), suggesting that, like the establishment of cemeteries, this is a practice which may increase in significance later in the sequence.

Veit (1993) argues that we should view burials in cemeteries and settlements as a totality. How are we to consider these burial rites in commemorative terms? Much depends upon the significance attached to the settlement. I have argued above that the construction of the Linear Pottery Culture longhouse and its location in a specific landscape setting was a commemorative act which indexed past practices. In this light, houses take on an increased significance because they form the cosmological focus of the Linear Pottery Culture world; longhouses function as a kind of mythological archetype, or 'ur-house', distantly related – conceptually, if not physically – to either the Körös or AVK house in the Great Hungarian Plain. The significance of myth in this kind of context has recently been emphasised by Alasdair Whittle (2003, 114–18). The burial of infants in and around the longhouse setting therefore places them at the centre or cosmological origin point of the Linear Pottery Culture world, a sphere to which they belong by virtue of their age. Adults, however, may be buried beyond the reach of the settlement. But here, too, the significance of the house is important. Cemeteries are located close to long-established settlements, places with histories. Given this, and the late appearance of cemeteries in the sequence, the establishment of cemeteries may be a process of cementing ties to a particular place. Cemeteries are not representative of the entire community (van der Velde 1997), but they do act as *representations of* the ideal of community. The common orientation of burials and houses suggests that cemeteries are representations of the settlement. The burial of people in cemeteries indexes an idealised notion of the settlement; the orientation of individuals towards their place of origin likewise indexes the past.

We can observe this point more clearly when we consider the deposition of certain specialised artefacts in burial contexts. The deposition of gastropods and the skeletal elements of animals are well documented for Linear Pottery Culture burials (Jeunesse 1997). The most well-known species deposited is the gastropod *Spondylus gaederopus*. *Spondylus* shells have their ultimate origins in the Aegean or Adriatic (Shackleton and Renfrew 1970), yet they were exchanged over immense distances throughout the Linear Pottery Culture network. Shells may be intact or fashioned into beads, bracelets, medallions, and belt-hooks. Notably in regions to the east *Spondylus* shells may be deposited in an intact condition, whereas towards the western edge of their distribution in northern France they tend to be deposited as fragments (all eight of the *Spondylus* finds from France are fragments; Jeunesse 1997), acting as tokens of distant places.

Other species of shells are also deposited. These include *Dentalium vulgare*, whose ultimate origin is likely to be the Mediterranean or Atlantic. Dentalium shells are usually perforated and are components of necklaces or headdresses. Dentalium shells are almost as widespread and are found in cemeteries in Bavaria (such as Mangolding and Aiterhofen), Alsace (such as Mulhouse-Est), and central and eastern France (such as Cuiry-les-Chaudardes and Larzicourt). Whatever the origin of Dentalium shells, their presence in regions such as Alsace and Bavaria also denotes long-distance exchange. Other shells with distant origins include *Columbella rusticata*, a Mediterranean species which accompanied a burial at Ensisheim, Alsace, and *Trivia monacha*, whose origins lie in the Atlantic or Mediterranean and which was also found in burials at Ensisheim and Cuiry-les-Chaudardes.

Distant places are also referenced by the burial of other animal species, such as the Sea Eagle talon which accompanied a burial at

Lingolsheim (Jeunesse 1997). Given the maritime habitat of this species and the inland location of the burial, the eagle talon must index a distant coastline.

It is not only distant places that are indexed by the deposition of animals and gastropods; local places are also referenced. For example, a number of burials contain fox teeth utilised in necklaces or ornaments, such as at tomb 13, Rutzing (Jeunesse 1997); deer antlers are occasionally deposited, such as the antler adze socket in tomb 129, Schwetzingen. Local shell species are also deposited, such as the terrestrial species *Ena detrita* associated with burials at Quatzenheim and Souffelweyersheim (Jeunnese 1997) or the river species *Theodoxus danubialis* deposited at Aiterhofen, Sengkofen, Mangolding, and Essenbach. I have argued elsewhere that because of their specific habitats, animal species are strongly bound up with place (Jones 1998). In the case of the Linear Pottery Culture burials animals and gastropods seem to be utilised in burial contexts to index both local and distance places and the connections between them.

The distinction between local and nonlocal origins is clearly indicated in recent strontium isotope studies on populations at the cemetery sites of Flomborn, Dillingen, and Schwetzingen in southern Germany (Bentley et al. 2002, 2003; Price et al. 2001). Those identified as locals were buried with a possible orientation towards the nearest adjacent settlement. Price et al. (2001) suggest that those nonlocals buried with a different orientation (often female) may have origins in hunter-gatherer populations. If so, the treatment of the dead is also an arena for indexing past events and social relations, of themes of movement, origin, and memory.

AFTER THE LINEAR POTTERY CULTURE – COMMEMORATION AND THE TRANSFORMATION OF THE HOUSE

Around 4900 BC the Linear Pottery Culture begins to fragment and we observe the emergence of a variety of local groups (Coudart

1998; Gronenborn 1999). Longhouses remained in use, although a plethora of distinctive local pottery styles emerge. Away from the *loess* on the fringes of Atlantic Europe monumental mounds begin to be built. Chronologically the two events are closely related in time; 'the creation of landscapes with prominent monuments occurs as the colonisation of the *loess* was reaching its limits' (Bradley 1998b, 37).

The relationship between the inhabitation of longhouses in the post-LBK period and the emergence of longmounds to house the dead on the fringes of Atlantic Europe is traditionally seen as being closely linked. A number of commentators have noted the close architectural similarities between longhouses and longmounds (Hodder 1984, 1990; Midgley 2005; Sherratt 1990, 1997). Ian Hodder (1984) lists eight connections between the two architectural forms, which include form, alignment, internal organisation, and the position of entrances. A key component of Hodder's argument lies in establishing continuity between the two types of architectural construction; he situates this overlap in the post-Linear Pottery Culture Lengyel phase of Poland, where we observe villages of longhouses with a trapezoidal ground plan, such as at Brzésc Kujawski (Hodder 1990, 145). These are preceded in the later Trichterbecher (TRB) phase by cemeteries of longmounds with trapezoidal groundplan of a similar orientation (Midgeley 2005, 77–98). Northwest Poland has traditionally been treated as one of the key geographical regions where this transformation from the architecture of the house to that of the tomb took place. However, recent excavations at Balloy, in northern France, reveal a situation where longmounds are stratigraphically superimposed upon the groundplans of earlier longhouses (Kinnes 1998; Mordant 1998).

This transformation from 'houses of the living' to 'houses of the dead' has often been discussed in rather an abstract fashion, as a component of the transformation of the 'idea of the house' or *domus* (Hodder 1990). However, if we wish to consider commemorative practices it is helpful to consider how this transformation may have taken place in practice. Crucially, Bradley (1998) situates this transformation in the materiality of the longhouse. Basing his argument on the projected use-life of houses at the settlement of Bylany (Soudsky 1973) and the well-documented sites of the Merzbach region he suggests an average life cycle for individual longhouses of between 14 and 25 years. Given the relatively lengthy occupation span of many settlements he suggests that many settlements will have contained abandoned houses as well as those in use. Such occupational continuity with abandoned houses still in existence close to occupied houses may explain the apparent order and lack of overlap in houseplans in most Linear Pottery Culture settlements. It follows that some houses remaining within the settlement were left to decay. Bradley suggests that it was the decayed houses which gave rise to the longmounds:

> . . . eventually as the process of decay increased, each of the houses would collapse, leaving a gap in the distribution of buildings marked by a long, low mound, much of it contributed by the daub which had covered the walls. The erosion of borrow pits might even have given the impression of side ditches. The very process of decay in the heart of the inhabited area might have given rise to the basic idea of the long mound. (Bradley 1998, 45)

The situation at Balloy is useful because it highlights that earlier longhouses existed as visible traces upon which later constructions took place. The significant point here is that it is the material presence of the physical traces of the past which provides the conditions for remembrance. In Bradley's terms the physical components of the longhouse provide the conceptual materials for longmounds; through decay the longhouse transforms itself into a longmound. This is a neat proposition – how was it considered conceptually? Again, much depends upon how the longhouse was conceptualised. Most commentators describe the physical transformation from longhouse to longmound as a transformation from the construction of 'houses of the living' to 'houses of the dead'. Such a transformation is likely to be an important context for myths of origin and change

(Whittle 2003, 118). This transformation may have been less of a conceptual change if we consider my earlier points relating to the cosmological significance of longhouses. If Linear Pottery Culture longhouses are reproductions of an idealised form then the 'houses of the living' are simultaneously also the 'houses of the dead' because they embody the ancestral ideals of the past. People inhabited the houses of their ancestors. The transformation from longhouse to longmound may have been *both physically and conceptually seamless.* The point I want to emphasize here is that the seamlessness of this transformation occurs precisely because the physical attributes of the house are treated as mnemonic traces. I now want to contrast this situation with the timber architecture of a region on the edge of Europe – that of lowland Scotland.

PLAYING WITH FIRE – FIRE AND THE SCOTTISH NEOLITHIC

The presence of Neolithic houses in the British Isles has been hotly debated (Barclay 1996, 2003; Cooney 1999; Thomas 1996b). Arguments have focused around the opposite poles of either a transitory settlement pattern based on Mesolithic settlement modes or a sedentary settlement system with recognisable houses. Part of the problem has been the relative absence of settlement structures in much of the south of Britain. However, evidence for Neolithic houses is relatively common in the north, while the development of commercial archaeology in Ireland has led to a Neolithic 'housing boom' (Armit et al. 2003). Over 90 Neolithic houses are now known in Ireland. The presence of Neolithic settlement structures in highland Britain and Ireland simply points up the regional variability in settlement patterns. I want to focus now on the timber constructions of the Scottish Neolithic.

The timber constructions have a passing resemblance to the timber houses of the Linear Pottery Culture. I discuss them here to draw out the differences in commemorative practices in central

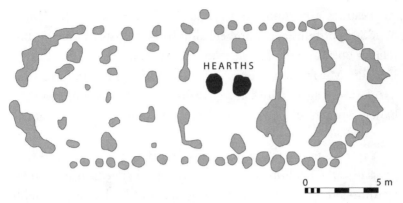

HEARTHS

0   5 m

10. Groundplan of the timber structure at Claish, Stirling region, Scotland (after Barclay et al. 2002, 101, fig. B).

Europe and Scotland. I explicitly focus on the role of fire in the use and abandonment of Neolithic buildings in Scotland.

At Claish, Stirling region, two features, F15 and F19, were located in the centre of the middle section of the post-built building (Fig. 10). These two features are described by the site's excavators as: 'pits with burnt deposits' (Barclay et al. 2002). It is worth considering them in some detail. F15 includes a series of deposits of Early Neolithic pottery, representing up to five pots, six burnt bones, 300 carbonised hazel nut shells, and grains of barley, emmer wheat, and bread wheat. The charcoal recovered from the upper fills of the pit includes birch, hazel, oak, and willow. The second feature, F19, includes portions of 12 pots, over 250 carbonised hazel-nut shells, and grains of barley, emmer, and bread wheat. Charcoal included birch, hazel, and oak. In the second feature the large quantities of pottery had been deliberately placed around the edges and base of the pit to act as a support for fire setting. The upper fills of both features have a series of layers of in-situ burning. Both features are contemporaneous with the structure as sherds from pots deposited in the hearths were also recovered from post pipes. The excavators suggest a possible function as a pottery-firing site. Although this interpretation is intriguing, I believe that these features also served as large communal hearths, evidently in use during the life of the structure.

Features very similar to those at Claish were detected by Magnetic Susceptibility at the timber hall at Balbridie, Aberdeenshire, but remain unexcavated. The recently excavated site at Crathes Castle, Deeside (Murray and Fraser 2005), also had two features in a similar position, again with large quantities of early Neolithic pottery, barley, emmer, and bread wheat and carbonised birch containers deposited at the site.

Hearths are therefore physically and symbolically central to a series of early Neolithic buildings in Scotland. The hearth provides warmth and is also the site of transformation. In the case of Claish pottery may have been fired in one hearth, as evinced by the presence of burnt clay. The processing of foodstuffs through heating is also an activity conducted around the hearth. The notion of the hearth as a cohesive feature of Neolithic buildings that helps bind people in communal activity is clearly observed when we note that the smaller dwellings of the Orcadian or Hebridean Neolithic are provisioned with a single hearth, whereas larger structures such as Claish have two large hearths, possibly indicating their use by more than one social group.

Fire therefore appears to be a catalyst for social cohesion. However, fire is used in a number of contrasting ways during the Early Neolithic. It is notable, for example, that the large timber buildings at Balbridie, Claish, and Crathes Castle were all burnt down. This is curious because this is also a major feature of mortuary monuments in Scotland.

At a series of Early Neolithic timber monuments – formally described as mortuary enclosures – there is also evidence of in-situ burning. These include sites such as Douglasmuir, Angus (Kendrick 1995), and Inchtuthil, Perthshire (Barclay and Maxwell 1991). At Inchututhil there is evidence that the smoldering posts of the final timber enclosure had been deliberately toppled into the enclosure interior (Fig. 11). Fire had also been used to destroy the cursus monuments at Dunragit (Fig. 12) and Holywood North, Dumfriesshire (Thomas 2000, 2004b), and the post alignment at Bannockburn, Stirling, region (Taverner 1987).

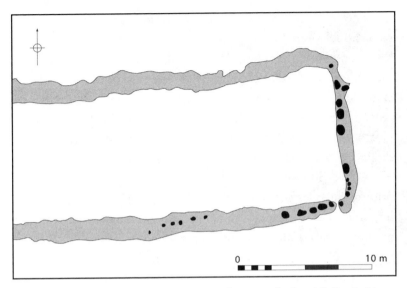

11. Groundplan of the long mortuary enclosure at Inchtuthil, Perthshire, Scotland, showing the position of burnt timbers (after Barclay and Maxwell 1991, 30).

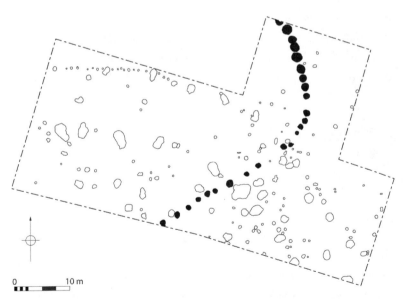

12. Groundplan of the post-defined cursus monument at Dunragit, Dumfries, and Galloway, Scotland, showing the position of burnt timbers (after Thomas 2004, 102).

The relationship between fire and mortuary monuments has wider associations. For example, the timber mortuary houses beneath long barrows at Dalladies, Aberdeenshire, Slewcairn, and Lochill, Dumfriesshire, Eweford (MacGregor and Shearer 2002), and Pencraig Hill, East Lothian, were all burnt down deliberately (Kinnes 1992). Fire is also used in the round barrow and ring bank burials of Northeast Scotland – at Boghead, Moray (Burl 1984), Midtown of Pitglassie, Aberdeenshire (Shepherd 1996), and Pitnacree, Perthshire (Coles and Simpson 1965) the old ground surface had been fired prior to the construction of the mound (Fig. 13). This is especially important because each of these monuments is associated with cremation burials. Indeed, firing on the old ground surface is likely to be the result of cremation pyres (Shepherd 1996).

Fire is not confined to timber monuments. It is also used in those areas with chambered tomb traditions – in Orkney a series of early Neolithic 'stalled' tombs built of stone bear evidence of repeated firings which must have filled the entire chamber of the monument. Given the absence of cremation in Orkney it seems likely that fire is here used as an agent of purification. Fire is also a feature of the chambered tomb traditions of western Scotland. Here too the interior of tombs may be fired, but cremation deposits are far more common in this region – particularly in the Clyde tombs of Arran.

◼ KEEPING THE FLAME

Fire acts as a catalyst of interaction and transformation. I want to consider this more fully by turning to the stone-built houses of Early Neolithic Orkney. Early Neolithic houses in Orkney are typically linear, and internal space is divided up with stone orthostats. At the Knap of Howar – as with other settlement sites – the hearth is located either at the centre or inner space of the house. Activities associated with the transformation of food occur around the hearth in both houses. Primary transformation occurs in the back space of

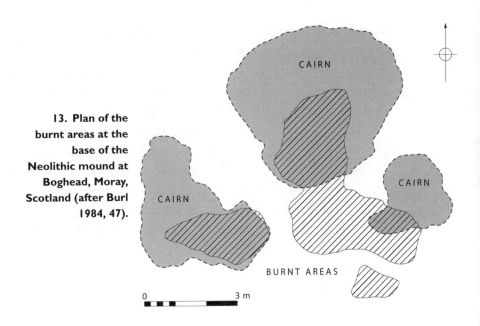

13. Plan of the burnt areas at the base of the Neolithic mound at Boghead, Moray, Scotland (after Burl 1984, 47).

CAIRN

CAIRN

CAIRN

BURNT AREAS

0   3 m

house 1, where a large saddle quern is situated. The spatial analysis of pottery from Knap of Howar indicates that a number of vessels were deposited around the hearth in house 2 (Ritchie 1973). Storage of foodstuffs is likely to have taken place in the back space of the two houses – provisioned with plentiful stone cupboards.

The hearth is therefore an axial point around which stored foods are transformed. That this takes place in the central and back space of the house is important because this practice acts as a spatial framework for understanding how the dead are treated in chambered tomb contexts (Jones 1999). The stalled tombs of Orkney are architecturally homologous to the settlement site. Analysis of the location of skeletal elements within a number of chambered tombs suggests that inhumations are interred in the central area of the tomb and, upon decay, selected elements of the skeleton are placed in the inner chambers of the tomb. Spatially and metaphorically the transformation of food and the transformation of the dead are linked. I have argued elsewhere (Jones ibid.) that the activities of food storage and production provide a metaphorical mechanism by which the process of death is both organised and understood, as the body is transformed through decay in the tomb interior and parts of the skeleton are stored in the interior of the tomb. In both cases fire plays a leading role as a transformative device in the cooking of food in the hearth in the house and the cleansing by fire of tomb interiors.

The high quality of the Orcadian evidence allows us to reconsider the role of fire in other regions of Scotland. I want to underline the point that fire plays a connective role; it links a series of social practices – the consumption of food and the treatment of the dead. In the form of the hearth, fire serves to provide a focus or anchor for the household and may be one place around which the household is organised. In some senses the hearth serves to reference the house itself by acting as a mnemonic reference for the house. Fire also acts as a mnemonic device in terms of its use in building destruction.

In the case of a series of timber monuments in SW Scotland, including the Dunragit and Holywood North cursus and Holm timber alignments (see Fig. 12), Julian Thomas (2000) has noted that fire acts as an agent of memory formation. He suggests that the periodic construction and firing of monuments is a form of continuous performance. The periodic and spectacular immolation of a building is a means of consigning an event to memory; this kind of memory formation is typically described as *episodic* – the form of memory constructed during traumatic or eventful experiences. The destruction of material culture and monuments – a culturally active process of forgetting – here creates a space for remembrance.

Rather than thinking of the timber monuments of the Scottish Neolithic as permanent structures we are perhaps best considering them as monuments in process, whose destruction by fire was a key part of their life cycle. This is particularly apposite for the timber structures beneath earthen long barrows and for timber alignments and cursus monuments. How are we to think of this process in relation to houses? Here I want to modify Hodder's insight that the durability of houses was one medium by which the idea of the house was transformed and perpetuated. Instead I want to suggest that the repetitive performance of the practices of building and destruction served as a means of reproducing the concept of the household or community.

I want to consider this in relation to the timber monuments of eastern Scotland. The timber buildings at both Balbridie and Claish are immense – 22 m long in the case of Balbridie and 24 m in the case of Claish. Their size has led to debate concerning their character as houses – are these the typical settlements of a sedentary population or are they gathering places for larger social groups? Are they indeed even houses? Their resemblance to the long timber mortuary enclosures is significant here. By examining the practices associated with the use and destruction of these buildings I hope to throw some light on their character.

As I noted, the twin hearths at Claish are focal to the building; they are the site of food production and may have been the focus of pottery production. As well as being the site of production, these hearths also formed a focus for deposition, as pottery was deposited in the base of both fire pits. The productive and destructive agency of fire is therefore represented by the use of the hearth as the focus of production and destruction. The destruction by fire of the productive capacity of agriculture is also observed at Balbridie, where over 20,000 grains of barley were charred in the deposits at the back of the building (Ralston 1982).

Similar notions of production and destruction are expressed in the building of these monuments and in their spectacular immolation. Fire is used then as an agent of production and destruction. Given the large scale of these monuments, the hearths may act as foci for more than one social group. The production and destruction of these buildings acted then as a catalyst bring together communities in acts of building and creating a collective memory upon their destruction. Their destruction by fire may represent the temporary or provisional nature of the social ties of these communities. Indeed, the deposition of artefacts and cereals within these buildings may commemorate the productive capacity of the communities who built them.

The community inheres, then, in acts of production and destruction and the idea of the house is therefore representative of this wider notion of community. The concept of community expressed in these cycles of building and destruction can be observed in the comparable ground plans and treatment of sites like Douglasmuir and Inchtuthil. Indeed, the building and spatial layout of these monuments commemorates the processes of house construction, as does their destruction by fire. Gordon Barclay notes, too, that the structures at Littleour, Perthshire, and Balfarg Riding School, Fife, represent a similar constructional vocabulary to that of Claish and Balbridie (Barclay and Maxwell 1998). These structures were not burnt down but instead rotted insitu, although the repeated firing of the interior of Littleour is suggested by the large quantities of charcoal in the upper fill of the post-holes (Barclay and Maxwell 1998). These structures resembled houses in their form and in some of the activities conducted in their interior. Indeed, their resemblance to houses is referenced some time later by depositional events, which mirror the hearth deposits in earlier structures. During the Late Neolithic, eight Grooved Ware vessels were deposited in a pit in the centre of Littleour and a cairn associated with Grooved Ware was built over the two Balfarg structures.

Repetitive cycles of construction are a feature of many of the monuments in eastern Scotland, for example, the pit defined cursus monuments at Balneaves Cottage, Kinalty, Milton of Guthrie, and Bennybeg, in Angus (Brophy 1999). The repetitive construction of monuments is seen in its most impressive form in the Cleaven Dyke bank barrow, Perthshire, constructed in four segments and running for a length of 2 km (Barclay and Maxwell 1998). These monuments are therefore perpetuating and exaggerating the architectural and social principles of construction observed in timber constructions such as Claish and Balbridie; physically and metaphorically these structures are aggrandised representations of houses. More importantly, like earlier houses, they act as a means of cohering communities together in the performance of construction. The idea of the house, through repetitive reenactment, is both referenced and transformed.

It is worth comparing these sequences of activities with those in Orkney and the Western Isles. In Orkney and the Western Isles houses are built of stone; they do undergo cycles of destruction, though this is not undertaken by fire. Houses are rebuilt in the same place, often forming settlement mounds; the dead in these regions are rarely cremated. This contrasts strongly with the evidence from eastern Scotland, where houses are destroyed by fire and we see little evidence of settlement continuity and the dead are more often cremated. It would appear that in each of these regions the materiality of architecture is intimately bound up with practices of commemoration and inhabitation.

Richard Bradley has recently drawn a distinction between the treatment of houses and the dead in England and Ireland (Bradley 2007). A similar contrast pertains here. In Orkney and the Western Isles we observe slow cycles of decay and long-term practices of inhabitation; in eastern Scotland the decay of the dead is accelerated by fire and the inhabitation of the settlement is relatively short term and shifting. This interpretation is supported by the observation that at Boghead midden material is being deliberately burnt with the bones of the dead (Burl 1984).

In Orkney, fire offers a means of metaphorically connecting the domains of everyday consumption and the domain of the dead. Houses are built of more durable substances. The very practices of settlement offer a means of remembering the past. In other areas, such as eastern Scotland, fire offers a way of metaphorically connecting the life cycle of houses with those of the dead and the monuments built to contain them. In these regions fire is essential to the formation of houses and to the transmission of the concept of community represented by houses. Metaphorically, people are 'keeping the flame', as fire connects different regions of practice and connects communities. The reiteration of processes of house building and destruction served to reproduce the notion of community in other material and architectural forms. In one case the durable house is organised around the central hearth; in the other, fire is a medium for determining the durability of social relations.

■ IMAGINED COMMUNITIES: COMMEMORATION AND THE PERSON IN THE NEOLITHIC OF CENTRAL EUROPE AND SCOTLAND

I now want to return to the Linear Pottery Culture to draw comparisons with the timber constructions of the Scottish Neolithic. I argue that there are major differences in commemorative practices in the two areas; two different 'traditions of practice' (Thomas 2004b, 175). In Scotland we observe repetitive cycles of burning which were active in the production of memory. In central Europe through the repetitive reproduction of an architectural ideal situated in the same kind of place people physically inhabited traces of the past. The physical presence of buildings and the artefacts – lithics, shells, and animals – exchanged over long distances provided tangible links with the past. I believe that these two different ways of 'performing' remembrance are indicative of different ways of organising time.

Both Chris Fowler (2003) and Josh Pollard (2004) have recently highlighted the point that social practices in Neolithic Britain suggest a pronounced interest in issues of decay and transformation. Pollard discusses the way in which decay produces a radical reconfiguration of substance, as the decayed bones of the dead were disarticulated and reconfigured in other forms in chambered tombs, and material culture was weathered and broken down in midden deposits and reassembled in pit deposits. Fowler observes that the temporal cycles of decay are important as they closely resonate with the human life cycle. The process of destroying a monument by fire is in essence an accelerated means of decay. If, as Fowler and Pollard suggest, decay is an important means of relating to the past, then we observe at least two contrasting ways of relating to the past in continental Europe and Scotland, which indicate two different ways of perpetuating tradition and producing or 'imagining' communities.

In the lowlands of Neolithic Scotland we see communities anchored around the production of immense timber buildings that are eventually burnt down. Communities are produced and reproduced through this repetitive process of building and burning. The act of burning provided a 'space' for remembrance, a practice highlighted in the cremation of the dead in northeastern Scotland. It would be wrong to say that Linear Pottery Culture buildings were never burnt; there is the well-known example of Zuaschwitz, Saxony, where a child burial was covered by the burnt remains of a house (Veit 1993). Cremation is also a feature of some Linear Pottery Culture cemeteries. However, the deliberate burning of structures is rare in the Linear Pottery Culture (it is one of the major contrasts with the settlements of southeastern Europe where burning is common; Stevanovic 1997; Tringham 2000). In the regions occupied by the Linear Pottery Culture, by contrast, houses are allowed to decay naturally. Communities are imagined through the physical ideal of the Linear Pottery Culture longhouse and the common orientation of longhouses in settlements. Communities extend well beyond the borders of the settlement; they are indexed by the orientation of longhouse doorways back to past regions of settlement and presenced by the exchange of raw materials and other artefacts. Community is also referenced in the commonality of burial practices. Indeed, the deposition of artefacts, such as Spondylus shells, in mortuary contexts highlights the significance of the mortuary domain as a place for emphasising the idea of community.

The performance of remembrance is related, then, to two different attitudes to time; in Neolithic Scotland we observe a high tempo of existence where fire seems to be used because it offers a means of accelerating the tempo of decay and connecting events together. This is underlined by the fact that the radiocarbon determinations for many of the timber monuments discussed above fall in the first quarter century of the fourth millennium BC. It is possible that these practices were strongly associated with the earliest Neolithic in Scotland. In central Europe, by contrast, we observe a slower tempo of existence, with past practices firmly presenced in contemporary existence conveying an impression of the timelessness of past and present practices. Cultural networks were also established in two different ways. In central Europe networks of relationships are created through the exchange of artefacts and the physical presence of long-distant traditions. In Scotland networks are formed by the repeated execution of certain dramatic events. In central Europe the past is physically present, whereas in Scotland the past is measured by the distance between certain significant events. These contrasting practices and their associated attitudes to time and memory will have concurred with two different ways of imagining the person.

The parameters of a person's life are measured in different ways. For the Linear Pottery Culture the history of the person is set against the history of the household; in turn, the history of the household is set against the longer term histories of settlements and the depth of cultural traditions. In central Europe the person was firmly embedded in a community where change occurred relatively slowly; they belonged to a wider imagined community. They were both grounded in place and tradition, yet they were also flexible to change; they moved through Europe and in doing so encountered and incorporated indigenous people into their community – if the strontium isotope data are interpreted correctly. They were both shaped by the forces of history and flexible to change (see also Jones 2005a). In Neolithic Scotland, however, the tempo of building and destruction is closer to the tempo of the human life cycle. The person was shaped by the forces of history, which were rapidly undergoing change, as represented by the treatment of both monuments and the dead.

Curiously, it is the simultaneous groundedness and flexibility of the Linear Pottery Culture which gives rise to the permanence of mortuary architecture in Atlantic Europe and the evanescence of monument construction in Neolithic Scotland; the conceptions of time, memory, and the person on the fringes of Europe are immanent to, or nested in, the conceptions of time, memory, and the person embodied in the traditions of the Linear Pottery Culture of central Europe.

Culture, Citation, and Categorisation

Regionality in Late Neolithic Britain and Ireland

Although culture has been discussed by successive waves of archaeological theorists, the culture-historical description of material culture has remained remarkably resistant to change. Siân Jones points out that despite the critique of culture-history made by New or processual archaeologists, culture-historical categories were retained as a component of the core methodology of archaeology (Jones 1997, 27). However, the same charge could be made of postprocessual archaeologists. A good example of this can be observed in Julian Thomas's *Time, Culture and Identity* (Thomas 1996a), where, despite a thoroughgoing theoretical discussion on the nature of culture and identity, the case studies retain category descriptions formulated under quite different theoretical principles; such is the case in the final chapter, where arguments concerning the restructuring of the Late Neolithic henge at Mount Pleasant, Dorset (Thomas 1996a, 212–22), depends upon an analysis of the deposition of beaker sherds of specific culture-historical categories (e.g., Wessex/Middle Rhine; European; Northern; Southern). We are left, then, with complex theoretical approaches overlaid onto a series of traditional culture-historical categories. There is little interrelationship here between theory and practice.

Culture-history appears to be a fundamental component of archaeological method. This is because it fulfils the need for archaeologists to organise past material culture into coherent categories; categories offer a useful heuristic device – they provide archaeologist with a common descriptive reference point – but linguistic categories simultaneously circumscribe. As Olsen (1990, 195) notes: 'the transformation from a material object (i.e., a piece of burnt clay with ornamentation) to meta-language ('this is a beaker'), involves a dramatic reduction of the object's possible signification. Given these problems, in this chapter I want to extend the discussion of artefacts as components of indexical or citational networks (see Chapter 4 for expansion of this idea) to the study of artefact categories.

CULTURE AND CATEGORISATION

I believe that if we are to move away from a view of culture as an autonomous object and embrace the notions of culture as a network of practical actions we need to critically reconsider how it is that we categorise archaeological materials. The traditional view of categorisation stems from the assumption that things have essences that are revealed by their visible properties. Things belong to natural categories that exist out there in the 'real world'; they behave in particular ways according to the possession of these properties and can be categorised on the basis of these properties. This belief in the existence of natural kinds then allows taxonomic groups of natural kinds to be formulated. As the psychologist George Lakoff (1987, 5) points out, the view that categories are based on shared properties is both a folk (or everyday) model as well as a technical or scientific model. This 'classical' model of categorisation is habitually applied to archaeology through the tabulation of the occurrence of objects bearing particular properties and their correlation with a normative notion of culture. Gordon Childe's famous definition of archaeological cultures as 'composed of series of material traits which reoccur repeatedly' allowed archaeological artefacts to be categorised according to the prevailing assumptions of the late-nineteenth-/early-twentieth-century natural sciences.

Problems with artefact categories arise because we treat objects as having a predetermined set of properties, as natural kinds. Apart from the philosophical problems inherent in this view (see Lakoff 1987, 12–57), a major problem with this view is that artefacts are not preexisting natural entities; they are humanly constructed. Robin Boast has addressed this problem in a series of articles on the categorisation of British beakers (Boast 1998a, 2002). Drawing on Lakoff, he treats various elements of beakers (morphology, fabric, decorative motifs) as components of 'fuzzy categories'. 'Fuzzy categories' are categories composed of two elements: artefacts which share a series of common features exist as core components of the category, whereas artefacts with only one or two features shared with the core components exist as a penumbra. Categories are polythetic, and one category may shade into another. From this analysis Boast shows the distinct elements making up categories of beakers pots in different regions of the British Isles. This approach offers a far more realistic treatment of the problems of beaker categorisation; however, the analysis remains confined to the archaeological category of 'beaker'. As an alternative I believe we can also consider artefact categories as components of indexical or citational networks. Just as we need not treat archaeological cultures as bounded and homogeneous, artefact categories need not be seen as bounded and homogeneous. If we are to consider how cultural change relates to the formation of novel categories of artefacts it is important to treat categories as open fields of interaction. I will do this by turning to a case study.

CASE STUDY: LATE NEOLITHIC/EARLY BRONZE AGE BRITAIN AND IRELAND

In this chapter I will examine two aspects of the Late Neolithic/Early Bronze Age in Britain and Ireland. The first thing I want to discuss is the nature of the relationship between the ceramics we describe as Beakers and Grooved Ware, and the second thing I want to examine is the nature of the relationship between different regions in Britain and Ireland during the Late Neolithic to Early Bronze Age. Both of these issues are linked by the problems that surround our understanding of the term *cultural interaction.*

Before I investigate these problems I will begin by quoting some of the literature that has dominated the discussion of Beakers and Grooved Ware over the past 30 years. The opening quotes come from David Clarke's magnum opus *Beaker Pottery of Great Britain and Ireland,* published in 1970. The final quote comes from Wainwright and Longworth's reassessment of the 'Rinyo-Clacton' or Grooved Ware culture from Britain, in the excavation report of the Late Neolithic henge at Durrington Walls, Wiltshire, published in 1971.

> We will begin with Clarke...'The first wave of Beaker expansion reached Britain between c. 2100–1900 B. C., bringing the All-Over-Cord and European Bell Beaker groups in quick succession to the East Coast, mainly from the Rhine delta. The Beaker groups influenced the indigenous regional Neolithic groups to a considerable extent but remained themselves largely unchanged. .... The Beaker settlement fundamentally altered the character of the rest of the British Neolithic cultures, providing the basis for the pottery traditions of the full Bronze Age'.

Clarke continues . . . 'The impact of the second wave is so strong, that the Final Neolithic groups universally abandon their ancient traditions of round based vessels, for flat based beaker-like forms'.

Wainwright and Longworth writing of Grooved Ware say . . . 'To replace the Rinyo-Clacton culture we would employ the term sub-culture to describe a stratum of the population bound together by a common mode of pottery manufacture and a strong tradition of ritual practice. That part of the population who manufactured Grooved Ware forms one strand of a complex society, whose other manifestations include users of Peterborough ware and Beaker groups'.

The viewpoints encapsulated in these quotations embody a series of implicit assumptions concerning material culture and cultural interaction, that:

1   The distribution of morphologically and decoratively similar material culture can be used to map the distribution of ancient populations. In other words, pots equal people.
2   The populations defined by material culture groupings are each considered to be hermetically sealed and distinct, just as materially we consider archaeological artefacts to be hermetically sealed.
3   There is a causal link between the presence or absence of material culture and certain social effects.
4   The influence of these social effects is considered to be unidirectional. For instance, Beakers have a positive effect on other Late Neolithic groups but not vice versa. These views seem to define a kind of colonial power relation in which one materially defined culture group imposes its influence upon another.

It is these assumptions that I want to challenge in the context of the archaeology of a series of regions of Britain and Ireland. These regions will include Orkney and the Western Isles in Scotland

and the eastern coast of Ireland. Comparisons of some of these regions have been made before under the aegis of the notion of peer polity interaction (Bradley 1984; Bradley and Chapman 1986). These analyses delineated certain core regions within Later Neolithic Britain, defined in the main by elaborate monumental traditions and complex artefacts.

A major reason for reexamining this material is that, archaeologically, the picture has changed since these articles were published. In his earlier analysis Bradley noted that there was no Grooved Ware in Ireland (Bradley 1984), whereas Grooved Ware has subsequently been recognised from a number of locations in Ireland (Brindley 1999). Meanwhile, recent excavations in Orkney have revealed the previously elusive presence of Beaker pottery in settlement contexts. The purpose of this chapter is to compare these regions afresh based on this altered picture of the archaeological evidence.

REWRITING NEOLITHIC AND BRONZE AGE HISTORIES: ORKNEY AND THE WESTERN ISLES

I begin my account in the Northern Isles of Scotland: Orkney. The Later Neolithic of Orkney is characterised by the construction of a series of monumental forms: passage graves, henges surrounding stone circles, and stone-built settlements. Colin Richards has analysed the nature of the relationship between these architectural constructions and argued for the operation of a common cosmological perspective (Richards 1993). This is manifested in an ordered architectural scheme that links each type of architectural construction, house, tomb, and henge. Importantly, he has also shown that these architectural constructions are all built in the same fluorescence of activity around 3300–3200 BC (Richards 1998).

Like their Irish counterparts, monuments such as passage graves are associated with art. The art takes two main forms: scratch art, a series of light linear incisions on the surface of stones, and pecked art, a series of curvilinear designs. The linear art is not confined to passage graves and is also found in contemporary settlements such as Skara Brae, Barnhouse, and Pool. Both curvilinear and linear designs are important components of Grooved Ware pottery, which is associated with passage graves, henges, and settlements.

Neolithic settlements in Orkney provide us with a stratified sequence of pottery from the early Neolithic to early Bronze Age because of the practice of depositing midden material in close proximity to houses. The earliest Grooved Ware forms are characterised by an abundance of complex curvilinear and linear designs. By the end of the Later Neolithic sequence we observe the appearance of simpler forms characterised by a series of horizontal incisions or cordons.

I want to examine the practices involved in creating a biography of ceramics in Late Neolithic Orkney by focussing on an analysis of the settlement at Barnhouse (Richards 2005). I have discussed the analysis of this pottery assemblage at length elsewhere (Jones 2000, 2002a, 2005b). Here I provide a brief overview of this analysis.

The settlement at Barnhouse has two broad phases of occupation (Fig. 14). The first is characterised by a series of circular stone built houses arranged in two concentric rings around a central space. The second major phase is marked by the construction of a monumental building that fuses the architectural features of house, henge, and passage grave (Richards 2005). Analysis of the Grooved Ware from the first phase of settlement suggests considerable complexity. Three sizes of vessel were produced, associated with quite different uses. The productive histories of these vessels differed depending on which area of the settlement they were produced in. Vessels tempered with shell were produced in the central area and used by those inhabiting the inner ring of houses. Those vessels tempered with rock were confined to the outer ring of houses. Vessels were made with individual recipes of tempering material specific to the house within which they were made. Despite this specificity of production all vessels were decorated in the same way. In the earliest phases of the Late Neolithic throughout Orkney Grooved Ware designs

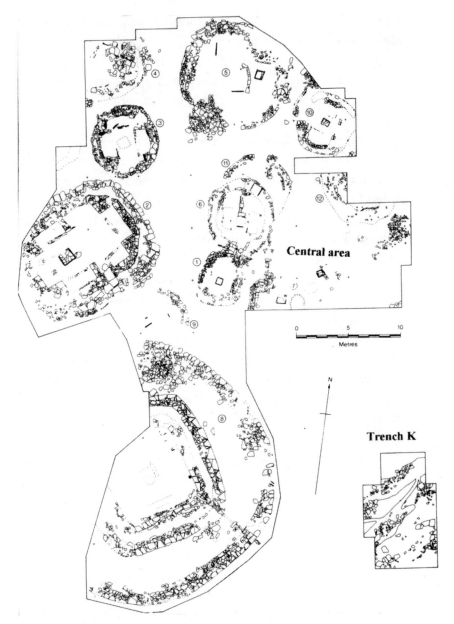

Central area

Trench K

14. Plan of the Late Neolithic village at Barnhouse, Orkney.

appear to be peculiar to specific settlements and seem to represent settlement-specific identities.

It was possible to determine by petrography and decoration that some of the Barnhouse vessels were eventually deposited in the ditch at the Stones of Stenness henge and the Quanterness passage grave (Jones 2002a).

Turning to the later phase of settlement, Grooved Ware is also associated with cooking activities on the platform and inner building of the monumental structure. The Grooved Ware in this context differs from the material in the earlier phase. Petrologically it contains all the rock sources that had been used in the earlier phase to distinguish distinct household identities. In terms of decoration the later pottery is composed of simple and repetitive horizontal cordons or incisions. These later Grooved Ware designs are identical to those used by all contemporary Later Neolithic settlements. The designs represent a communal Orcadian notion of identity.

Grooved Ware ceramics are flat based and, importantly, those from Orkney are the earliest flat-based ceramics in Britain, despite Clarke's assertion in the quotes at the beginning of this chapter concerning Beaker pottery and flat bases. At a few Orcadian settlement sites, including Barnhouse, we also find material that we might describe as Beaker pottery.

One infamous pot described by Childe as 'the most degenerate Beaker in the British Isles' was found in the house fill deposits at the settlement of Rinyo. It is characterised by a series of curvilinear designs executed with cord impressions. Recent excavations at the settlement of Crossiecrown have also revealed the presence of sherds of Beaker pottery within a Later Neolithic house (Fig. 15). Grooved Ware is also associated with the house and midden, whereas Beaker material was also found in the wall core and within the house structure itself. The Beaker was decorated with a series of horizontal cord impressions (or All-Over-Cord).

It is worth reviewing the sequence associated with Grooved Ware and Beakers in Orkney. The earliest forms of Grooved Ware are decorated in a similar fashion to designs in the passage grave art repertoire.

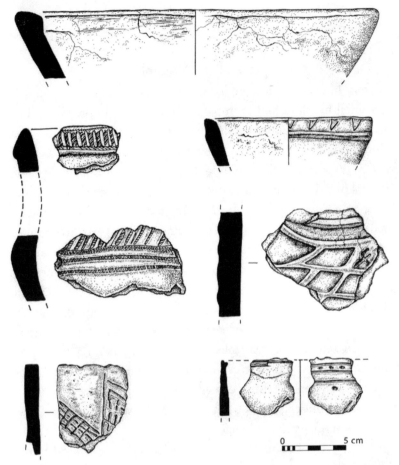

15. Grooved Ware and Beaker pottery from the Late Neolithic settlement at Crossiecrown, Orkney.

These designs are unique to individual settlements. My analysis of the Barnhouse Grooved Ware assemblage suggests that certain vessels are associated with the expression of settlement-specific identity. Towards the end of the Late Neolithic the production and use of Grooved Ware alters and designs are used that are common to all settlements in Orkney. In fact, so common are these designs that they are also found on some of the few Grooved Ware sherds found at Sumburgh on the Shetland Isles some 50 miles distant by sea. Over the course of the Neolithic, pottery decoration alters from something that denotes certain settlements to something that denotes the entire community.

During the later phase of the Neolithic we also observe two different kinds of technique used to decorate fine vessels: multiple horizontal incisions and multiple horizontal cord impressions. The first marks out vessels we would conventionally describe as 'Grooved Ware', and the second vessels we would call 'Beaker'. These 'Beaker' vessels are used alongside Grooved Ware and they are used in the same cultural practices. Given the communal and expansive nature of the later phase of pottery decoration and the parallel use of techniques of incision and cord impression it may be most appropriate to consider the late use of 'Beaker' pottery in the Neolithic sequence of Orkney as an attempt to produce 'Beaker' within the technological framework associated with Grooved Ware. Beaker decoration techniques are therefore indexed or cited by potters producing Grooved Ware. In this light it may be less important to think of Orkney beaker pottery as 'degenerate' and more realistic to see it as part of a process of innovation in which new ceramic forms were indexed and cited rather than being slavishly copied. This highlights the point that we need to understand the relationships between artefacts in an historical framework of change.

One of the curious aspects of the Later Neolithic of Orkney is the predominance of Grooved Ware ceramics and the relative absence of Beaker. To provide a contrast to this situation I want to briefly consider the nature of the Later Neolithic and Early Bronze Age of the Western Isles of Scotland. When we turn to examine the archaeology of the Western Isles we see a quite different picture emerging. The earlier Neolithic of the Hebrides is characterised by similar pottery traditions to Orkney, with the presence of Unstan pottery alongside so-called Hebridean Ware. However, the Later Neolithic is represented by a relative absence of Grooved Ware, the only examples being from the chambered tomb of Unival (Fig. 16) and the ceremonial monuments at Callanish (Armit 1993).

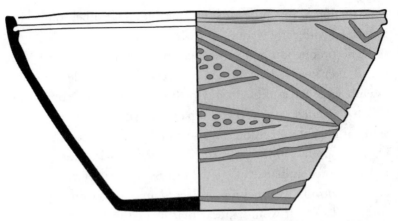

16. **The Grooved Ware vessel from the chambered tomb of Unival, Hebrides, Scotland (after Henshall 1966, 72).**

When we examine the nature of the settlement evidence for the Western Isles we observe a predominance of houses and middens, such as those at Dalmore, Northton, the Udal, Alt Chrysal, and Rosinish, associated with the use and deposition of Beaker pottery. Like the Orcadian Neolithic sites many of these sites appear to have an occupational history that began in the Earlier Neolithic (Armit 1993).

Like at Orkney, stone circles, chambered tombs, and settlements are associated with the deposition of pottery. However, the history of the use of each of these monuments is less unified and more complex. Chambered tombs of passage grave form were constructed during the Earlier Neolithic, but, unlike at Orkney, they are not associated with passage grave art (Henshall 1972). These monuments are continuously used from the earlier Neolithic onwards and we find Earlier Neolithic bowls, Grooved Ware, and Beaker associated with them. The construction of stone circles, such as the example at Callanish initiated around 3000 BC, overlaps with the construction of chambered tombs. This complex is associated with Grooved Ware alongside pottery decorated with cord impressions. The passage grave that forms the centre of the Callanish complex was built after the construction of the stone circle and avenues. Like other tombs, it is associated with early Neolithic bowls and Beaker.

The production and subsequent deposition of Grooved Ware and Beaker involved a continuum of techniques. While settlement assemblages such as those from Northton and Rosinish consisted of vessels decorated with the predominant use of cord and comb impressions, at Northton incision was also employed. Likewise, the assemblages of pottery from mortuary and ceremonial contexts appear to have a predominance of incised techniques (Armit 1996). However, we do observe incision and cord impression on the vessels from Callanish. It would appear that incised pottery, or 'Grooved Ware', was most appropriate for deposition in ceremonial and mortuary contexts, whereas comb/cord impressed 'Beaker' was used and deposited most appropriately in settlement contexts.

Our problems arise in analysing these contrasting situations since we place considerable emphasis on the material form/decoration of both Beakers and Grooved Ware, and we view these forms as conforming to an idealised and widespread Beaker or Grooved Ware culture. Instead, in these contexts we need to realise that at various points towards the end of the third millennium BC a continuum of decorative techniques and morphologies were employed as a mean of shaping and decorating ceramics; contrasting pottery styles were indexed and cited in different ways by different communities of potters. Importantly, we need to understand how pots bearing these techniques were deployed in the context of existing cultural practices and thereby understand how it is that ceramics were categorised through use rather than solely through the rigid definition of morphology and decoration.

In effect what I am saying is that, in Orkney, communities who produced Grooved Ware index or cite Beaker decoration and the products of this interaction were used in the same way as Grooved Ware. By contrast, in the Western Isles communities who produced Beaker pottery index or cite Grooved Ware decoration and the products of this interaction were used in a similar way to Beakers.

In each regional context the significance of the production techniques, uses and depositional practices that refer to Grooved Ware and those that refer to Beaker will be quite different because they reference cultural practices whose histories have unfolded in different ways in each region. Orkney has very few examples of Beaker pottery because Beakers were deployed within a technological framework shaped by the use of Grooved Ware. The Western Isles, however, deployed Beaker ceramics more extensively. Prior to this, or around the same time, Grooved Ware was also used; however, its use was restricted to nonsettlement contexts.

GROOVED WARE AND BEAKERS IN IRELAND

To further illustrate my argument, I want to examine the nature of cultural practices associated with Beakers and Grooved Ware in the Final Neolithic of Eastern Ireland. Here it is worth noting that both Grooved Ware and Beakers appear to have been adopted in Ireland at around the same time, 2500–2400 BC. If we are to understand the nature of Grooved Ware and Beaker in this region we also need to examine their contexts of deposition.

Let us deal with Beakers first. The notable aspect of Beaker ceramics in Ireland is that they are not used within single grave burials as they are in many areas of Britain and the Continent. Rather, they are used within settlement contexts and in the context of communal activities at timber circles, which I discuss below.

When we come to examine Beakers from settlement contexts we note that they are often large, decorated with comb and cord as at Dundrum, and fingernail impressions and incisions as at Dalkey Island. Beakers are notably also associated with the use of timber circles erected outside the passage tombs at both Newgrange and Knowth (Eogan and Roche 1999).

Grooved Ware is found in very small numbers in settlement sites such as Dalkey Island; however, it predominates in the context of timber circles such as Knowth, Bettystown, and Ballynahatty. It is also found in small numbers in the post-holes of the Newgrange timber enclosure (Brindley 1999).

It is worth examining the Grooved Ware and Beaker material from Knowth and Newgrange together. Petrological examinations of the Beaker and Grooved Ware from Newgrange and Knowth indicate similar techniques of manufacture (Cleary 1983). At both sites we observe a continuum of decoration and morphology. For instance, at Knowth many of the upright bucket-shaped vessels conventionally described as Grooved Ware are decorated with cord impressions, whereas the Beaker material was often decorated by incision. Moreover, at Newgrange (Fig. 17) we find pots with out-turned profiles much like conventional Beaker decorated with incisions (see Brindley 1999).

Interestingly, at Knowth we find a Beaker pot placed with a cremation in passage tomb 15 and a Grooved Ware pot placed with a cremation in passage tomb 6, while a further Grooved Ware pot was deposited in passage tomb 18 (Eogan 1986; Eogan and Roche 1999, 104). These depositional practices echo earlier mortuary practices, associated with Carrowkeel ware. At Knowth the timber circle outside the eastern passage of passage tomb 1 is predominantly associated with Grooved Ware, although Beaker and Grooved Ware are deposited together in the spread of material known as concentration A.

Similarly, at Newgrange, we appear to observe a distinction of activities in some areas with Grooved Ware and Beaker in the platform and entrance area of the passage tomb and Beaker predominating in the timber enclosure assemblage. At Newgrange and Knowth we observe structured deposition occurring within the continuum of material we describe as Beaker and Grooved Ware. At certain locations these categories of material overlap, whereas at other points they are kept apart.

The distinction in each category is illustrated by the contrasting use of the pottery technologies at Knowth and Newgrange. In both cases we observe the construction of timber enclosures. At

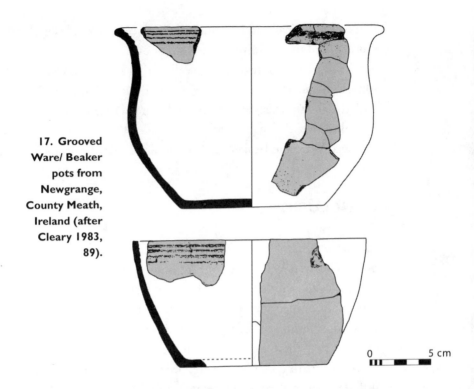

17. Grooved Ware/ Beaker pots from Newgrange, County Meath, Ireland (after Cleary 1983, 89).

0   5 cm

Newgrange a massive timber enclosure is associated with the large-scale consumption of food. Practices that may once have taken place within the passage tomb interior are now brought to the exterior and enacted in a more visible location. These are associated with Beaker and small quantities of Grooved Ware. At Knowth, the timber enclosure is also a context for similar kinds of feasting activity, although the nature and scale of this activity is much reduced and restricted compared to Newgrange. Its restrictive nature is underlined by the location of the timber enclosure in front of the entrance to the eastern tomb and its small size (comparable to the interior of the passage tomb). The more restricted activities associated with this monument are associated with Grooved Ware.

There are two ways in which we can consider the Beaker and Grooved Ware material associated with the final use of the Irish passage tombs. We can create rigid categories that appear to fit a unified or normative vision of culture, or we can embrace the fact that technologically and decoratively both ceramics index each other but are used in contrasting social situations.

In the Irish context it is revealing that Grooved Ware was for some considerable time categorised as Beaker. Although I do not wish to deny the existence of Grooved Ware in Ireland, it is important to realise that the manufacture and use of the pots we describe as Grooved Ware and Beaker draw on similar kinds of cultural practice.

CONCLUSION

As I have demonstrated through this detailed analysis of the Barnhouse Grooved Ware, the concept of a unified Grooved Ware culture belies the subtle ways in which artefacts are bound up with the expression of identities at a local scale (Jones 2000, 2002a, 2005b). If we consider this at the regional and interregional scale it becomes obvious that there never was a unified and homogenous Grooved Ware culture or a Beaker culture. Rather, as I have demonstrated in different regional contexts, ceramic technologies are used to create quite different categories of pottery, which are used in quite different contexts. When we consider the time depth involved this should not be viewed as problematic. The cultural histories associated with the use of Grooved Ware in Orkney are different to those bound up with the use of morphologically similar forms of pottery in southern Scotland, southern England, and eastern Ireland some hundreds of years later. In other words, there is no unified set of concepts associated with Grooved Ware over this time period. Similarly, the use of Beakers unfolds over a considerable period of time and is not consistent over all geographical areas.

Importantly, we need to view the adoption of ceramic technologies as a socially mediated exercise. The approach I adopt here is to view ceramic techniques to be components of complex citational and indexical fields. Each artefact is positioned in a nexus of indexes and is in effect a 'hybrid' that indexes or refers to a host of influences. In this chapter I have shown how by taking account of these contrasting influences it is possible to write nuanced histories of the adoption and use of pottery technologies free from overarching schemes of culture-historical development. I have tried to show how these influences are historically motivated, how indexing differing technologies may be a reference to either the past or the future or simply to the distant and the exotic.

The use of Grooved Ware in Orkney was strongly related to the expression of a widening regional and interregional identity and it is within this context that Beakers technologies were employed. In the Western Isles, the technologies associated with Beaker ceramics were employed to define continuity with previous occupation practices. Grooved Ware technologies were deployed to mark out ceramics used only in specific ceremonial contexts. Both ceramics were deployed in existing mortuary practices.

In eastern Ireland the adoption of the ceramic technologies associated with Grooved Ware and Beakers occurred at an important juncture of change when we observe a shift in ritual action away from the secretive activities of the interior of the passage tomb to the more inclusive arena outside the tomb. The technologies were deployed as a means of differentially demarcating arenas of open and closed display.

I take it as read that exchange was taking place around the Irish Sea during the Late Neolithic/Early Bronze Age, indeed in many cases exchange relations are easily demonstrated (Cooney 1999). The questions we should be considering are not whether there was contact but rather how local and regional identities were expressed and in what context and through what materials relationships were expressed. We are required to write more fine tuned and detailed histories of regions through an understanding of the nature of the cultural practices distinct to each region rather than simply cataloguing bodies of material and looking for similar material traits across regions.

There are no codified bodies of cultural practice associated with the use of Beakers or Grooved Ware that we can apply blanket fashion from above onto regions. Rather, each region deploys material culture according to its own specific frameworks of understanding. Rather than taking up a view of regions and regional identities as if occupying a view from afar by cataloguing similarities and differences in material culture we instead need to consider the way in which regions play out distinct historical trajectories related to the expression of distinct cultural practices and distinct kinds of identities.

In this chapter I have considered how through production artefacts act as nodes in indexical networks or fields and how by indexing or citing other technologies or decorative styles the production of artefacts draws on historically contingent factors. In Chapter 7, I continue to examine artefacts by considering artefact assemblages as indexical fields.

7

Chains of Memory

The Aesthetics of Memory in Bronze Age Britain

As shown in the previous chapter, artefact categories have often been treated as 'natural kinds' that can be categorised in much the same way as animal and plant species. As a result archaeologists have long assumed a relatively passive relationship between artefacts and their producers. For instance, we see little attention paid to the influence one artefact has upon the producer in the production of further artefacts. Instead we prefer to classify groups of artefacts morphologically and decoratively according to their cultural affinity. One means by which archaeologists compare artefacts is through the medium of the corpus, a printed volume with illustrated examples of artefacts that can be compared one to the other, almost as clients would compare one pattern with another in the pattern books of the eighteenth century. In this chapter I argue we need to divest ourselves of the comparative approach engendered by the archaeological corpus if we are to understand how memory is reproduced in prehistory. As I show at the end of this chapter the aesthetics of memory promoted by the printed page of the corpus, and the aesthetics of memory engendered by prehistoric mortuary practices, are of a wholly different nature.

The culture-historical method provides the impulse for the creation of the corpus of artefacts. Such an approach assumes a relatively passive role for culture. The possession of culture is here assumed to have an effect upon the morphology and decoration of artefacts, and this effect is often treated as if it were passive. However, the influence of culture is dependent upon an unexamined assumption about social practices. If we consider that culture only exists inasmuch as it is manifested in social interaction then we need to consider the nature of the social interaction instantiated through artefact production. We tend to forget, then, that the artefacts depicted in the corpus were once embroiled in the social lives of past populations.

There are a number of alternate ways in which we can discuss the relationships between people and artefacts. One common approach has been to consider the ways in which the lives of artefacts are entangled with the lives of people by examining the course of the cultural biography of artefacts. This approach has been adopted in various forms elsewhere (Hoskins 1998; Jones 2002a, 2002b; Gosden and Marshall 1999; Meskell 2004; Thomas 1996a; Tilley 1996). Alternatively, we might examine the connections between artefacts and the way these are used to make and reinforce connections between people. For example, John Chapman (2000a) examines the relationship between artefacts in terms of fragmentation, arguing that in the context of the Neolithic and Copper Age of the Balkans the physical breakage and sharing of artefacts created enchained relationships. However, enchained relationships between people may be expressed in ways other than physical breakage. For example, we can think of the indexical relationships between artefacts as a form of enchainment; where artefacts are related by physical similarity or contiguity.

BRONZE AGE ARTEFACT ASSEMBLAGES

Examinations of Bronze Age material culture tend to implicitly employ the passive notion of causality described above to organise material culture into chronologically and geographically distinct horizons or cultures (Burgess 1980; Needham 1996). In these studies the morphological, decorative, and contextual similarities or differences amongst artefacts are assumed to provide links between artefacts and so aid in their temporal and spatial classification. I also want to examine these morphological and decorative traits and, further, in terms of their relationship to each other. But first I wish to reconsider the nature of these relationships.

I want to suggest, following Gell (1998: 221–58), that we examine artefacts as part of an *oeuvre* or network. The concept of protention or retention evident in artefact traits is implicit to archaeologists' attempts to understand the cultural classification of artefacts. For instance, we assume two artefacts to be temporally or spatially coextensive if they appear the same. I do not wish to challenge this assumption; rather, I want to analyse this in terms of the social relations encapsulated by this relationship. Rather than assuming a spurious cultural relationship to exist amongst groups of artefacts, I want to examine groups of artefacts in terms of the social relationships that arise from relations of similarity or difference. Moreover, I will examine the relationship between the ordering of these social relations and particular conceptualisations of memory.

To paraphrase Gell (1998: 250): each object is a place where agency stops and assumes material form. Artefacts objectify the social relations binding people together, and we can trace these social relations spatially or temporally by examining dimensions of difference and similarity in the material and contextual nature of artefacts.

AESTHETICS, DEPOSITION, AND BURIAL IN THE BRITISH BRONZE AGE

At this point I want to examine the nature of the connections between various aspects of Early Bronze Age material culture in a particular region – eastern Scotland. The purpose of this is to draw out both the similarities and differences between the material practices of deposition and the consequences these have for our understanding of issues of aesthetics and memory. I want to examine the archaeology of this area at two scales of analysis. Firstly, I examine the relationship amongst the decoration of pottery, metalwork, and adornment at a broad level. Secondly – through a detailed analysis of selected mortuary deposits and hoards – I examine the contextual differences between the deposition of metalwork and pottery and the consequences they have for issues of remembrance.

The earlier Bronze Age archaeology of eastern Scotland is particularly rich. For the period under consideration we observe the deposition of pottery vessels in mortuary contexts, either alongside an inhumed individual or as a container for one or more cremated individuals. For the period from 2500 to 2000 BC beaker pottery is often deposited in mortuary contexts, whereas food vessels, either placed with an inhumation or containing a cremation, overlap with the currency of beaker use and continue to at least 1500 BC. Beyond this period, from 1500 to 1000 BC, the deposition of cremated human remains continues in large cordoned or collared urns.

In eastern Scotland we find both beaker and food vessel burials in isolated stone-built cist graves, in small cemeteries of two or three cists sometimes in a mound, or occasionally in cemetery complexes such as Borrowstone, Kingswells, Aberdeenshire (Shepherd 1986), or Barns Farm, Dalgety, Fife (Watkins 1982). Beaker graves are especially concentrated in northeastern Scotland

(Shepherd 1986), whereas food vessel graves are more widespread through eastern Scotland. Eastern Scotland is also well known for its impressive deposits of earlier Bronze Age metalwork (Burgess and Schmidt 1981; Coles 1969; Cowie 1988). Large concentrations of bronze axes are deposited in Aberdeenshire, Banffshire, and Moray. These objects are found either singly or in axe hoards, such as that at the Pass of Ballater, Aberdeenshire, or at Durris, Kincardine (Cowie 1988).

Traditionally beakers and food vessels have been treated as chronologically overlapping. Although there are some difficulties with regional (Shepherd 1986) or national (Needham 1996) chronologies, I want to pay less attention to the chronological distinctions between these ceramics to concentrate on their decorative similarities. Moreover, I want to examine these similarities in relation to metalwork and adornments, also concentrated in mortuary contexts in eastern Scotland (Callander 1916; Shepherd 1985). One important point I wish to emphasise when examining decoration is the relatively restricted range of motifs deployed on a number of Earlier Bronze Age portable artefacts (Fig. 18). These motifs include lozenges, chevrons, triangles, and cross-hatching. That these motifs are indeed restricted and deliberately drawn from a wider suite of other possible motifs is evinced by the comparison of these motifs with the repertoire of motifs found at contemporary rock art sites. Here circular motifs such as cups, rings, and rosettes predominate. Given that circular motifs are found on earlier ceramic traditions, such as Late Neolithic Grooved Ware, the appearance of linear motifs on Earlier Bronze Age artefacts should be seen as a deliberate choice.

Although it has long been noted that certain motifs are held in common between beakers and objects of adornment such as gold lunulae (Eogan 1994; Taylor 1970, 1980), it has not been widely appreciated that the same motifs are also often held in common between jet necklaces and food vessels. Moreover, an examination of the occurrence of these motifs on these artefacts reveals a striking correlation – both gold lunulae and jet necklaces are typically decorated with lozenge or triangular motifs on their spacer-plates or upper section. Similarly, where we observe lozenge or triangular motifs on beakers and food vessels they are typically executed around the upper zone of the vessel (in the case of beakers this is often mirrored by decoration near the base). The correlation between the decoration of pottery and the decoration of articles of adornment is striking. The spatial patterning of motifs on these objects also appears to correspond to one another (see Fig. 18).

Although much metalwork remains undecorated, where we do find decoration on metal artefacts such as axes we also observe the same motifs (Bradley 1990: 82–7). Again, the range of motifs are fairly restricted (Fig. 18), and again we observe chevrons as well as cross-hatching and linear zoning (Megaw and Hardy 1938). Where these motifs occur on metalwork they are not necessarily patterned in horizontal zones from the top of the object to the bottom as we observe with pottery and body adornments; more often they run vertically down the length of the artefact. In this instance the decoration works with the form of the artefact.

There seems, then, to be a close relationship between the decoration of the body and the decoration of contemporary ceramics. Moreover, these decorative motifs extend to metal objects such as axes. Through decoration we see a referential or citational field established across different categories of objects: metalwork, pots, and various form of adornment. It would be possible to posit a metaphorical relationship amongst pots, metal objects such as axes, and the human body. However, this equation may be too literal. I do not believe we need to conceive of pots and axes as bodies; rather, we need to think of them as 'of the body' – they have bodylike qualities and in certain contexts these qualities are brought to bear in the construction of meaningful action. I prefer to think of decoration in each of these contexts as a means of material 'citation' in which traces on each artefact establish relations of similitude within a wider matrix of similarities and differences.

The concept of citation is especially important at a more detailed level of analysis, such as in a mortuary context, where each depositional episode involves drawing on previous actions (Mizoguchi

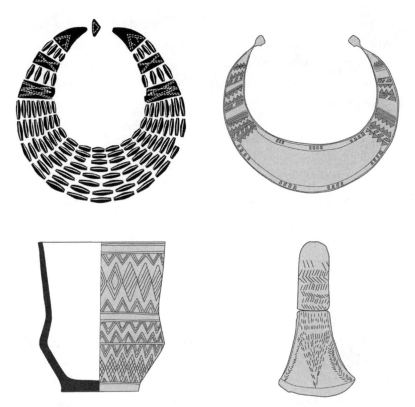

18. Comparison of the position of decorative motifs on a variety of artefacts from the Early Bronze Age. (Top left) Jet spacer plate necklace; (top right) gold lanula; (bottom left) beaker pot; (bottom right) bronze flat axe.

1993). Mizoguchi notes that people are situated in time and space by the consequences of previous practices and bring these to bear in the articulation of existent mortuary practices. Rather than perceiving this process in terms of constraint I examine how various media are rearticulated (or cited) to create fresh categories of material culture.

Chapman (2000b) discusses these concepts in his examination of the construction of identities in cemetery contexts in Late Neolithic/Copper Age Hungary. Importantly, he moves between the nature of material expression in single graves and material expression with regard to the cemetery as a whole. I intend to utilise this insight in my discussion of Earlier Bronze Age mortuary practices while also drawing on the wider regional picture. While Chapman concentrates on the body and its accoutrements I also focus on (1) morphology, (2) design structure, (3) decorative motifs, and (4) context of artefacts. I explore these in two mortuary contexts and two metal hoard contexts.

■ A TALE OF TWO CEMETERIES

At North Mains, Strathallan, Perthshire, we observe a complex series of Earlier Bronze Age mortuary practices (Barclay 1983). The Earlier Bronze Age activities are concentrated in two zones of the site: in relation to a Late Neolithic henge and a barrow. The henge is reused during the Early Bronze Age and contains 16 inhumations or cremations (Fig. 19), associated with beakers, food vessels, and urns. The barrow contains 10 inhumations and cremations, some associated with food vessels. Central to the henge is the inhumation of a 20- to 25-year-old female with a food vessel in a deep cist (burial B). The food vessel is of bowl form and is decorated by opposed incision and stab motifs. The vessel contained a cereal-based food or liquid flavoured with *Filipendula* (meadowsweet). The significance of this is discussed below in the section 'Powerful Pots and Magic Metal'. Deposited either side of this burial is an adult inhumation also placed in a deep cist (burial C); difference is here signalled by the absence of any vessel. Burial D is in a shallow cist and consists of inhumation with a small cremation deposit. A food vessel was placed in the corner of the cist. The food vessel has a similar profile to the one in burial B, although its whipped cord decorative motifs signal difference, as does its shallow depositional context and unusual relationship to both cremation and inhumation. A further inhumation (burial E) was placed in a shallow cist, like burial D, but this burial was inserted into the henge bank outside the main cemetery. This burial was accompanied by a broken food vessel. The shape of this

NORTH MAINS HENGE

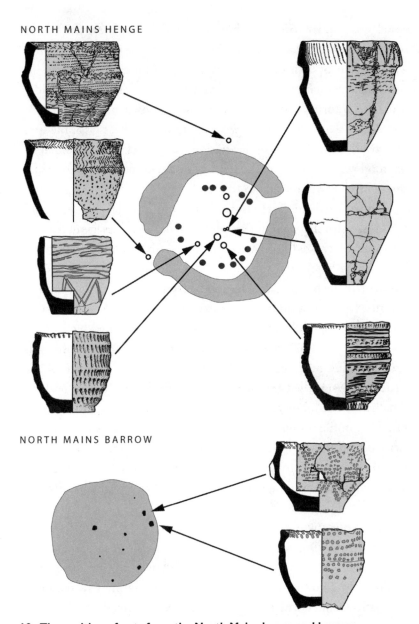

NORTH MAINS BARROW

19. The position of pots from the North Mains henge and barrow.

vessel was similar to that in burial B, and decoratively the use of zoned stab motifs is also similar. However, on this vessel these zones were broken by twisted cord as well as incisions. Burial F was an adult male cremation and was accompanied by a struck stone and a squat vessel formally described as a beaker (Cowie in Barclay 1983: 155–6). In shape the 'beaker' is similar to the food vessels at the site; moreover, the technique of decoration used – incision – is similar to the food vessels. However, the decoration is composed of a zone of a zigzag or chevron unusual to the food vessels.

Three burials are also found in urns. One (burial K) is an enlarged food vessel urn that contains an adult female. This vessel is decorated by zones of twisted cord chevrons above the shoulder and bone impressions below the shoulder. These decorative techniques are redolent of techniques on the food vessels from burials B and E described earlier, although their execution differs. Another urned burial (J) of an adult male and child was accompanied by a struck stone. The urn was undecorated although its bipartite profile was similar to the other urns on the site, whereas the presence of the struck stone signalled a similarity to the cremation with the 'beaker'. Finally, we also observe a collared urn containing an adult (burial H). The profile of this urn was similar to that of the others and had twisted cord zigzag on its collar area and fingernail motifs below this. Internally it was decorated by linear twisted cord around the rim. The technique and design structure of this urn is similar to that of the enlarged food vessel.

The construction of the barrow at North Mains is initiated by a central post ring with a series of fence divisions radiating from the centre. These radial features were followed by the deposition of different colours of soil in sections of the mound to compose the barrow superstructure. The mound was capped with a stone layer. A series of cists and pits were inserted into the mound at various points during its construction (Fig. 19). Two of these were inhumations placed close together at one edge of the mound. The inhumation of a child was placed in a cist grave with a food vessel and a flint scraper. The food vessel was decorated with zones of bone-end impressions on the upper body, whereas the rim was decorated with whipped cord impressions. The second inhumation was deposited with a food vessel and a jet necklace. In this case the food vessel differed in shape from the first, but decoration was also executed by bone-end impressions in horizontal zones across the body, rim, and base. Six further cists were constructed in the body of the barrow and each of these contained between two and eight cremated individuals, and some of these were also associated with flint implements, such as knives. Finally two cremation deposits were placed in the upper area of the barrow.

A series of citations are articulated between vessels in different mortuary events. Citations are made spatially between henge and barrow, where we observe similar techniques of decoration on vessels. However, the network of citations also extends through time as elements of mortuary practice relate the earlier beaker cremation deposit with the later bipartite urn cremation deposit. In the case of both henge and barrow the nature of deposits are simultaneously used to define differences in mortuary practice. In the henge, food vessels are used to define inhumations, whereas beakers and then urns are used to define cremations. In the barrow food vessels define inhumations, whereas cremations are defined by the absence of ceramic deposits.

By way of comparison, I now want to examine the citations between depositional practices at another cemetery. The cemetery at Gairneybank, Kinross-shire (Cowie and Ritchie 1991), consists of five cist burials inserted into a low gravel ridge running NW-SE in a linear fashion (Fig. 20). The most northerly cist contained a flexed inhumation with a small bronze knife-dagger and a small pottery bowl. The bowl has four lugs, and the rim is decorated with bird bone impressions. The body is decorated with a complex design of twisted cord impressions encircling whipped cord maggot impressions. The second cist contains a crouched inhumation with a food vessel. The vase-shaped food vessel is decorated with zones of alternating linear and diagonal twisted cord impressions, therefore, the same technique as used on the bowl in cist 1. The third cist also contained a crouched inhumation with the right humerus, radius, and ulna from a pig. There were two further cists associated with pottery vessels, although we have no skeletal data for these deposits. The first vessel is a beaker decorated by incisions with two zones of opposed triangles containing cross-hatched infill. The second vessel is a food vessel with zones of alternating twisted cord and bone-end impressions. As with North Mains we can observe a series of citations occurring within the context of the cemetery. The small pottery bowl – treated as anomalous by the excavators (see Cowie and Ritchie 1991: 105–7) due to its problematic form and decoration – is related, by decoration and depositional context, to the two other food vessels. Similarly, although the beaker stands out morphologically and decoratively it is also zoned like the food vessel and possesses a cordon very much like food vessels.

What the analyses of these cemeteries indicate is that each cemetery is composed of individual deposits that are made with reference to the wider cemetery structure. Rather than categories of artefacts and depositional contexts being constructed at a synoptic level, instead we observe that each cemetery has its own internal logic. Categories are constructed 'from the ground up' with reference to previous contexts and categories of burial. Each burial act therefore cites previous burial events in its construction. What I consider is how artefacts mediate the reproduction of burial practices and to what degree particular conceptualisations of aesthetics and memory have a part to play in this mediation.

Before considering what these citations have to tell us about the nature of memory I examine the nature of depositional practices in relation to contemporary metalwork hoards (spanning the period 2200–1500 BC). One of the most spectacular hoards from the region is that at Colleonard Farm, Banffshire (Burgess and Schmidt 1981; Cowie 1988). Here seven bronze axes were deposited blades upward in a food vessel, which was protected by two stones. Six of these axes are decorated (Fig. 21). Three had repeated zones of 'raindrop' motifs – a series of punched incisions into the surface of the metal. Another three of the axes had relief decoration running down the length of the blade. A further two of these axes were decorated with

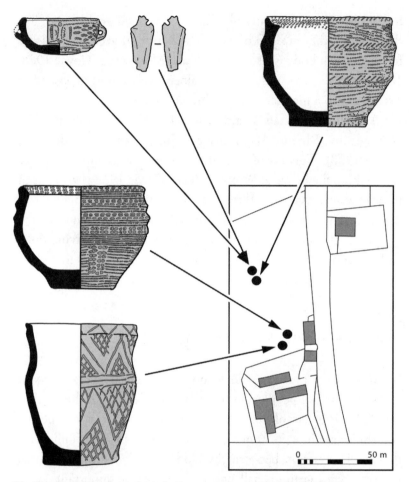

20. The location of artefacts in the cemetery at Gairneybank, Kinross-shire, Scotland.

a short linear motif dotted around its outer sides. Notably the food vessel that contained them cited some of the decorative motifs found on the metalwork with a series of short stab motifs around the belly of the vessel, while the upper edge had a series of short linear motifs. The metalwork is worn and two axes were broken. A series of citational practices link these objects. The groups of axes decorated in a similar way cite each other, while the food vessel signals its relationship to the axes. The context of this deposit draws on or cites contemporary mortuary practices; the axes here seem to stand for the cremated human bones more commonly deposited in food vessels, and, like these bones, they are also broken. The notion of axes as surrogates for the human body is also cited at Sluie, Morayshire (Cowie 1988: 18), where two axes and a copper halberd were found deposited in a stone cist in a manner akin to a human burial.

A further important hoard of metalwork comes from the Hill of Finglenny, Rhynie, Aberdeenshire (Burgess and Schmidt 1981; Cowie 1988). This hoard of seven axes was placed under a stone overlooking the henge at Wormyhillock (Cowie 1988: 19). Four of the axes were intact, while three had been deliberately snapped across the blade (Fig. 21). Interestingly, although the axes were undecorated they were all tinned (see Needham and Kinnes 1981), giving them a silvery appearance. Due to this process each axe indexes the others as they constitute part of a set.

POWERFUL POTS AND MAGIC METAL

Both mortuary practices and hoards constitute deliberate acts of burial: the first of people and things and the second of things. At a simple level the act of burial constitutes a process in which people and things are hidden from view and removed from visibility. It is the simple equation between the hidden and forgetting in burial practices that I want to challenge here. One of the important points to have arisen from my analysis of the two cemeteries was the inter-relationship between ceramics and mortuary practices deposited on the same site over a considerable period of time. I described this in terms of citation, in which fresh categories of mortuary practice are created through the creative manipulation of previous mortuary practices (Mizoguchi 1993). But how are we to understand these citational practices? How are mortuary and other depositional practices reproduced?

Here it is important to examine the coherence between memorial practices and notions of aesthetics. We need to reassess the nature of the materiality of decoration amongst other sensual dimensions

FINGLENNY

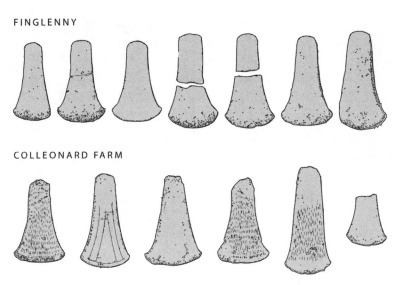

COLLEONARD FARM

21. The axe hoards from the Hill of Finglenny and Colleonard Farm.

of Earlier Bronze Age depositional practices. There remains a tendency to view aspects of an object's materiality such as decoration and colour as an addition to the central function of the object (Boast 1998b). Often decoration is considered in terms of its role in signalling identities (Wobst 1977). Although this may be a dimension of the nature of decoration, we need to examine how decoration operates as such and, moreover, how this relates to mnemonic processes. Here Gell (1996, 1998) makes some crucial points. He discusses the visual and sensual dimensions of art objects in terms of their abilities to affect the viewer or recipient. It is this aspect of an object that imbues it with its ability to extend the cognitive influence of the object's maker spatially and temporally. Objects are able to perform this function due to their decorative or aesthetic immediacy, captured in terms of their decoratively complex, colourful, or sensually striking material form (see Gell 1996). One of the important aspects of this process is that the efficacy of objects is determined not simply by their immediate effect upon observers but also by the afterlife of that effect; in other words, the manner by which that effect is retained in memory.

It is important then to explore the modalities by which the aesthetic dimensions of Earlier Bronze Age depositional practices are related to the production of memory. I want to argue that a number of features of Earlier Bronze Age depositional practices are bound up with the creation of memory. One of the obvious modes by which this may operate is through decoration and colour (Jones 2002b). Investigation by the author of a range of beakers from Aberdeenshire, Banffshire, and Kincardineshire held in Marischal College Museum, Aberdeen, indicated three important aspects of beaker decoration. Firstly, the zoning, which is characteristic of Northeastern Scottish beakers, meant that the surface of the beaker alternated between undecorated smooth burnished zones and roughly textured zones of decoration. Secondly, decoration is visually complex and the interrelations of zones of decoration disrupt the easy visual inspection of the beaker surface. Finally, a number of beakers exhibited a degree of whitening in the decorated zone. While this aspect of beaker has been remarked on previously, if it can be accepted in the case of the northeastern Scottish beakers, then this also serves to emphasise the visual contrast of decoration. Although these effects are found on beakers the effect of decoration in certain extensively decorated food vessels is even more pronounced. While decoration on food vessels by no means occurs in all cases, many food vessels are extensively decorated on rim, body, and base, as we have seen with the examples from North Mains and Gairneybank.

It is interesting at this point to note the difference between the occurrence of decoration on ceramics and on metalwork. Whereas the vast majority of Earlier Bronze Age ceramics are decorated, the majority of metalwork remains undecorated. This pattern differs when we examine the occurrence of decorated metalwork in hoard contexts where the incidence of decorated metalwork rises (see Needham 1988). While metalwork is largely undecorated there are other dimensions which make it sensually striking, especially its colour and brilliance. As we have seen, the axes from the Hill of Finglenny were tinned sometime prior to deposition, giving them an especially luminous surface. Early Bronze Age artefacts in eastern Scotland are marked out by their decorative complexity and colour.

A further sensual dimension of Earlier Bronze Age depositional practices relates to taste and smell. I noted earlier that the food vessel from burial B at North Mains henge contained a cereal-based substance flavoured with meadowsweet. However, the association between food and drink and the deposition of meadowsweet is a more widespread practice in this region of Scotland. Tipping (1994) notes examples of pollen from *Filipendula* sp. (meadowsweet or dropwort) in graves from Sketewan, Perthshire; Beech Hill House, Angus; Loanleven, Perthshire; and Ashgrove, Fife. A further example comes from Dalgety Bay, Fife (Whittington 1993). The majority of these samples are from the floor of the cist and probably represent a carpet of flowers on the base of the grave. The examples from North Mains (Bohncke 1983), Beech Hill House (Tipping 1994), and Ashgrove (Dickson 1978) are more likely to constitute flavoured food or an alcoholic drink such as mead (see Dickson 1978). The prosaic interpretation – that flowers were employed to disguise the stench of decay – is insufficient because *Filipendula* is found in graves containing both inhumations and cremations. Instead, I believe that we need to emphasise the embodied nature of mortuary practices. Smell and taste are constitutive of memory, especially in the context of mortuary practices (Eves 1996; Foster 1991; Siegel 1983). The smell and taste of *Filipendula* is apt in this context because the plant is seasonal, flowering in early summer. Its smell would be redolent of the season and may relate to the temporality of the mortuary practices. The smell of *Filipendula* would serve to evoke the memory of the burial when the flowers came into bloom on subsequent years.

Each of the instances I have discussed relates to the embodied nature of mortuary and other depositional practices during the Earlier Bronze Age. I would argue that in each context the embodiment of the senses is productive of memory (see also Hamilakis 1999). In relation to mortuary practices, both the objects surrounding the corpse and the smells and tastes associated with the mortuary ritual are related to notions of consumption. As the consumptive abilities of the deceased are disrupted so, through smell, taste, touch, colour, and decoration the image of the deceased is consumed by the mourners. The sensual dimensions of mortuary rituals therefore act as agents of memory; the senses integrate the memory of the deceased with that of the mourners. The memory of the deceased is extended beyond the grave through the medium of artefacts and other forms of material culture.

The impact of decoration on pottery is another critical dimension of the extension of memory. Notably, in mortuary contexts pots are generally deposited whole. In those contexts in which pots are placed in proximity to the body the pot is used as an adjunct to the equally powerful visible reminder of the human body. In some cases, as at North Mains barrow burial G, the body is adorned with a necklace which also serves as a visual reminder of the deceased (see Jones 2001b). The close relationship between pot and person is referenced through similarities in decorative motif. This is especially true of cremation burials where the pot stands for the deceased. Indeed, with the use of urns in burial we observe the upper area of the vessel – the area traditionally reserved for adornment on the person – becoming the focus for decoration. The most obvious instance of this is with collared urns in which decoration is generally above the collar.

As Barrett (1991) notes the variability of pottery from the Earlier Bronze Age may relate to the need to emphasise different categories of people. The mnemonic capacities of pottery decoration may be implicated in this process. At the moment of burial the pot acts as a visual index of the person and therefore the potential of the pot to act as reminder is increased. In this context pot and person are fused. The decoration of pottery serves to experientially define the memories related to the individual deposited.

In the context of metalwork deposits we observe fewer incidences of decoration and a far greater number of broken objects. Whether we consider metalwork deposits to be the result of exchange cycles or mortuary deposits, decoration and colour here serve as a means of presencing absent social actors. As such the fragmentation of metalwork serves to divide social ties while also being productive of fresh relationships of exchange, as broken segments may be shared or circulated in fresh exchange relations (Chapman 2000a). In this context decoration does not signify particular individuals as in the mortuary context but indexes the relationship between individuals.

TECHNOLOGIES OF REMEMBRANCE: CITATION, AESTHETICS, AND MEMORY IN THE PAST AND PRESENT

I now want to draw out the distinct nature of Bronze Age technologies of remembrance in contrast to those of the present. To do this I return to the notion of indexical fields or citational fields, discussed in Chapter 4. The notion of citation, encapsulating as it does the reiteration of previous practices and the creation of fresh categories, is concerned with the reproduction of memory. As Connerton (1989: 6–40) notes, all acts contain an element of recollection as previous practices are continually drawn on and reworked in the formulation of present practices. What I want to discuss in this instance is the role of aesthetics in the mobilisation, transference, and transformation of memory, comparing the Bronze Age with the present.

From the outset it is important not to draw hard and fast distinctions between present aesthetic regimes and those of the Bronze Age. One obvious point of similarity is that in both cases memories are materialised – in the present in the form of printed matter, books, compact discs, and other forms of digital storage technology. In the Early Bronze Age in the form of pots and metalwork. In each case memory is manifest in material traces (Mines and Weiss 1993). The real differences lie not in the distinction between embodied or disembodied mnemonic practices but in the *material nature of their transmission.*

During the Earlier Bronze Age memories are evoked through sensual immediacy, and the citations that are drawn on in the formulation and reformulation of mortuary practices are retentions of remembered practices generated through the intense sensual atmosphere of previous mortuary practices. In the case of both metalwork and pottery the destruction or burial of artefacts constitutes a commemorative act, which is generative of fresh memories. The memory of the absent social actor (or the deceased) is extended beyond the existential plane and ultimately rematerialised in the form of pottery and metalwork and through other means. Indeed, it is the repetitive nature of cycles of deposition during the Earlier Bronze Age (see Bradley 1990) that is actively generative of memories. Memories are evoked materially and sensually by the presence of three-dimensional objects and through immediate embodied sensual horizons, such as smell, taste, texture, and colour (Jones 2004). The reproduction of memory requires the immediate attention of the embodied subject. The citational field or *oeuvre* available for the reproduction of memory is therefore limited to the sensual environment of the subject.

Fields of citation do exist at various levels, beginning with the cemetery and extending to wider spheres of exchange relations, and they also extend between conventional categories of material. While citational fields are fairly restricted spatially I argue that they are temporally extensive, because earlier artefacts and practices are implicated by citation in later artefacts and practices. In this case the *oeuvre* associated with artefacts can be seen as a unity of discrete but related 'events' distributed in time. Crucially the aesthetic dimensions of artefacts and practices are bound up with the mnemonic process of creating and expressing the *oeuvre*.

Of course, contemporary practices of memorialisation are also materialised aesthetically. Memory is still evoked through the conduit of the materiality of the artefact (see, for example, Edwards 1999 on photography and materiality) and the evocation of memory occurs at the same embodied scale as in the Bronze Age. However, the technology of print renders a difference between the printed page and the Bronze Age artefact. Printing renders three-dimensional objects into two-dimensional objects. Although this transposition may involve a degree of loss of sensual immediacy it simultaneously expands the citational field. In this instance the citational field has *spatially* expanded, as through the medium of the page objects are easily circulated. In this case the *oeuvre* – the entire corpus of a given artefact – is laid before the reader. Just as the book provides us with spatial extension it contracts the temporal field as the printed page aestheticises memory as a form of static temporal trace. The *oeuvre* is atemporalised. Here aesthetics are not so much implicated in memory production; instead, memory is aestheticised two dimensionally on the printed page.

The reduction of certain senses coupled with the optical expansion of citational fields is a product of a particular way of knowing in which the 'jural' process of visual witnessing came to the fore (Shapin and Schaffer 1985). This process is not unique to the medium of the printed page and there are plenty of historical antecedants for this visual materialisation of knowledge. For example, Evans has recently discussed the use of archaeological models in the early stages of the discipline (Evans 2000). However, the visualisation of knowledge through models and through illustrations on the printed page is distinguished by the two-dimensional nature of the page.

We observe a distinction, then, between the printed volume and the Bronze Age artefact. The printed page captures certain qualities of the archaeological artefact while losing others. It is not my intention to draw distinctions between a prelapsarian sensually rich aesthetic and a postlapsarian sensually impoverished one (see Ingold 2000a: 243–87), rather the main point I want to draw out in this chapter is simply that *particular materialities are associated with specific conceptualisations of memory.*

8

The Art of Memory

Memory, Inscription, and Place

Prehistoric societies are often referred to as societies without texts, societies before written history. I have yielded to the overarching distinction between prehistory and history as all the prehistoric examples I have discussed so far have focussed on the nontextual and implicit use of artefacts in commemorative practices. In Chapters 8 and 9 I shift my focus to inscription as a possible form of explicit commemorative practice.

The appearance of writing has traditionally been seen to accompany a shift in social organisation. Childe (1981 [1950]) considered writing to be one of the defining components of civilisation; a corollary of the 'urban revolution' (Childe 1981[1950], 144–5). However, the simplistic relationship between writing and the emergence of states is called into question by the existence of the *quipu* or *khipu*, a knotted cord artefact used to convey information, in use by the Inka state. As Salomon remarks: 'the fact that some huge states got along without writing should invite searching questions about whether grammatological or anthropological understandings of writing are really up to the task of explaining relations among language, inscription, social practice and socio-political integration' (Salomon 2001, 1). Another example comes from the use of writing in the Shang period of China c. 1500–1045 BC. Written scripts are found on the plastron (lower shell) of tortoises, which are subsequently burnt and fragmented. It is likely this early script was used on these 'oracle bones' for the purposes of divination rather than administration (Highham 2005, 558–9). The presence or absence of written texts need not imply anything about levels of sociopolitical organisation; if we are to delve deeper into explanations for writing, we need to consider the possible use of systems of inscription in prehistory and, further, how such systems relate to wider social practices.

WRITING WITHOUT WORDS

Much has been made of the disjunction between oral and literary traditions, with many commentators proposing a radical alteration in cognitive capacity and social organisation with the emergence of text (Donald 1998; Goody 1977; Ong 1982). I discussed this in Chapter 1. Here I reprise this discussion to emphasize two points. The first point, as Dewey and Childs (1996, 61) note, is that 'complementary modes of remembrance operate at the same time: "inscriptive" ones such as oral and textual recollections interact with "performative" or "embodied" modes.' As we shall see this point is important because it allows us to consider the way in which inscription (in the case of the next two chapters, the production of 'art' carved on stones) occurs as a component of embodied and place-centred commemorative practice.

The second point is that we are mistaken in solely treating text as a form of external symbolic storage, whereby texts represent an externalised historical 'truth' distinct from the frail mnemonic abilities of humans. On the contrary, I believe that in certain historical contexts texts are also treated as performative and embodied and, as such, are open to the invention and reinterpretation inherent in performance. They merely provide cues for remembrance rather than existing as absolute and inviolate records of historical events. The grammatologist Roy Harris (1995) distinguishes between what he describes as 'telementational' theories of human communication and 'integrational' theories. Telementational theories (of which Saussure's theory of the sign is one) 'envisage two individuals (A and B) attempting to resolve the problem of transferring a thought already formulated independently in one mind (that of A) to the other mind (that of B). Communication is achieved if and only if the transference is successfully achieved, that is, if the thought B's mind receives is indeed the thought A's mind formulated' (Harris 1995, 21). This is remarkably similar to the principle of communication underlying Donald's theory of 'external symbolic storage' (see Fig. 1). A similar approach to written notation can be observed in Houston's review of the archaeology of communication technologies (Houston 2004).

By contrast, what Harris describes, rather forbiddingly, as 'integrational semiology' views human communication as consisting of the contextualised integration of human activities by means of signs. This approach resonates with the notion of citation and cultural performance I developed in Chapter 3. This approach to sign making indicates that writing is no less performative than other forms of inscription and makes no *a priori* assumptions about the relationship between inscription and memory. As Harris (1995, 14) observes, the demotion of writing to a mere set of mnemonic devices renders it inert from a philosophical point of view, because it sidesteps the issue of whether writing is the actual mode of *transmission* of knowledge or a possible source of the *production* of knowledge. Instead, writing is simply treated as a repository or store for knowledge. Harris' integrational approach, which I intend to adopt here, is remarkably similar to the more general approach to images adopted by Melion and Küchler (1991). They note that remembrance is performed and, as an active component of this process, images don't so much represent memories as help to create them (Melion and Küchler 1991, 3–4). Support for this view of writing and imagery comes from Carruther's (1990) analysis of the theory and use of memory in the Medieval period. Texts served as cues for remembrance as they were orally recited. Although the written page was understood to be a mnemonic device, it was reading as opposed to writing that was regarded as an activity of the memory. Once again, we need to consider how artefacts facilitate remembrance as well as how they are employed in practices of remembrance rather than treating them simply as externalised stores for memory.

Rather than defining writing as a de facto mnemonic device related to the administration of higher order political organisation, and thereby removing it from the ambit of prehistory, an integrational approach to writing seeks not to arbitrate on what does or does not constitute writing; instead the aim is to analyse the semiological mechanisms of different forms of communication (Harris 1995, 72). It should make little difference then whether a system is semasiographic (a system of writing without words, using only abstract marks or symbols) or whether a system is glottographic (a system in which writing represents components of speech). We can therefore consider mark making of a variety of forms and consider how such marks might integrate past, present, and possible future activities, which is the basic function that writing serves. I now want to consider how mark making might be organised spatially to promote remembrance.

INSCRIPTIONS AND PLACE

The art of memory of the ancient Greeks and the memory theatre of the Renaissance are well documented (Yates 1966). The 'memory theatre' of Guilio Camillo Delminio and the 'memory palace' of

Matteo Ricci – two Renaissance contemporaries – are based on the relationship amongst memory, image, and place. In Chapter 3, I discussed the close relationship between artefacts and place. This cognitive relationship is exploited in the Renaissance with the construction of the 'memory theatre' and 'memory palace' and before this in the *ars memoria* of the ancient Greeks (Yates 1966). Contemporary accounts by Viglius suggest that Camillo's 'memory theatre' was a building of wood, big enough to contain two people at the same time. It was:

> marked with many images and full of little boxes; there are various orders and grades in it. . . . All things that the human mind can conceive and which we cannot see with the corporeal eye. . . .may be expressed by certain corporeal signs in such a way that the beholder may at once perceive with his eyes everything that is otherwise hidden in the depths of the human mind. (quoted in Yates 1966, 136)

A further quote from the fifteenth-century 'De Memoria Artificiali' of Thomas Bradwardine indicates that antique models of memory were adapted in the high Medieval period and provide a link between the mnemonic practices of the ancients and those of the Renaissance:

> For trained memory, two things are necessary, that is, firm locations and also images for the material; for the locations are like tablets on which we write, the images like the letters written on them; moreover, the locations are permanent and fixed, whereas the images are now inked on like letters and are then erased; and the locations are fundamental to the images, just as I earlier said of them. With regard to these locations, then, six matters are distinguished, that is size, configuration, characteristics, number, order, and distance-away. Each location should be of moderate size, as much as one's visual power can comprehend in a single look, such as a small garden or arcaded space (like a cloister). Indeed

memory is most powerfully affected by sensory impression, most strongly by vision; wherefore something occurs in memory as it customarily occurs in seeing. (quoted in Carruthers 1990, 281)

Again we observe that the spatial ordering of objects is seen as an essential component for the trained memory. Through the medium of images the trained memory effectively takes a walk around and connects places together with images. The connection between image and place thereby facilitates recall. The principle of ordering memory spatially, and often architecturally, is not only familiar from Greek Antiquity, the high Medieval period, and the Renaissance but is also documented in a number of ethnographies. For example, in her account of memorial practices amongst the Luba of Zaire, Roberts (1996) describes the use of memory boards or Lukasa. Lukasa 'provide a framework for history while permitting multiple interpretations of it. Court historians associate memories with particular loci on a lukasa. The rectangular or hourglass shape that represents the Luba landscape, the royal court, human anatomy, and the emblematic royal tortoise (symbol of time and longevity) all at once, the memory board embodies multiple levels of information simultaneously. Beads, coded by size and colour and incised or raised ideograms provide a means to evoke events, places and names in the past' (Roberts 1996, 117). The Greek art of memory, the Renaissance memory theatre or palace, and the Luba memory boards all work because of the simple metaphorical relationship between place and memory which is activated by images, ideograms, or objects. The key point about the Luba memory board is that this sophisticated mnemonic system is made possible by the spatial metaphors established by the form of the memory board, the layout of the royal court, and of the Luba landscape itself; each resembles, and therefore recalls, the other. Memories associated with specific locations are linked and are recalled by the spatial positions of the beads on the memory board. The Lukasa of the Luba are used mainly to remember the genealogies of kings and

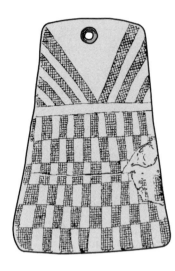

22. An Iberian plaque from Folha da Amendoeira, Beja, Portugal (after Lillios 2003, 133).

nobles. The precise spatial positioning of abstract images is therefore critical.

SYSTEMATISING MEMORY: THE CASE OF THE SLATE PLAQUES OF PREHISTORIC IBERIA

A semasiographic system (system of writing without words) has been proposed for the decorated slate and schist plaques of prehistoric Iberia by Katina Lillios (2003, 2004). Plaques are produced of a variety of metamorphic rocks, including slate, schist, and amphibolite, during the Late Neolithic and Copper Age (3000–2500 BC) of southwestern Iberia (Fig. 22). Crucially, the rock sources from which these artefacts are made are restricted in location, mainly outcropping in the Evora and Portalegre regions of Portugal (Fig. 23).

The plaques themselves are typically deposited with the bones of the dead in megaliths, caves, rockshelters, rock-cut tombs, and corbel-vaulted tombs (Lillios 2004, 129). In these contexts the plaques are found in association with undecorated pottery, flint blades, and unused polished stone tools (ibid.). Plaques display a degree of consistency in form (see Fig. 22). They are generally trapezoidal, roughly 10–20 cm in height, and approximately 10 cm

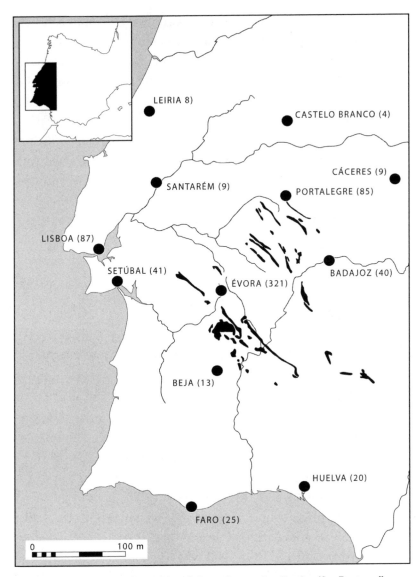

23. Distribution map of number of slate plaques by district (for Portugal) or Province (for Spain) with outcrops of amphibolite marked in bold (after Lillios 2003, 132).

in maximum width. According to Lillios (2003, 131), approximately 30% of the plaques share a common compositional structure. This 'classic' group of plaques has a bipartite composition, which consists of a narrow one-third at the top and a wider bottom two-thirds at the base. The top is often perforated with one or two holes. The top has an empty triangular field in the centre with bands of decoration, either horizontal or vertical. Occasionally a space separates the top and base; this may remain undecorated or may be decorated with cross-hatching, triangles, or other geometric designs. The base of the plaques is where the decorative elements are concentrated and we find one or more of six repeating geometric motifs: checkerboard, vertical bands, triangles, chevrons, herringbone, and zigzags. The checkerboard and triangles are organised along horizontal registers, whereas the chevron and herringbone are organised along vertical registers. Zigzag and vertical bands use the entire base as their compositional field (Lillios 2003, 133).

The designs used on the plaques are found in a number of other contexts. Both Lillios (2004, 146) and Harrison (1974) before her argue that the geometric designs on the plaques – as well as on contemporary beaker ceramics – were copies of textile weaves. Lillios establishes that all of the designs on the plaques are basic textile weaves reproducible by card or tablet weaving or on a simple loom. The existence of loom weights and spindle whorls attests to the existence of a thriving textile tradition in Late Neolithic and Copper Age Iberia. In addition, there are two surviving fragments of preserved textile. Two pieces of linen – one painted with horizontal bands like the plaques – have been found covering metal axes in two Portuguese Copper Age Burials (Lillios 2003, 134). In addition geometric patterning in the form of horizontal rows of triangles is echoed in other forms, such as the large engraved stelae or standing stones found in western Iberia (Bueno Ramírez 1992). The geometric designs are associated, then, with monuments to the dead and with textile and clothing. However, as Lillios (2003, 134) argues, the key to understanding the use of these plaques comes from the fact that a number of plaques are anthropomorphic; they represent individual people, as they are indeed deposited with the bones of the dead. The form of plaques is metaphorically related to the person, and the clothing on the person. The primary function of the design on the slate plaques, as with clothing, was to communicate the deceased individual's membership within a social group (Lillios 2003, 135–6). This interpretation is supported not only by the context of the plaques, which are placed alongside or on the chest of individuals, but also their regular compositional structure and the relatively small numbers of decorative elements. To test her hypothesis Lillios devises five conditions (Lillios 2003, 136):

1   There should be no relationship between the number of registers and the size of the plaques.
2   There should be more plaques with high numbers of registers and fewer with low numbers of registers.
3   Plaques with low numbers of registers should be found over a small area, and those with larger numbers should be more widely dispersed.
4   Assuming tombs and tomb groups housed related people over many generations, there should be plaques in continuous sequences of register numbers, by motif, within these tombs or tomb groups.
5   Those plaques with higher number of registers should postdate those with lower numbers of registers, by motif.

In each test case the conditions were positively met with. There is no relationship between plaque size and number of register. Some large plaques had very few registers, while in the case of some smaller plaques registers were squeezed into the available space (see condition 1). In the case of all four motifs there is an increase in the number of plaques as the register numbers increase (condition 2); plaques with low numbers of registers are restricted, while those with higher numbers are more dispersed. In fact in Portugal this spread seems to have an east–west gradient, possibly reflecting the movement of peoples east to west along the major river valleys of the Sado and Tejo (condition 3). Sequences for tomb groups (condition 4) can be detected at a number of sites, especially in the Évora region of Portugal at Anta Grande do Olival da Pega, Anta 1 do Cebolinho, Brissos, and Escoural and in sites in Badajoz and Lisboa (for further details see Lillios 2003, 145). Only condition 5 could not be met due to poor dating sequences for the plaques. The distribution and iconography on the plaques does, however, strongly indicate that they were used as genealogical records.

We can go further by noting that the plaques satisfy the condition of all inscribed notational forms by being composed of tokens and emblems. As Harris indicates (1995, 71), writing would be impossible if human beings were incapable of distinguishing between tokens and emblems. Tokens are signs based on one-to-one correlations between single items. Emblems are signs based on one–many correlations, in virtue of which the many are regarded as forming a single class. Emblems obey the logic of replication: ideally, a given emblem always takes the same form. Typical emblems include signatures, proper names, potters' seals, logos, and manufacturers labels and trademarks. Tokens obey the logic of cumulation: what matters is not that tokens should be alike or different, but they should be discrete and denumerable. Typical tokens include notches on a tally stick, beads on an abacus, or crosses on a list. Importantly, while tokens and emblems may be discrete they also often function as what Harris (1995, 76) describes as 'duplex' signs which combine the function of both tokens and emblems. Harris uses the example of names in a directory which lists names like this:

JONES, Adam
JONES, Andrew
JONES, Augustus
JONES, Colin

This requires us to read the term *JONES* as having a dual function. The number of its occurrences corresponds to the number of persons listed: the sign functions as a token. It also functions as an emblem because it distinguishes this group of individuals from other groups in the directory with different surnames. In a similar sense the number of registers on the Iberian plaques act as tokens distinguishing generational time, while the existence of distinct motifs might transform plaques into emblems, distinguishing them from motifs used by other social groups. Plaques would therefore act as 'duplex' signs. As a semiotic sign the act of notation – the production of notched implements – is a simple form of a token-iterative system which stretches back to the Upper Palaeolithic, if not earlier (D'Errico 1998; Marshack 1991), whereas the appearance of other marks on antlers dating from the Upper Palaeolithic from La Marche, France, indicates the early use of emblems (d'Errico 1998, 46). Notational systems which include both tokens and emblems therefore have a deep antiquity.

This simple system of notation constitutes an important example of explicit commemoration, which functions because of the close metaphorical relationship forged amongst places, material culture, and individuals. Place is important here for two reasons. The raw materials used to make the plaques are place specific, being made of amphibolite quarried at a specific location in the region (see Fig. 23). Likewise the deposition of the plaques is closely associated with place as they are deposited in specific family tomb contexts. I want to explore this further in the next case study. Lillios's discussion of abstract imagery and its use as mnemonic device raised the possibility of the relationship between the iconography of plaques and that on standing stones or stelae. I examine this further by analysing the case of Irish Passage tomb art. My discussion focusses on the well-documented monuments of the Boyne Valley, County Meath, eastern Ireland.

STASIS AND PROCESS: REMEMBERING PASSAGE TOMB ART

My starting point for this discussion is the remarkable practice of overlaying motifs in certain Irish Passage tombs, as discussed by

George Eogan (1997). This practice is clearly observed on decorated stones from the western tomb at Knowth, County Meath. My example is orthostat 45; this stone is decorated with angular incised motifs followed by angular picked motifs, dispersed picking, picked ribbons, and close area picking (Fig. 24). The stone is covered with a total of five overlays of motifs. How are we to understand this phenomenon? Traditional accounts tend to emphasise each set of motifs as distinct chronological styles (Eogan 1986, 1997) and thereby overlook the cultural specificity of this practice.

Many of our problems with passage tomb art arise because, when examining these images, we tend to privilege form over process. One consequence of the subordination of process to form is the tendency to dislocate panels and motifs from their contexts. For example, in the classic corpus of megalithic art Shee Twohig (1981, 107, 137, see also corpus catalogue) presents both motifs and panels in isolation. In part, this is a precondition of academic discourse; motifs and panels are transferred to the medium of paper so that we can compare and analyse them (see previous chapter for a discussion of this phenomenon).

Nevertheless, a consequence of this is that images then appear to us as spatially and temporally static. For this reason we often overlook the context of motifs and feel compelled to compare motifs that are spatially and temporally disparate (see Kinnes 1995). It is this strategy that lies at the heart of schemes of cultural interaction (Bradley and Chapman 1986, 132; O' Sullivan 1993, 10–11; Shee Twohig 1981, 137) and chronologically based narratives of art styles (e.g., Eogan 1986, 1997; O'Sullivan 1986). Interestingly, although endogenous interpretations of passage tomb art (Bradley 1989; Dronfield 1995a, 1995b, 1996; Lewis-Williams and Dowson 1993) provide an understanding of how motifs and panels may have functioned in terms of the human nervous system, these schemes are also reliant on a notion of temporal stasis. This is particularly true of Dronfield's statistical analyses, which depend upon the incorporation of all panels into a single atemporal scheme (Dronfield 1996). As Cooney (1996, 60) notes in the comments to Dronfield's article such analyses

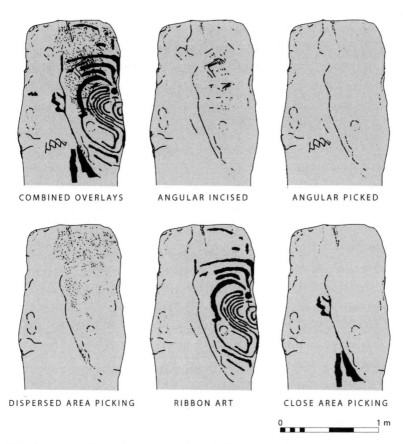

COMBINED OVERLAYS   ANGULAR INCISED   ANGULAR PICKED

DISPERSED AREA PICKING   RIBBON ART   CLOSE AREA PICKING

0   1 m

24. Orthostat 45, western tomb, Knowth illustrating the succession of decorative techniques beginning with angular incised motifs (after Eogan 1997, 1).

depend upon the visibility of panels which were not easily accessible during the use of the monument. Cooney's point underlines the fact that this methodology, and the mode of representation to which it is allied, is synoptical and tends not to take account of the position of the viewing subject. Effectively – as archaeologists – we are beguiled by formal similarity at the expense of a deeper investigation of the context of the production of images. What might the study of passage tomb art look like if we focus on process rather than form? If we are to do this, then it is critical that we consider the relationship between images and memory. Although the relationship between the two is not immediately apparent, it is important because, in focussing on *making* images, we are simultaneously examining the effect both the images and the act of production have on cognition.

Like other forms of inscription, such as writing, scholars have tended to treat images as the products, or traces of, prior mnemonic functions. The production of images is treated then as an expression of memory. This presents a passive model of *images* in which visual images simply reflect memory or act as surrogates for memory (Melion and Küchler 1991). Such a view presupposes a static model of *memory* in which memories are hermetically retained or stored. I have thoroughly criticised this view elsewhere in this volume. The issue here is that static models of images and passive notions of memory are embedded in the stadial concept of 'art styles'.

As discussed earlier, I propose an alternative view of the relationship between visual images and memory. Instead of speaking in terms of discrete stored memories, we need to consider memory as a continuous and interactive process of engagement between person and world. The relationship between image production and remembrance should then be viewed as a dynamic process, in which the production of visual images shapes the form of remembrance. The act of producing images is therefore responsible for projecting memory, while the visual traces of image are mnemonics for the act of production. Images therefore have a dual function in terms of their relationship to memory. If we are to consider images as active participants in the production of memory we need to consider how it is that images function. How do the material qualities of images visually affect the viewer?

MAKING AND REMAKING PASSAGE TOMB ART

With this question in mind, I will now turn to passage tomb art. Instead of examining distinct art styles, or abstracted motifs, in the passage tomb art repertoire I intend to examine the *practice* of motif production and reception. I am not interested in defining the meaning of art motifs; rather, I examine how art functions in certain architectural and social settings (see also Bradley 1989; Thomas 1991, 1992). In doing this I wish to provide an interpretative framework for understanding the observations and insights of Muiris O'Sullivan (1986) and George Eogan (1997). This account is of course indebted to their prior observations.

I will confine my analysis to the well-documented passage tombs from the Boyne Valley, County Meath, eastern Ireland.

I will examine three aspects of image production:

- The location of superimposed images versus nonsuperimposed images, and the technique used in their production.
- The location and technique employed on reused panels in the construction of monuments.
- The significance of the material qualities of the stones on which art is executed.

Superimposition, Location, and Technique

Let's start by looking at the nature and location of superimposition in the exterior and interior of the great passage tombs of the Boyne Valley. The best evidence comes from Knowth site 1 and the main mound at Newgrange, although some evidence for superimposition can also be gleaned from Dowth. At the outset we distinguish between incision and picking as distinctive techniques (see O'Sullivan 1986; Eogan 1997).

We begin with an investigation of Knowth. Faintly incised angular motifs are rare on the exterior kerbstones at Knowth. They are found on only 6 stones, or 7% of the total (Eogan 1986, 150); these motifs are always superimposed by other picked designs, usually of a curvilinear form. O'Sullivan (1986, 77) identifies a further stage of superimposition of picked ornamentation on 15 stones, or 16%, of the kerbstones. It would appear that two, occasionally three, episodes of superimposition occurred on the kerbstones at Knowth;

in some cases superimposed designs cross-cut previous designs, such as K52, where a picked spiral was cut by picked ribbons. In most cases, however, subsequent picked designs seem to enhance previous designs.

When we come to examine the interior of Knowth the first thing that strikes us is the intense degree of superimposition. Faintly incised angular motifs are more common in the interior of the monument and are on a total of 30 stones in the chamber and passage of the eastern tomb and 11 stones in the chamber and passage of the western tomb. Like the kerbstones, incised stones also seem to have superimposed picking on their surfaces. This picking takes a number of forms: angular, formless loose area picking, formless close area picking, and broad picked lines in ribbon/serpentiforms (Eogan 1997, 221). If we include the incised motifs, five episodes of superimposition can be identified in the interior of the passage tombs at Knowth. These episodes appear to follow in temporal succession and they both relate to and cross-cut previous motifs. On some occasions the primary angular incised designs are used as guidelines for subsequent angular picking, as in corbel 37/38 (Eogan 1997, 225); on other occasions, as in orthostat 41, incised and picked angular motifs are cross-cut (Eogan 1997, 226).

Other forms of picking often appear to cross-cut subsequent designs, this is especially true of the loose area picking and ribbon designs. Close area picking seems to often be used to sculpt areas of decorated stones not otherwise covered by previous designs.

This distinction in the number and intensity of episodes of activity is also a feature of Newgrange. Incised angular motifs are absent from the visible surfaces of exterior kerbstones at Newgrange (C. O'Kelly 1982). Most stones have picked angular and curvilinear designs, and there is less absolute evidence for secondary picking, although O'Sullivan (1986, 79) suggests that K1, K52, and K67 – the most elaborate of the kerbstones – may have been enhanced with secondary picking.

The interior of Newgrange is quite different. Here we see a small number of stones with incised angular motifs (six in total), but more importantly a great many stones have evidence of superimposition, with at least four episodes of superimposition, in particular of picked angular motifs and loose and close area picking. In some cases this reworking is extensive. Indeed, O'Sullivan (1986, 79) notes that loose area picking is found on nearly all the stones of the passage. Close area picking at Newgrange is particularly spectacular because it is used to sculpt the form of the stone – clearly seen in stones R21 and R22 flanking the transition between passage and chamber.

At Dowth (O'Kelly and O' Kelly 1983), the evidence is more partial, particularly on the exterior where the original number of kerbstones is unknown. All kerbstones with evidence for art have picked curvilinear designs. There is some possible evidence for loose area picking on K16 (ibid., 163); however, there appears to be only a single episode of working on the exterior of the monument.

This contrasts with the tombs in the interior. There is evidence for incised angular motifs on orthostats C2, C7, and C8, north tomb (O' Kelly and O' Kelly 1983, 169–71), and on recess orthostat C12, south tomb (ibid., 177). Curvilinear picked motifs are present on many of the structural stones of the interior, and there is evidence for the reworking of picked motifs, especially on orthostat C19, north tomb, where a picked radial design cross-cuts an earlier picked curvilinear design (ibid., 172). Loose and close area picking are also evident. Loose area picking is evident on C1, C7, C19, north tomb, and R1, the lintel of the recess, south tomb. Evidence for close area picking is most apparent on the recess orthostat C12, south tomb, where it is used to both obliterate earlier picked designs and accentuate incised designs (ibid., 177).

At each monument we appear to observe numerous episodes of reworking in relation to artistic production, with distinctions in the amount of reworking in monument interiors and exteriors. Eogan has noted that there are distinctions in the design of motifs at Knowth, with curvilinear art predominating on the exterior kerb and angular motifs in the interior (1986, 188–9, 194–5). At Dowth the exterior of the monument consists of curvilinear designs, whereas the interior has a propensity of angular designs. A similar pattern can be observed at Newgrange, where the exterior of the monument has both curvilinear and angular pecked motifs (ibid., 193). Again, these are more often executed as a single episode, as distinct from the multiple episodes of reworking identified in the interior.

If we combine this observation with the observed distinctions in the practice of reworking, it follows that the exterior curvilinear art is largely the result of a single episode of in-situ execution and on each stone is executed as a holistic design, often covering the entirety of the stones' surface. This is in contradistinction to the interior panels, where motifs are executed over a lengthier period of time, and where the execution of motifs follows a pattern from faintly incised motifs to boldly realised pecked motifs. In this case the position of motifs on stones is more haphazard and often covers only certain sections of the stone. In both cases, the mode by which the motifs on the exterior and in the interior operate visually is quite distinct, and this relates to the manner of their execution.

The Incorporation of Art

The practice of artistic reworking is related to the incorporation of art within the body of monuments. At Knowth, a series of panels with art are hidden within the fabric of the monument. These include orthostats 17, 18, 74, and 81 in the western tomb. A number of panels of art are also difficult of access, especially those used in the corbelling of the central chamber (Eogan 1986).

At Newgrange the corpus of hidden art includes the back of kerbstones K13 and K18 (Fig. 25), the roofstone of the east recess, art placed on the back of the roof of the passage RS3 and RS7 as well as stones X, Y, and Z. Furthermore, panels of art are also a feature of three of the structural stones of the famous roofbox, which permits the access of sunlight into the darkness of the tomb at midwinter (C. O'Kelly 1982). At Dowth, hidden art is found on the back of Kerbstone K51 (O'Kelly and O'Kelly 1983, 164–6).

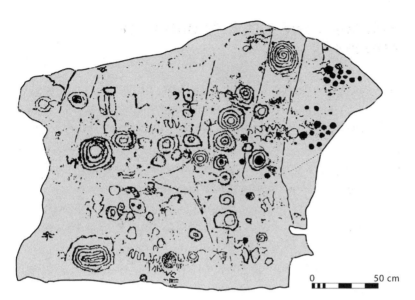

25. An example of the 'hidden' art from the back of kerbstone K13 at Newgrange. Note the haphazard nature of the design (after C. O'Kelly 1982, 42).

Interestingly, this hidden art appears to consist of both incised and picked techniques – this is especially evident in the panels hidden on the back of kerbstones K13 and K18 at Newgrange. On K51 at Dowth there is a distinction in the manner of execution on either side of the panel with the hidden motifs being haphazard in their overall effect, in contrast to the more ordered designs on the front of the stone. Picked angular motifs are also a feature of the corbelling of Knowth and the art on the roofbox at Newgrange. Obviously some of these panels have been incorporated from elsewhere bearing pre-existing art motifs (especially the stone used in the eastern recess and the kerbstones K13 and K18 at Newgrange); in other cases, as with the art found on the Knowth corbels and Newgrange lightbox, this is more likely to have been executed in-situ. Eogan (1998) suggests that much of the hidden art from both Knowth and Newgrange may have been derived from a now dismantled monument standing in the position of the present Knowth 1.

▩ PASSAGE TOMB ART, PERFORMANCE, AND PLACE

How are we to understand these processes of reworking? They are difficult to comprehend if we subordinate form to process; because of the spectacular visual nature of passage tomb art we simply assume the art was made to be viewed. If we are to reevaluate this aspect of passage tomb art, we need to contextualise the processes of reworking alongside other contemporary activities at passage tombs.

We know that the two major passage tombs at Knowth and Newgrange were constructed of materials from several widespread sources (Mitchell 1992). At Knowth and Newgrange, quartz from County Wicklow and granodiorite, granite, and siltstone from Dundalk Bay were used in the construction of the facade. The greywacke, sandstone, and limestone used in the construction of both Newgrange and Knowth were probably quarried some 25–40 km from the sites (Fig. 26). As Gabriel Cooney (1999, 135–8) cogently argues, the use of both local and nonlocal stone is significant because each material embodies a sense of place which is then rearticulated in the form of the passage tomb (see also Scarre 2004). Moreover, places of significance are embedded in monuments, as Knowth incorporates both an earlier settlement and a subsequent passage tomb (passage tomb 16).

In a sense these individual components are *material citations* or *iterations* of the significance of place and identity. Nowhere is this more apparent than in the construction of the curious circular stone settings outside the entrances of Knowth and Newgrange (Fig. 27). The Newgrange setting was a stone pavement bounded by low uprights of schist; the setting contained two pieces of flint and an unusual piece of polished sandstone and was subsequently covered by a mound composed of fragments of quarried quartz, water-rolled quartz, and grey granite pebbles (M. O'Kelly 1982, 75–6). At Knowth, stone settings were abundant outside both the eastern and western tombs (Eogan 1986, 46–8, 65). The largest of these outside the eastern tomb was edged with glacial erratics and ironstone. The

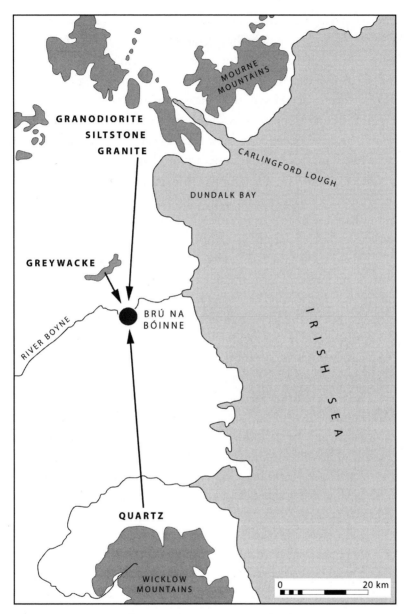

26. The source of the lithic materials used in the Boyne Valley tombs (after Cooney 1999, 137).

internal paving was covered by two successive layers of quartz chips. Like the use of materials in the passage tombs themselves, these stone settings reiterated and rearticulated the significance of place through the successive deposition of materials of differing origins. Similar features occur on the top of passage tomb 16 at Knowth (Eogan 1984) and beneath the passage tomb at Townleyhall II (Eogan 1963).

The formal connection between these circular features and the curvilinear images in contemporary art has been highlighted by Bradley (1998b, 104–9). However, I believe that these circular features and the curvilinear designs of passage tomb art are related by more than just formal similarities. They are also connected by their association with a specific form of cultural practice.

To begin with, the circular stone settings give us a critical insight into an understanding of the perceived qualities of stone. Stone is a material that embodies the significance of place. Its use in the construction of the passage tombs is a citation of this significance. What is more, as we see with the stone settings, the significance of the relationship between stone and place is reiterated or replenished through repeated episodes of deposition.

The process of reiteration that characterises the use of stone in both the monuments and the stone settings also occurs in relation to passage tomb art. In some instances panels of art are incorporated into the body of the monument, possibly from earlier monuments, just as stones from differing sources are incorporated in the mound construction. Likewise, in the interior of the monument, the connection between the significance of place and identity is reiterated by the episodic replenishment of images on stones. Here the process of superimposition is of the utmost importance because the execution and repetition of images is a visible citation of events of prior significance, as fainter images are pecked over, or drawn attention to, by subsequent pecking. Moreover, images are executed in sympathy with the material qualities of stone. Rather than thinking of images being carved onto stone, then, perhaps we need to consider images to be drawn *out of* stone; this is of particular significance when we

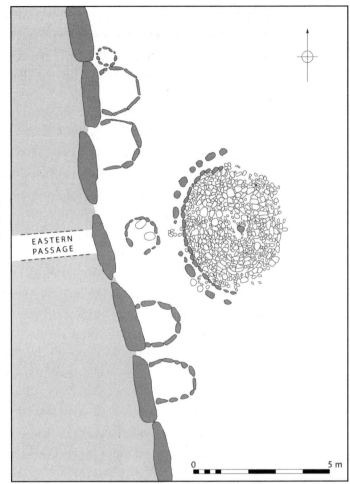

27. Stone settings outside the eastern tomb at Knowth (after Eogan 1986, 47).

EASTERN PASSAGE

0   5 m

think of the sculptural qualities of later pecking. Once we consider this, alongside the observation that the execution of images within the passage tomb produces an acoustic effect, it becomes clear that it is the *work* of image creation that is critical to the reception and meaning of passage tomb art.

Like the repetitive registers of images on the (broadly contemporary) Iberian slate plaques discussed above, the motifs in passage tombs act as tokens distinguishing successive events in time. Unlike the Iberian plaques the motifs are not differentiated spatially; instead, each overlays the other. Like other systems of notation, the successive execution of motifs serves to integrate the past with the present and the future. The evidence for the Iberian slate plaques as form of genealogical record is convincing. It is less easy to argue in the case of Irish passage tomb art, although there can be little doubt that the process of recarving also records the succession of temporal events. The significance of recording repeated calendrical events is under- lined by the existence of the roofbox at Newgrange which allows the light from the midwinter sunrise to shine directly down the main passage. For around 15 minutes on this particular day the sunlight floods the floor of the passage and burial chamber (M. O' Kelly 1982).

Rather than simply recording genealogy, art in the great passage tombs of the Boyne valley records the cosmological link amongst stone, place, and identity. In some ways we can think of the art as activating and reactivating this link. That images are indeed active is evinced by the location of images on the structural stones of the Newgrange roofbox – itself a conduit for the episodic source of solar energy – and on the external surfaces of the great basin stones at Knowth and Newgrange, which may have been used to contain the remains of the dead (Sheridan 1986).

Images are active in a number of different ways, depending upon the nature of their composition and their overall visual effect in rela- tion to the viewing subject. On the exterior of the monument images are easily available for visual inspection and are composed as a whole. The images on the exterior kerbstones are executed in-situ, proba- bly during the monument's construction; as such these images are architectural – they are an integral part of the monument – and as a whole they act to visually define the perimeter of the monument. One consequence of their composition as a continuous whole is that the images are visually complex, and the involutions of spiral and concentric curvilinear designs serve to cognitively captivate the viewers, drawing them into the design. This is especially interesting

because many of the most complex compositions are on the kerbstones at the entrance to the passages of Knowth and Newgrange
and K52 and K67 at Newgrange (Bradley 1989; Thomas 1991).
Might this art be so placed on the perimeter kerbstones to provide a
visual barrier, drawing the viewer's attention to the art rather than the
activities occurring inside the monuments? Interestingly, M. O'Kelly
(1982, 72) notes that complex panels of art such as K52 at Newgrange, placed diametrically opposite K1 at the entrance, may have
created an apparent visual axis for the monument. Indeed, the concept of art as a visual cue defining points of transition in and around
monuments has been discussed in the context of the contemporary
settlement of Skara Brae, Orkney (Richards 1991), and the passage
tombs at Loughcrew, County Meath (Thomas 1992).

The art on the interior of the tomb works quite differently. In the
interior of the monument images are encountered in semidarkness as
the subject moves down the passage and into the chambers. Notably
the art of the passage at Newgrange is heavily pecked, whereas pecked
ribbons dominate the Knowth passage, making the encounter of
the art a partially textural experience. Images in the chambers and
recesses are often placed in inaccessible places making their visual
appreciation difficult; this is especially true of the incised images. At
the outset these images did not visually captivate the viewer; rather,
the presence of images actively shapes the production of successive
images, each made with (either negative or positive) reference to
the primary image. Over time, as earlier images were embellished,
the art became more visually arresting. Like the exterior motifs, it
is so placed in the recesses of the chambers to draw in the viewer.
Through repeated performance, images are visually drawn out of
the rock. The successive production of images in the interior acts
as tokens recording the succession of events and remaking the link
between stone and place, while the use of fresh motifs acts as emblems
and the marks of successive individual carvers over time. In a similar sense the successive deposition of pebbles in the stone settings
at the entrance of the passage tombs also act as tokens. Here the

link between stone and place is physically and tangibly indexed by the use of pebbles with specific geological and geographical origins.

I have argued that we need to consider the passage tomb art of the Boyne Valley monuments as a form of technology executed to instantiate the relationship between place and identity. On both the exterior and interior art acts as a 'technology of remembrance' because it is executed to memorialise the significance of place and identity; in both cases images act as visual cues for remembrance. Due to their spectacular manner of execution, images on the exterior simply elicit remembrance visually; in the interior, images also act as cues for remembrance, as remembrance is materially expressed through the repetitive action of image making. We can think of the great passage tombs of the Boyne Valley as forms of living archives; the execution of images serves to record the significance of place and in so doing provides a directive for future action. Rather like the growth rings on large trees, the ever-changing character of the images on the passage tombs could be read as indexes of deep historical time, each monument was effectively living and as it grew it acquired more elaborate images.

CONCLUSION

The image I have just presented of the gradual growth and alteration of the art in the great passage tombs of the Boyne Valley encompasses a very different view of inscription from that normally associated with texts or images. As noted in the introduction to this chapter texts and images have often been treated as fixed entities, a form of external symbolic storage. As shown in this chapter the inscription of images and texts, whether those of the Renaissance, the high Medieval period, the Luba, or prehistoric Iberia or Ireland, act as *aide memoires* for other things – places, people, artefacts, ideas. However, these forms of inscription are not static; rather, it is the act of inscription (writing and image making) that produces the mnemonic relationship between image and thing. Although image making of this sort might provide a framework for history (or a record of events), such histories are not static but are always being reinterpreted through the act of image and mark making. It is the role of production in the act of mark making, and its influence on the creation and telling of narratives, that I deal with in Chapter 9.

Tracing the Past

Landscape, Lines, and Places

I n Chapter 8, I discussed the role of art or inscription as a
mnemonic for place. In the case of Irish passage tombs distant places were referenced by incorporating materials into
monuments or by the deposition of stone. The significance
of place was made reference to by the repetitive embellishment of the interior of tombs. In this chapter I again want
to consider the relationship amongst inscription, place, and
remembrance. I do this by considering the case of prehistoric
rock art placed in open air landscape settings. How images
in the landscape resonate with the landscape around them
is an important topic of archaeological and philosophical
enquiry (see Heyd 2005). Open air rock art differs from
Irish passage tomb art because it does not simply refer to

place but is 'in' place. We examine the ways in which rock art depictions bring into focus different understandings of 'place' in landscapes. What is the relationship between rock art and 'place', and to what extent is such a relationship the product of memory? Is rock art in fact a form of 'writing without words'?

I want to consider these issues by thinking about the materiality of memory in more depth. As I indicated earlier, there is an intellectual problem in tacitly treating inscription as a form of memory storage. The claim that writing or inscription acts as a means of storing memory takes no account of the medium on which inscription takes place. When discussing the role of the book as a technology of remembrance, inscriptions generally appear as representations of ideas, information, or as symbols encoding culture placed on the surface of the page in preparation for the future. Page surfaces usually emerge as blank substrates onto which thoughts are imposed in the form of inscriptions. This view of inscription may be unhelpful in the case of rock art. We need to rethink the relationship between the act of inscribing and the materiality of the rock surface if we wish to consider the mnemonic potential of rock art in the round.

The point I wish to make regarding surfaces is a phenomenological one and regards the way in which inscriptions – as manifestations of human thought – are imposed upon the world. The approach I wish to take here – as I have done throughout this book – is to examine the way in which, through practice, person and world are mutually entangled. As we shall see, the treatment of surfaces as interfaces between the natural and cultural emerges as an intellectual problem whether we are looking at the microtopography of a rock carving surface or the macrotopography of the landscape.

To begin thinking around the problems associated with the notion of surfaces as interfaces between the cultural and natural it is helpful to consider the practice of line making. Both the tracing of lines on a writing medium such as paper or stone and the tracing of lines of movement around a landscape are linked because we traditionally treat them as movement across a surface. Is it realistic to treat lines as being traced upon a surface or paths as being traced upon the surface of the landscape? I want to argue that to treat rock surfaces and landscapes simply as natural or unaltered substrates is to efface the dimension of time and the activity of social practice from our accounts of inscription and landscape. I believe this promotes a false view of inscriptions and landscape features as static and leads to the view that each act as static components of an external symbolic storage system. To reconsider the way in which inscription and landscape are conceived in relation to surfaces is to reconsider the mechanism of remembrance; instead of being the simple mechanical retrieval of static images or places situated on the surface of writing medium or landscape, remembrance becomes an active process of discovery and re-discovery caught up in the current of social practice. I consider this point in further detail later in the sections on British and Scandinavian rock art as I deal with the role of surfaces in accounts of landscape and inscription. As with the previous chapter I emphasise that without a consideration of process our accounts remain decidedly 'flat'. By asserting the importance of time we begin to produce a more nuanced three-dimensional (as opposed to a two-dimensional) view of past social practices.

I want to continue considering this issue by focussing on lines or tracks in the landscape. A good starting point for this discussion is maps. Maps come in all shapes and sizes and need not be two dimensional in form. Here for the sake of argument I want to focus on Western techniques of mapping landscapes. Maps of landscapes contain inscriptive traces – the marks of natural lines of movement, such as rivers, and humanly produced lines of movement, such as roads, railways, and canals. Despite the lines of movement described on maps, the geographer Doreen Massey notes that maps give the impression that space is the 'sphere of completed horizontality' (Massey 2005, 107). The notion of the map as a spatial surface seems to remove the element of time, so essential to us if we want to consider the role of remembrance in the constitution of the landscape. An alternative might be to consider landscapes as palimpsests. Palimpsests likewise embody the idea of inscription; the word is derived from the Greek for a class of writing material or manuscript in which the original writing has been effaced to make room for a second, a little like the mystical writing pad beloved of Freud. The term has likewise entered the archaeological lexicon to denote a landscape in which the traces of a former landscape are not so much effaced but buried beneath the present landscape. In searching for a term that embodies the gaps and erasures in maps, Doreen Massey rejects the term *palimpsest* as 'too archaeological' (Masssey 2005, 110) because it seems to embody the notion of an accretion of layers; for her 'the heterogeneous multiplicity of space is imaged as a series of layers which seem to simply refer to the history of a space rather than to its radical contemporaneity. Coevalness is not established through the metaphor of the palimpsest' (Massey 2005, 110). Maps tend to produce an image of space at a frozen moment in time. Time is excluded and the existence of multiple elements from different periods of history is likewise excluded.

As I argued in Chapter 4, the stratified vision of history as a series of discrete and successive epochs or periods which sweep all before them is untenable, we instead need to develop a view of history as a series of intercutting events, which cut across and materially impinge upon one another. Just as I argued for a network of referentiality for cultural practices, so the same goes for landscapes. Any given landscape will contain numerous traces of past activity from multiple periods of history. The task of the archaeologist is to examine how these different elements interact or coexist, not treat them as a series of discrete elements buried under the strata of history. As Barrett (1999, 255) points out with regard to the Iron Age treatment of Earlier Bronze Age monuments: 'the construction of monuments is always an interpretation of a pre-existing world'.

This discussion about how features of the landscape from different periods of history impinge upon one another returns us to the general problem of how landscapes are imagined. The way in which we conceptualise landscape depends a lot on the way we conceptualise the dimensions within which movement occurs. Maps produce an image of movement across a surface from point to point and thereby the line of movement occurs in two-dimensional space and tends to exclude time. We need to reassess the temporal character of the landscape. In his essay 'The Temporality of the Landscape,' Tim Ingold (1993) characterises the landscape not as a plane upon which meanings are attached but as a relational field in which places are gathered from within the landscape and are indivisible from the whole.

The act of inhabiting the landscape is therefore an embodied activity, in which the form of the landscape is generated through a process of incorporation whereby forms are not so much inscribed upon the landscape but are rather generated out of interaction. Tasks and activities conducted with landscapes are constitutive of place, and the occupation of landscapes occurs at a series of tempos or rhythms. Landscapes and what Ingold (1993) defines as 'taskscapes' emerge within the same current of activity. That landscape is processual in character is emphasised by Barbara Bender's point that 'landscape is time materialising. Landscapes like time never stand still' (Bender 2002, 103). The process of engagement and reengagement is underlined by her remark that:

> Human interventions are done not so much to the landscape as with the landscape, and what is done affects what can be done. A place inflected with memory serves to draw people towards it or to keep them away, permits the assertion of knowledge claims, becomes a nexus of contested meanings. (Bender 2002, 104)

The material correlates of activity are especially important here, because the act of inhabiting the landscape involves an intimate perceptual engagement with an environment imbued with traces of the past. To remember is to actively deal with these traces. To interpret these traces involves discovering meaning rather than reading meaning into landscape. Landscape forms are then clues to meaning rather than carriers of meaning (Ingold 1993). In a Peircean sense they index the past.

In a further essay Ingold (2000b) distinguishes between 'cognitive maps' and 'wayfinding' as examples of Rubin's (1988) distinction between memory as a 'complex structure' or a 'complex process'. The notion of cognitive maps posit that an individual has copied into his or her mind a comprehensive depiction of the objects, features, and locations contained in a landscape before setting out on a journey. Movement, then, becomes an almost mechanical act of executing the prescribed course. Here the simple process of bodily movement is harnessed to the complex structure of the cognitive map. Wayfinding, however, posits a complex process which imputes little prestructured content to the mind. Wayfinding is a skilled performance in which the traveller 'feels their way' towards their goal, fine-tuned by previous experience (Ingold 2000b, 220). Wayfinding, then, involves remembering previous journeys taken and involves a response to traces or indices of the past. Each place holds within it memories of previous arrivals and departures, as well as expectations of how to reach it or other places from it (Ingold 2000b, 237). Wayfinding does not posit a view of landscape as a process of looking down upon a surface and mapping it; instead, it promotes the perspective of moving *through* an environment, which changes and unfolds as the beholder moves within it. We shift, then, from a perspective in which movement is characterised as a predetermined progression from one spatial location to another across the surface of a landscape to a movement in time through a landscape in which the environment offers mnemonic cues as to how to progress. As Ingold (2000b, 238) notes, such a movement is more akin to playing music or storytelling than reading a map because it requires continuous response to the given conditions of the moment; landscapes are in effect 'improvised'. As we shall see this view has important resonances for our analysis of prehistoric rock art.

▣ THE ANALYSIS OF IMAGES

Barbara Bender's view of landscapes as 'time materialising' har-
monises nicely with Melion and Kuchler's (1991, 3) discussion of
the role of memory in image production, discussed in Chapter 8.
Rather than treating image production as a process enabled by memory, they argue instead it may be more appropriate to think of it as
a process that enables mnemonic transmission. Just as landscapes
are time materialising, so, too, are images a means of materialising
remembrance. This critical aspect of human cognition is produced
with and by images, and the act of producing each visual trace will
affect the production of the next. Like places, images will also inflect
memory and draw people towards or away from them.

How does this view accord with archaeological accounts of
images? I believe there are a number of problems with the archaeological analysis of visual culture. There is a tendency for form to
be privileged over process; and the visual is elided with and subordi-
nated to representation. I have argued elsewhere that this is partly a
precondition of the discourse of typology in which visual forms are
transferred to the medium of paper to aid in comparison and analysis (Jones 2001a). As I noted in Chapter 8, this perspective presents
images in a decontextualised format and tends to treat them syn-
optically as static entities. Although these procedures are related to
a specific disciplinary discourse the treatment of prehistoric art as
static images suspended or 'floating' upon the surface of the printed
page pervades other interpretative frameworks.

The form of the image is especially emphasised in semiotic
interpretations of art. For example, discussions of the menhirs of
Neolithic Brittany have focussed mainly on the ascription of meaning based on the interpretation of images as visual symbols (e.g.
Thomas and Tilley 1993; Whittle 2000), as have semiotic interpretations of Scandinavian rock art (e.g., Nordbladh 1978; Tilley 1991).
Arguably, these interpretations arise out of a static conceptualisation
of the image and do not encompass the full materiality (or visuality) of prehistoric imagery. In a sense by foreclosing on the visual

in this way, these interpretations circumscribe both what we define as art and narrow what can be legitimately said about prehistoric visual forms. The underlying representationalist logic of the analysis of archaeological art (in which the purpose of art is understood to be a device for representing other things) tends to exclude the analysis of artistic practice in image production (see Bolt 2004 for a wider analysis of this problem). Images are almost exclusively conceptualised as two dimensional, and there has been little analysis of the relationship between line and surface.

Many of our problems with the ascription of meaning arise due to distinctions made between surface and depth. Problems with the relationship between surface and depth are voiced by Barbara Stafford (1996), who traces the subordination of surface to depth to Plato. She rails against the treatment of images as mere surface appearances as they become what she calls 'decorporealised signs' and highlights the overarching desire in the analysis of visual images to reduce communication to a process of inscription. Similarly, in posing the intriguing question 'What do pictures really want?', Mitchell (1996, 82) states that pictures want equal rights with language, not to be turned into language. For Mitchell, images are not by-products of social reality but are actively constitutive of it. Mitchell's view of images seems to resonate with Ingold's view of landscapes. Just as we saw that landscapes should not be treated as static two-dimensional surfaces of the kind routinely represented in maps but as lived networks of places produced and conjoined by experience, we likewise need to begin to consider how – through production – images participate in a process of creating or forming experience. To consider this further I examine the question of prehistoric rock art.

LINES IN THE LANDSCAPE: THE STUDY OF PREHISTORIC ROCK ART

Problems of the kind described above emerge with the analysis of rock art because we treat rock art production as a form of inscriptive practice in which meaning is laid upon a blank surface. Rock art is at least partly defined by the nature of human action on matter. Matter is seen as substrate, and the human mind is imposed through action on matter. Culture is literally sculpted onto mute materials. This perspective is beginning to alter as archaeologists increasingly take account of the role of the rock surface on the composition of images (Bradley et al. 2003; Hauptmann Wahlgren 1998; Helskog 1999; Tilley 2004). These perspectives have generally focussed upon the microtopography of the rock surface. In what follows I want to consider the way in which surface and line interplay in the production of rock art. Rather than treating rock surfaces as blank substrates upon which images are overlain, I believe it may be more fruitful to consider rock surfaces as open to interpretation. Just as we discussed wayfinding around the macrotopography of landscapes, the microtopography of rock surfaces will also offer cues for action to be responded to in the production of rock art images. The way in which rock surfaces are treated will differ depending upon how the rock art tradition is conceptualised in cosmological terms. Much will depend upon how rocks themselves are conceptualised, whether they are treated as inert, inanimate materials to be quarried and traded in an abstract form as commodities or as active and animate components of the lived landscape (see Boivin and Owoc 2004; Bradley 2000 for overviews of cultural perceptions of the mineral world). If rocks are understood as inert substrates, then the surface of the rock is unlikely to be implicated in rock carving; however, if rocks are treated as manifestations of supernatural entities then their surfaces are far more likely to be objects of attention. In these cases the very location of images on specific rocks in the landscape, as well as the surface, may be singled out for special treatment. One well-known interpretation of South African rock art treats the carving surfaces as a form of permeable membrane enabling access to the spirit world beyond (Lewis-Williams and Dowson 1990). This example demonstrates that the cultural significance of rocks has an important impact on the role of rock art in commemorative practices.

David Robinson (2004) provides an excellent example from the rock painting tradition of the Chumash of the Vandenberg region of California. He highlights the significance of the indigenous concept of 'atiswin. 'Atiswin is a complex concept having no analogue in English: it seems to stand for supernatural beings and the quality of power they embody. It also stands for powerful substances, items, or talismans (Robinson 2004, 96). Robinson goes on to discuss two rock shelters – Beehive shelter and Rattlesnake shelter – decorated with smears of red pigment. He suggests that the surface of these sites embody manifestations of 'atiswin. This is because they have crystalline mineral bands folded through their matrices lending them reflective properties. The production of images on such surfaces – especially the smearing of pigment across these surfaces – was a way to acknowledge and activate power (Robinson 2004, 97). Both the qualities of the pigment and of the rock were implicated in the activation of power. In this case remembrance was expressed in action, through the application of pigment.

In the discussion below I want to examine the role of surface and landscape as a means of considering the significance of place and remembrance in two different rock art traditions in prehistoric Europe: northern Scandinavia/Russia and Britain.

PREHISTORIC ROCK ART OF NORTHERN SCANDINAVIA/RUSSIA

The prehistoric rock art of northern Scandinavia and Arctic Russia is of considerable antiquity. The well-dated images from Alta, Norway, date between 4200 and 1800 BC. The rock art traditions of this region are mainly representational and consist of images of animals, humans, and objects, such as boats. I want to consider how representational images interact with the rock surfaces upon which they are carved as a means of reproducing cosmological narratives. This topic has been recently discussed in a number of publications by Knut Helskog (1999, 2004), which I shall draw upon here. The populations that made this rock art were hunter-fisher-gatherers, and Helskog argues that in terms of belief there are many similarities with the beliefs recorded ethnographically from other circumpolar cultural groups, such as the Evenk and the Tungus (Helskog 2004). Judging from the ethnographic evidence, it is likely that the landscape was animate and alive (Helskog 2004, 268) and populated not only by people and animals but also spirits. A dominant belief in this region is the idea that the universe is divided into three worlds: an upper world of the spirits, a middle world inhabited by people, and an underworld of the spirits of the dead, often accessed through water.

There are striking patterns in the location of the rock art in this region. The strongest association is its location close to water or the seashore. Indeed, the consistency of this association has allowed researchers to estimate the date of much rock art in this region according to its elevation above sea level, in accordance with known sea-level changes in the past. Knut Helskog (1999) argues on the basis of this locational pattern that rock art panels are deliberately carved at the juncture between land and water, the place in which cosmological worlds meet. The relationship between rock art and the belief in a tiered cosmology helps explains the location of rock art sites in the wider landscape; it also offers a way of reconsidering the images and their relation to the rock surfaces upon which they are carved.

Helskog makes a strong case for treating northern rock art as images of stories (Helskog 2004, 266). In semiotic terms many of these images act as icons – the way they work as signs depends upon their resemblance to a natural object, such as an animal. Because of the iconic nature of this rock art it is possible to observe that time is embodied in these stories in the form of animals and the activities taking place at different seasons. Due to the seasonal specificity of animal appearance and behaviour we can say, for example, that the depiction of reindeer without antlers indicates late winter–early spring; herds of reindeer with large antlers indicate summer, possibly males before the rutting season. An elk depicted without antlers but

with a large beard will be an image of a male elk during midwinter. Elk without beards and antlers are female at any time of year
and when in a herd represent winter. The depiction of bears suggests spring, summer, or autumn because they hibernate during the
winter. Beluga whales depicted in the White Sea region of Russia
indicate early spring to late autumn (Helskog 2004, 271–2).

Helskog discusses rock art in a number of regions in the Arctic north of Scandinavia and Russia, at Alta, Norway, Nämforsen,
Sweden, and Zalavruga in the White Sea region of Karelia, Russia
(Fig. 28). His major insights concerning the role of narrative and storytelling in this art come from his analysis of the site at Bergbukten I
and Kåfjord, Alta, Norway (Helskog 1999). The panel at Bergbukten
I is from the earliest phase on the site and is dated 4200–3300 BC.
It is smooth and glacially striated. It is undulating with surfaces of
various sizes and orientations. There are pools of rainwater caught
in cracks in the rock surface. Depictions of a bear are central to
the interpretation of the panel. The bear is depicted on a slightly
slanting surface leaving its den (place of hibernation). Bear tracks
lead upwards, downwards, and horizontally. After leaving the den in
the spring the bear walks horizontally along the bottom of a shallow
depression in the rock surface to emerge, towards autumn (signified
by the size and shape of the bear), on a sloping surface where they are
surrounded by armed human figures and attacked. The tracks from
the den also go down into a rainwater pool in the rock, connecting
the bear (via water) with the spirits in the lower world. Tracks also
lead upwards to higher parts of the terrain, such as mountains, to
again contact spirits in the upper world. The topography of the rock
surface therefore represents the topography of a landscape through
which bears walk. This is a landscape which connects the different
components (the upper, middle, and lower worlds) of the universe.

Similar depictions are observed in the panel at Kåfjord, dating
from the same period (Fig. 29). This composition includes depictions
of two bears in dens around 8 m apart. These bears are connected
by their tracks. In the den to the left the bear faces the opening
as if leaving in spring, whereas in the other it is facing the back as

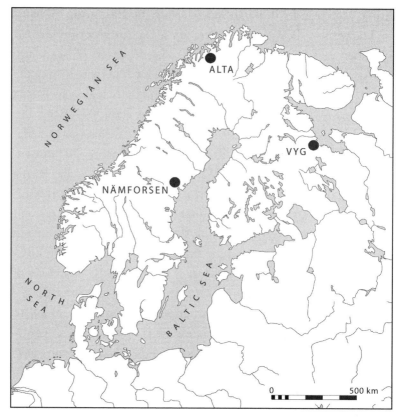

28. The Location of the three major rock art sites in northern Scandinavia and Russia (after Helskog 2004, 272).

if entering in late autumn. The bears are also different shapes; the 'spring' bear is thin, as if it has just lost body fat during hibernation, and the 'autumn' bear is larger, as if storing body fat in preparation for hibernation. Tracks, perhaps from the same bears, from between sun and moon symbols higher up on the rock surface connect to the track between the two dens and continue downwards into a basin which today fills with water. Above the symbol of the sun and moon there are depictions of a reindeer and an elk facing each other. These depictions are inverted, as if the two animals are standing in opposite dimensions to each other.

Human figures at Kåfjord dance under the sun and moon, representing an associated ritual, which possibly acts out the return of

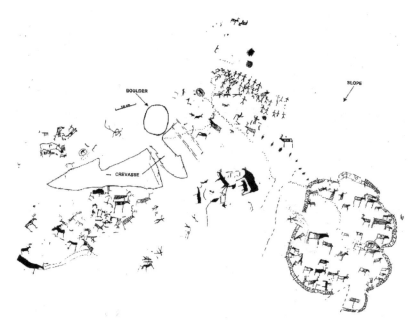

29. The rock art site at Kåfjord, Alta, Norway. Reproduced with kind permission by Knut Helskog.

the bear (and of life) in the spring. To the right of the bears is a reindeer corral, representing autumn. A similar corral of reindeer is found at Bergbukten I. Both panels depict scenes in a story where the bear moves through time and space, and in which the rock surface signifies part of the landscape in the story.

These remarkable depictions of seasonal and cosmological narratives are paralleled at other sites in the Arctic north, such as Old and New Zalavruga on the mouth of the River Vyg in the White Sea region of Karelia, northern Russia. The panels at Zalavruga date between the last half of the fourth millennium and into the beginning of the second millennium BC, making them broadly contemporary with the sites at Alta. At New Zalavruga one scene depicts elk hunted by three human figures on skis. The surface of the rock plays an important part in this composition. The ski tracks appear on the highest part of the rock surface to the left as marks of walking on a horizontal surface, then sliding on a sloping surface, then walking, and again sliding depending on the slope of the surface. The tracks are made by three hunters who have followed the elk for some distance. The elk walk in a group single file through the snow before being separated and killed. One hunter spears an elk in the back, while the other two are shooting elk with bows and arrows. The story depicts an elk hunt in a winter landscape. An elk at the far right of the panel is facing a Beluga Whale that has been harpooned from three boats. It seems as if the composition depicts two stories taking place at two times of year: the elk hunt at winter and the whale hunt in the summer. At other points on the panel other times of year are depicted as if several landscapes and several stories intersect.

A panel at Old Zalavruga depicts a group of human figures on skis, each with a ski pole. Some of these skis leave tracks, and others do not. The surface of the rock is flat and probably depicts figures moving through the flat landscape of Karelia. The colour of the rock and its slope and orientation are especially conducive to viewing the figures. The stories in the panels at Old and New Zalavruga depict three landscapes: the land as signified by elk hunts and human figures on skis, the sea as seen in depictions of whale hunts and boats, and the sky represented by compositions with birds.

These three worlds are also depicted at the well-known site of Nämforsen on the Ångerman River, northern Sweden. Today the sites at Nämforsen are located on small islands in the middle of the river, although 5700 years ago with an alteration in sea level they would have been located on the shore of the Bay of Bothnia. The sea-level data provide a maximum date for the carvings, underlined by the late Neolithic date (c. 3000 BC), the Iron Age date derived from the discontinuous occupation of the settlement associated with the site (Tilley 1991, 49). The main animal species depicted at Nämforsen is elk. Human figures with elk-headed poles suggest a ritual where the elk represents a cosmic being of some sort (Helskog 2004, 278).

Small groups of elks, which signify winter, are frequently depicted in compositions. Winter is also indicated by the absence

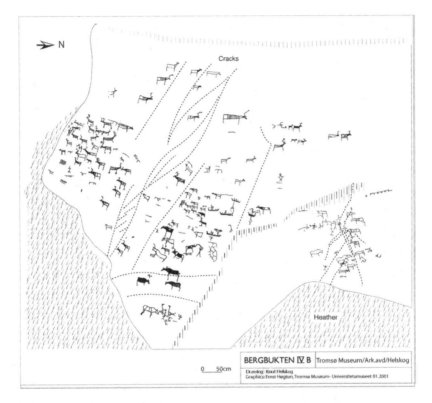

30. The rock art site at Bergbukten IV, Alta, Norway. Reproduced with kind permission by Knut Helskog.

of antlers on male elk, which are also distinguished by their large beards. Some of the compositions include female animals only, while the depiction of a female and calf signifies spring to autumn. Like the other sites discussed many of the compositions appear to depict stories, but the directionality of stories is less obvious.

The three concentrations of rock art discussed by Helskog (2004) are the largest groups of carvings in northern Norway, Sweden, and Karelia, Russia. They probably represent the most important ritual places in each region. What kinds of places are represented by these carvings? The carvings appear to represent liminal places where spirits and people meet to maintain social order and reinforce relations, specifically to distribute rights to resources between coastal and inland populations (Helskog 1999, 2004, 282). Importantly, in this example the carving surface is implicated in the production of rock art images, and the rock surface is imbued with significance as it plays an important role in the creation of narratives. Both the macrotopographic location and the microtopography of the rock surface are significant. In this case both the carvings in the landscape and the landscape in the carvings (Helskog 2004, 284) are important. The rock surface provides a series of mnemonic cues, indexes around which the narrative is created in iconic form; this rock art tradition meshes together index and icon to produce a denser (and more meaningful) narrative. I will discuss the role of place and memory in this rock art in more detail below.

■ BRITISH PREHISTORIC ROCK ART

Having examined the use of index and icon in the representational rock art of northern Scandinavia I now want to turn to a different rock art tradition to look at how rock surfaces are implicated in the production of meaning. Unlike Scandinavia, the case for representational images is difficult to make in the rock art traditions of Britain.

Curvilinear and geometric motifs are an important feature of the Late Neolithic and Early Bronze Age period in Britain, approximately spanning the period 3000–1500 BC. Their date is equivocal, but the floruit of these images is most likely to be during the Late Neolithic. Images of similar character are found on Late Neolithic Grooved Ware pottery (discussed in Chapter 6) and on a series of specialised portable artefacts. As we saw in the previous chapter, similar images are also found on the kerbstones and interior of passage tombs, such as those at Knowth, Newgrange, and Loughcrew in eastern Ireland. Although these images have a wide currency, their location in open air contexts is restricted to northern Britain and northwest and southwest Ireland.

Work by Richard Bradley on the topographic location of images has demonstrated that they are often placed in prominent landscape positions, often with extensive views over inland valley route ways or coastlines (Bradley 1997).

Although the recognition that particular images are executed in particular places is clearly important, the interpretation of these images presents problems. Early researchers in the field attempted to enumerate the possible functions and meanings of these abstract motifs, as representative of natural elements such as water ripples to the use of cups and rings for arcane practices (Morris 1977). More recent researchers, such as Bradley, have recognised the opaque nature of these images. Richard Bradley (1997b, 10) acknowledges that we will never understand the meaning content of these images. However, observing that images of greater or lesser visual complexity occur in different regions of the landscape he draws on Howard Morphy's analysis of Yolungu art of Northeast Arnhem Land, Australia (Morphy 1991), to suggest that images are likely to contain inner and outer meanings, depending upon their audience (see also Bradley 2000).

On the face of it this analogy appears reasonable, but problems arise when we compare the materiality and periodicity of production of Yolungu art with that of British prehistoric rock art. The former is produced for specific occasions or events where it is explicitly manufactured for the transmission and communication of knowledge. Knowledge is controllable precisely because of the restricted life of the medium bearing motifs, whether sand, bark, or body painting. By contrast the rock art of Britain, by its very nature, is permanent and as such the control of knowledge transmission could occur only through the restriction of imagery, or the location of images in inaccessible locations. Should we analyse these images as semiotic signifiers or, as the anthropologist Maurice Bloch (1995b) discovered when asking about the meaning of Malagasy house carving, is this a question not to ask of art? Bloch found that the carvings in Madagascar did not carry meaning content in the semiotic sense; rather, the embellishment of house posts by carved designs was meaningful in and of itself because it represented the closer marital ties of the couple occupying the house.

By emphasising process and visuality the aim then is not to consider the meaning content of British rock art, but – keeping in mind Mitchell's comments about art discussed previously – the aim is to explore how the production and reception of rock art is meaningful, as a socially constitutive activity.

IMAGES AND LANDSCAPE IN THE PREHISTORIC LANDSCAPE OF KILMARTIN

I want to consider some of these issues in relation to the Neolithic and Early Bronze Age monument complex (dating from 3000 to 1500 BC) of Kilmartin, Argyll, northwest Scotland, an area in which I have been conducting fieldwork over the past few years. The region is situated on the west coast of Scotland and consists of a main steep-sided, flat-bottomed valley from which lead a series of upland valleys. Laminated vertical strata of sandstones and schists dominate the valley sides.

With over 250 individual decorated panels Kilmartin is a major rock art landscape (RCAHMS 1999). The art mainly consists of abstract cup and ring images pecked into rock outcrops or boulders. Importantly a number of other motifs are found in the Kilmartin valley. These include motifs commonly associated with Irish passage tomb art such as 'rosettes' and horned spiral motifs. These are found both on open air rock surfaces and on upstanding monuments such as the southern stone circle at Temple Wood (Scott 1989). Images are used to refer to contact with places, such as Ireland, beyond the confines of the landscape. Contact is evinced by the exchange of artefacts between Argyll and eastern Ireland.

The most complex rock art sites are found in upland locations at the junction or entry points into valleys and these have extensive views into the valley. Less complex sites are found on the lower terraces of the valley overlooking monuments and in the upland hills (Fig. 31). The execution of images of differing visual complexity therefore defines distinct topographic zones within the landscape.

In the valley bottom a series of monuments are located, including chambered cairns, round cairns, stone circles, and standing stones (Fig. 32). Each valley appears to have discrete clusters of monuments, and in each case cairns and standing stones seem to direct the axes of movement through valleys. This is particularly evident with the major monument complexes at Kilmartin and Ballymeanoch. At Kilmartin a linear cemetery of cairns runs down the axis of the valley over a distance of four miles. This is accompanied at the northern end of the complex by two stone circles and by a linear alignment of standing stones.

Likewise, at the southwestern end of the monument complex at Ballymeanoch there is a small linear cemetery of cairns which incorporates a Late Neolithic henge reused as a burial cairn. It too has an impressive double avenue of standing stones.

Rock art is not confined to natural outcrops, as many of the standing stones in the region are also decorated with cup and ring marks. A number of Bronze Age cairns also incorporate decorated stones.

Detailed analysis of the major rock art panels in the region reveals that, contrary to expectation, images are executed on cracked and fissured rock surfaces (for full details see Jones 2005c). Field survey in the surrounding area indicated that smooth (and perfectly serviceable) rock surfaces were ignored in favour of surfaces cracked and scoured by glacial action. Moreover, rocks with specific systems of fissures or cracks were carved on. Three main types of surface were utilised: surfaces with dense criss-crossed lozenge-shaped cracks, surfaces with widely spaced rectangular cracks, and surfaces with widely spaced lozenge-shaped cracks.

There are clear distinctions in the complexity and type of motifs on each type of panel. Panels with dense triangular/lozenge criss-cross cracks were decorated with complex motifs, often with unusual

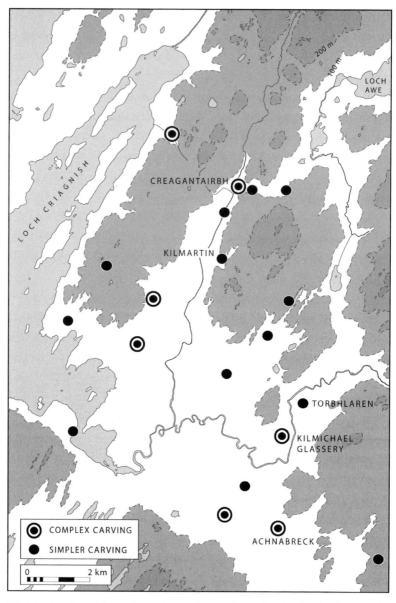

31. The location of simple and complex rock art sites in the landscape of Kilmartin, Argyll, Scotland.

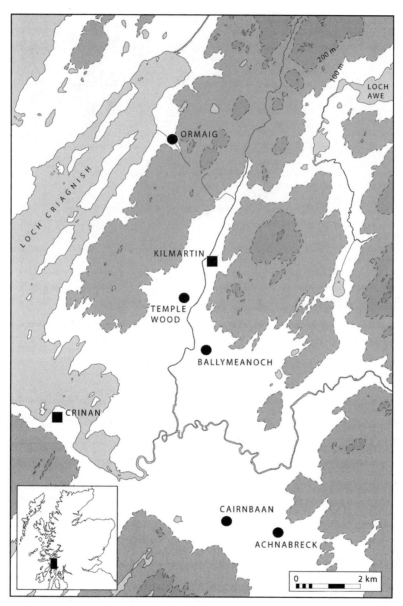

32. Map of the landscape of Kilmartin, Argyll, Scotland, showing the location of sites mentioned in the text.

33. Rosette motifs at Ormaig. Note the way in which the motifs are fitted between natural cracks in the rock surface. Photo: the author.

motifs found in the passage tomb art repertoire (Fig. 33). Panels with large rectangular or lozenge-shaped cracks are decorated with complex motifs with multiple rings (Fig. 34). Panels with small lozenge or rectangular-shaped cracks are decorated with simple motifs, cups with one or two rings, and tails (Fig. 35). In the first case these images are often placed over systems of cracks, in the other cases cracks frame the images. Distinctions also occur at the regional level as analysis of sites in the side and upland valleys indicate that each valley employed distinctive types of motif.

The relationship between rock surfaces and images is not confined to cracks and fissures. At a number of sites the form and orientation of natural glacial runnels are paralleled by the form and orientation of the 'tails' of rock art images. In other cases carved cup marks mimic natural hollows in the rock (see Jones 2005c). In a great number of cases the tails of motifs are used to join motifs

34. Rock art at Cairnbaan (upper panel). Note the way in which the motifs are fitted between broadly rectangular cracks in the rock surface. Photo: the author.

to the natural fissures of the rock and appear to 'enter' the rock via these cracks.

How are we to conceptualise the relationship between the geological features of the rock and rock art? What kind of relationship was being expressed through the execution of rock art motifs? At one level the relationship appears to be mimetic. Images enact mimetic resemblance because of their correspondence with natural features of the rock surface, they also enact a form of mimetic contact whereby images incorporate components of the rock surface. This relationship is emphasised by the physical contact made between natural features and carvings. Curiously, the organisation of motifs on lozenge-shaped panels of rock closely resembles the organisation of motifs on other media, especially the infilling of motifs between lozenge-shaped panels on Late Neolithic Grooved Ware pottery and the practice of superimposition found in the interior of Irish Passage Tombs (as discussed in the previous chapter). Because of this I believe that rock surfaces are anything but blank substrates upon which to carve. Rather, rock surfaces are being addressed as surfaces upon which the traces of ancestral or prior images are already visible (see also Jones 2005c).

Seen in this light the production of motifs is therefore a repetitive, mnemonic act that treats the rock surface as a surface upon which previous images are present. A sense of the repetitive act of production is gained when we consider the nature of the activities associated with rock art sites. Recent excavations around the rock art sites at Torbhlaren revealed a stone-built platform encircling one rock art site. On this platform were a series of layers containing hundreds of quartz artefacts (mainly hammerstones) and pieces of smashed quartz, which are likely to represent the residue of several rock art production events.

The repetitive nature of rock art production can also be observed at the largest panels, such as Achnabreck, where differential weathering suggests the successive carving of images. In a sense the carving of complex visual images attract others to the rock (Bradley 1997b, 128–9). These complex panels, numbering in excess of 100 images, are situated at entry or exit points into different valleys (see Fig. 31).

How do images work visually? Critically the size of images is proportional to the distance between fissures in the rock. Visually the images are either suspended between these frames or are executed over cracks. Through the production of the sinuous tails connecting image to fissure the entire rock becomes an indivisible visual whole. Images are woven into the fabric of the rock surface. Crowding images together produces a sense of indivisibility between rock and image. Like Wittgenstein's famous duck-rabbit figure, through spatial crowding and juxtaposition with the rock the images become multistable: are images distinct from the rock? Are they in fact distinct from each other? Figure and ground oscillate as the viewer moves around the rock.

35. Simple rock art motifs at Cairnbaan (lower panel). Photo: the author.

The indivisibility of figure and ground is important, because it visualises a sense of the fusion between image and place. The production of images in the landscape draws attention to significant places in the landscape; however, images themselves can also iterate or draw together places. This is especially significant when we consider that, by carving motifs found in the passage tomb art repertoire, images *presence* places outside the immediate landscape.

This process of condensing the significance of other places through image production is critical to understanding the treatment of other elements of the prehistoric landscape. I now want to consider the significance of images on standing stones and in cairns.

If we are to understand standing stones we need to consider their spatial and temporal contexts. Field survey around the valley sides has located the likely source of many of the standing stones. An exposed cliff face above the standing stones at Ballymeanoch consists of stones of identical size, shape, and lithology. In the neighbouring Kilmichael

Glen a standing stone quarry was identified overlooking a complex of standing stones and rock art. The vertical and laminated nature of these outcrops suggests that these natural standing stones are literally being prized off, walked down the valley sides and reerected in rows or as solitary stones in the valley bottoms.

Analysis of the position of rock art motifs on standing stones suggests they were decorated during or after erection. Motifs are located at the base of the stone and are large and fairly simple making them highly visible. Unlike images on outcrops, no visual reference is made to natural fissures on the stone.

The removal of stones from the valley sides and their decoration performs a number of important functions. Stones placed in the valley bottom direct movement through the valley, they are aligned on routes through the landscape yet their sides are oriented back towards the valley sides from whence they came. Overall they are involved in the creation of a visible sense of order (Fig. 36). Stones are both part of and other than the landscape. Their rough texture offers a clue to their origin. The presence of rock art on many of the stones acts as a citation or reference to the rock art located on the valley sides. However, the massive form of the stones and the size and visibility of the rock art motifs also denote that they are distinct from landscape.

Because of the tension between the timeless and the transitory or altered landscape embodied in their form, location and decoration, standing stones have fluid biographies. During the Early Bronze Age (2200–1500 BC) selected standing stones were broken up and reused in the burial cairns of the linear cemetery that runs through the valley. At Nether Largie North, excavation indicated the stone holes or former locations of standing stones beneath the burial cairn (Craw 1931). Indeed, a large stone incorporated into the central burial is decorated, with an undecorated portion at its base suggests that it formerly stood upright (Bradley 1993, 92).

The carving executed on reused stones differs from the execution of motifs in the landscape. Motifs on burial cists are generally

36. The Standing Stone alignment at Ballymeanoch. Photo: the author.

geometric lozenges or curvilinear rings. At three sites there are also representations of bronze axes (Fig. 37). Motifs on burial slabs operate in a number of ways. The execution of lozenges and curvilinear motifs reference the rocks upon which images are carved in the surrounding landscape, as well as the images carved upon them, and they also cite the decoration on portable artefacts from the Late Neolithic and Early Bronze Age. The execution of axe motifs is also referential as the process of producing the image of an axe in stone corresponds to the process of pecking out the stone moulds used

37. Axe motifs in the burial cist at Ri Cruin. Photo: the author.

to produce EBA metal axes. There is a technological equivalence to the process of image production that evokes and memorialises the productive capacity of metalwork (Jones 2001b). Motifs on burial slabs are on smooth surfaces and often cover the surface of the stone. Stones exhibit evidence of a number of episodes of recarving and it is likely that – due to the construction of the stone burial cists – they remain open and accessible for a period of time prior to final burial. On burial, images that were visible elements of the landscape are now removed from visibility; the site of burial becomes marked by an immense mound of stone and earth (Fig. 38). The position of these cairns along the axis of the valley mirrors the axis previously occupied by stone alignments.

The decorated faces of the fragmented stones placed in burial cairns are always turned to face the dead. Because of the origin of the stones the dead are in a sense enclosed by the valley sides.

38. The Glebe Cairn, Kilmartin Valley. Photo: the author.

TEMPORALISING THE LANDSCAPE OF KILMARTIN

In effect images operate at two different temporal registers; the first involves a process of decorating living rock in the wider landscape. The placement of images in the landscape provides a means of ordering the landscape and orientating the subject. As visual traces of past activity they draw attention to features of past and future significance. By reading natural fissures and cracks as ancestral traces and responding to them with the repetitive production of images people were temporally situating themselves in a landscape perceived as timeless. The production of images is a form of poeisis, a way of weaving a sense of belonging and place, just as images are visually woven into the rock surface. More than this, it is a way of objectifying or visualising the relationship between people and place.

Images are at once static and mobile, binding and connecting. Their placement on static rock panels in the landscape enacts a process of binding. However, images are also simultaneously connective as their production may presence distant places. In terms of the immediate landscape of Kilmartin the production of images weaves skeins of significance across the landscape binding one place to another. The production of images at geographically important points such as valley junctures are the nodes or 'knots' which tie this network of connections together. Images are elements of a relational indexical field, their purpose is to visualise and mobilise a sense of place. Images act as an *oeuvre* in the sense defined by Gell (1998) and discussed in Chapters 1 and 4.

The grounding of images in the landscape offers a platform for the use of images in a quite different temporal register involving standing stones and burial slabs. Images were not so much woven onto standing stones; rather, standing stones were mediums for mobilising or presencing images at other places in the landscape. Standing stones occupy an ambiguous temporal position, as immense sculptural forms placed in the valley bottom they act as figures against the ground of the landscape; however, as erstwhile components of the landscape they also merge with that landscape. Are they placed there by people, or are they an indissoluble part of the landscape? The ambiguous nature of standing stones is drawn attention to by images which in their size point up the alterity of the stones, but which also refer to their natural origins in the hillsides.

The alterity of the stones is emphasised by the execution of images on burial slabs, which evoke their former status as elements of the landscape and also evoke cultural artefacts. In a sense the treatment of standing stones and their subsequent burial echoes the human life cycle. In the valley bottom the stone intervenes materially and bodily with the life of humans; on burial its material presence is removed from view. Now images bind the person rather than the landscape. Their removal from circulation creates a space for remembrance, materialised by a cairn.

Images offer a way to visualise events of different temporal duration: one the timelessness of the landscape and the other the duration of the human life course. By addressing living rock as if it were the traces of past events and carving upon it, people situated themselves historically in the landscape. The provision of a timeless temporal and spatial framework created by carving images on living rock provided the ground for people to comprehend their own temporal spans and the capacity to alter the landscape through the production and destruction of standing stones and cairns. The production of images at each stage of these events provided a way of tracing the history of events.

ROCK ART, SEMIOTICS, AND PLACE

We have now compared rock art traditions in two different regions of prehistoric Europe. The images discussed by Helskog in northern Scandinavia and Russia are mainly iconic in character. In a semiotic sense they work because they resembled animals and human activities in the wider landscape. The rock surface was taken as both index and icon. At a fundamental level as indexes the rock surfaces provided visual cues around which narratives were constructed, but the surfaces were implicated in this narrative in an iconic sense: pools of water in the rock were taken to be larger bodies of water (lakes, seas) into which the characters of the story entered to communicate with the spirits, and the slope of the rocks were treated as if they resembled the slope of the land surface on which human figures skied.

British rock art traditions – as we saw with the example of Kilmartin – are mainly indexical in character. The rock surface was taken as an index, a visual cue around which images were woven. The significance of these images lies less in what they resemble and more in the physical act of their production and in the relationships they index with other images.

Curiously, in terms of their relationship to place, both rock art traditions work in similar ways: they act as nodes or knots tying together places in the wider landscape. I argued that the visual citation of other places in the Kilmartin landscape meant that images functioned to give the landscape temporal and spatial coherence, enabling people to 'place themselves' in the landscape. The rock art of northern Europe did the same thing, albeit in a different way.

There the production of images referenced multiple worlds, real and mythical, and conjured other times and places.

ROCK ART, REMEMBRANCE, AND PLACE

It is helpful at this juncture to consider the differences between the relationship to place formed by rock art production and the relationship to place we observed in the case of Irish passage tombs and the Iberian slate plaques. In the case of Irish passage tombs and Iberian slate plaques, place was a mobile and fluid concept. Passage tombs embedded raw materials from other places in their construction; Iberian slate plaques were made out of materials from significant places and were deposited in significant places (family tombs). The inscription of imagery embellishes or highlights the significance of these place-inflected relationships. Places were presenced or indexed in material form. As we have seen from this chapter rock art sites also presence or index other places, but rather than performing this by material citation, the carving of images performs the same action. Other places are presenced and juxtaposed in images. As a 'writing without words' the production of rock art performed or crystallised the relationship between places and images. Remembrance was then produced by the activity of carving rock art at significant places in the landscape. In Scandinavia we can observe that such acts of remembrance took the place of formalised seasonal and cosmological narratives. In the case of Kilmartin remembrance took the form of tracing relationships to places and previous activities as images were interwoven with the fabric of the landscape.

10

Coda

Central to the approach I have established throughout the book is the significance of participation and engagement. My principal cue for this comes from Merleau-Ponty's 'reversibility thesis' (Merleau-Ponty 1962). Merleau-Ponty argues for a perceptual connectivity between person and world. People are positioned in relation to the world they perceive; objects in the world reflect the position of the person. We can touch and be touched, see and be seen, act upon things and at the same time be acted upon by them – all this is due to our common fabric as 'flesh' (Olsen 2003, 98). Memory occurs as the person engages with the objects they encounter in the world they perceive; people remember as they are remembered by things. The habitual encounter with the phenomena of the world generates meaning, as the other philosopher of engagement, Charles Sanders Peirce, makes clear. The role of engagement lies at the heart of the philosophy of pragmatism: the meaning of things is determined by our perceptual engagement with them. While perceptual engagement is critical to remembrance, my approach to memory is essentially ecological in the terms described by David Rubin. Rubin (1988) argues that there is a psychological distinction between structure and process. We can consider accounts of memory as either 'complex structure' accounts or 'complex process' accounts. The problems arise when psychologists mistake complex processes for complex mental structures – effectively mapping events and processes that go on outside the mind onto the structure of the mind; as if real world events can be copied into, and then later explained, by the structure of the mind (Rubin 1988, 375). The approach I adopted in this book is to shift from the treatment of memory as a complex mental structure to the analysis of remembrance as a complex process incorporating the interaction between mind and material world.

RE-MEMBERING THINGS

How does focussing upon the philosophy of engagement help us consider material culture? If we are to take seriously Bjørnar Olsen's call to 're-member' things, to recall the physicality of the stuff that was once a component of past peoples lives and is now the meat and drink of archaeological studies, it is important that we do not forget that things are solid and material and not just signs, symbols, or metaphors. In short, we need to return to Durkheim's notion of artefacts as social facts (Olsen 2003, 97). Material culture provides a solid framework – like a spider's web or a scaffold – around which we weave ourselves and with which we articulate or organise ourselves. If we wish to take further the point that 'technology is society made durable', then we need to consider how objects are implicated in the process of producing durability. Objects are crystallised intentions, the physical memories of former actions. In this I believe Donald (1991, 1998) is partly correct to argue that artefacts are a form of external symbolic storage. Objects do act as external elements of society. But this point is not unproblematic; objects are not simply 'read' as symbols. Rather it is in the repetitive process of sensual engagement and re-engagement that remembrance occurs. Julia Hendon (2000) makes this clear in her study of storage systems in Mesoamerica and Neolithic Europe. She argues that the physical space of the house and its itinerant storage facilities provide a kind of solid physical framework for mutual knowledge; in some cases stored produce acts as a physical embodiment of the ties between people (Hendon 2000, 46). The placement of objects in storage does not mean that they are continuously part of the social fabric as envisaged in Donald's scheme. Rather, the act of putting objects in storage and bringing them out of storage provides a platform for a punctuated process of engagement and reengagement and provides the means for inequalities in the possession of socially important knowledge (Hendon 2000). This underlines the point that, although the material world provides a framework for remembrance, it is the social practices in which artefacts are engaged which determines how remembrance is socially experienced and mapped out. In this sense we can consider the object world as a kind of 'distributed mind', not only spatially distributed, but also temporally distributed. In taking this line of argument, the concept of the index is critical because it allows us to consider how things are related.

THE SIGNIFICANCE OF THE INDEX: ARTEFACTS, ASSEMBLAGES, PLACES, LANDSCAPES

The treatment of the physical world as an index allows us to consider in more depth how relationships are composed as artefacts, and places and landscapes are envisaged as components of indexical fields. If we consider the relationship between things as indexical in nature it enables us to reconceptualise the nature of artefact categories; artefacts can be seen as 'hybrids' composed of a series of indexical relations. Artefacts can also be treated as components of indexical fields in other ways: the notion of the index enables us to conceptualise the links between assemblages of artefacts, whether physically located in one place like caches or hoards or as cultural assemblages distributed across a landscape.

The concept of indexical fields also enables us to reconsider the relationship between places. As shown in Chapter 8, places may be circulated and their significance may be embellished by inscription. Physically, places need not be static; they can be mobilised, and their significance can be enhanced by reference to other places. This can be achieved by the physical circulation of fragments of place, as we saw in the case of Iberian stone plaques, and in the diverse geological sources used to create the great Boyne Valley passage tombs in Ireland. The significance of a given place can be amplified by reference to other places. Again the Boyne Valley passage tombs amply demonstrate this. However, reference to the significance of place can be made without recourse to the physical circulation of parts of other places. It can also be achieved by inscription. The elaborate carving of the Boyne Valley tombs demonstrates the point that the significance of places can be reiterated by repetitive embellishment. However, other places can also be conjured and evoked by the inscription of images as we saw in the case of the rock art of northern Scandinavia and in the landscape of Kilmartin. In the case of northern Scandinavia other places and other times, both real and mythical, were indexed. In the case of Kilmartin other places were evoked, and the indexical fields generated by marking the landscape were an important component of the way in which the landscape was organised.

Each event, whether the production of an artefact, its deposition, the act of building monuments, or the act of inscription, is an index related to other events as part of an indexical field. Indexical fields are each nested in other indexical fields. It is possible then to conceptualise landscapes as densely packed networks of indexes. Unpacking the relationships between indexes and indexical fields is a project for future research, although concentrating upon indexical relationships offers the chance for a fully situated contextual approach to archaeology.

References

Adams, B. (1990) *Time and social theory*. Polity Press: Cambridge.

Adkins, L., and Adkins, R. A. (1989) *Archaeological illustration*. Cambridge University Press: Cambridge.

Alcock, S. E. (2002) *Archaeologies of the Greek past: Landscape, monuments and memories*. Cambridge University Press: Cambridge.

Allen, C. J. (1998) When utensils revolt: Mind, matter and modes of being in the pre-Colombian Andes, *RES* 33, 18–27.

Alpers, S. (1983) *The art of describing: Dutch art in the 17th Century*. University of Chicago Press: Chicago.

Armit, I. (1993) The Hebridean Neolithic, in Sharples, N., and Sheridan, A. (eds.) *Vessels for the ancestors*. Edinburgh University Press: Edinburgh, 307–321.

Armit, I. (1996) *The archaeology of the Western Isles*. Edinburgh University Press: Edinburgh.

Armit, I., Murphy, E., Nelis, E., and Simpson, D. (2003) Irish Neolithic houses, in Armit, I., Murphy, E., Nelis, E., and Simpson, D. (eds.) *Neolithic settlement in Ireland and western Britain*. Oxbow: Oxford, 146–148.

Bachelard, G. (1964) *The poetics of space*. Beacon Press: Boston, MA.

Barclay, G. (1983) Sites of the third millennium bc to the first millennium ad at North Mains, Strathallan, Perthshire, *Proceedings of the Society of Antiquaries of Scotland* 113, 122–281.

Barclay, G. (1996) Neolithic buildings in Scotland, in Darvill, T., and Thomas, J. (eds.) *Neolithic houses in northwest Europe and beyond*. Oxbow: Oxford, 61–75.

Barclay, G. (2003) Neolithic settlement in the lowlands of Scotland: A preliminary survey, in Armit, I., Murphy, E., Nelis, E., and Simpson, D. (eds.) *Neolithic settlement in Ireland and western Britain*. Oxbow: Oxford, 71–83.

Barclay, G., and Maxwell, G. S. (1991) Excavation of a Neolithic long mortuary enclosure within the Roman legionary fortress at Inchtuthil, Perthshire, *Proceedings of the Society of Antiquaries of Scotland* 121, 27–44.

Barclay, G., and Maxwell, G. S. (1998) *The Cleaven Dyke and Littleour: Monuments in the Neolithic of Tayside*. Society of Antiquaries of Scotland Monograph 13: Edinburgh.

Barclay, G., Brophy, K., and MacGregor, G. (2002) Claish, Stirling: An early Neolithic structure in its context, *Proceedings of the Society of Antiquaries of Scotland*, 132, 65–137.

Barrett, J. C. (1987) Contextual archaeology, *Antiquity* 61, 468–473.

Barrett, J. C. (1991) Early Bronze Age mortuary archaeology, in Barrett, J. C., Bradley, R., and Green, M. (eds.) *Landscape, monuments and society*. Cambridge University Press: Cambridge, 120–124.

Barrett, J. C. (1994) *Fragments from Antiquity: An archaeology of social life in Britain, 2900–1200 BC*. Blackwell: Oxford.

Barrett, J. C. (1999) The mythical landscapes of the British Iron Age, in Ashmore, W., and Knapp, A. B. (eds.) *Archaeologies of landscape*. Blackwell: Oxford, 253–265.

Barth, F. (2002) The anthropology of knowledge. *Current Anthropology* 43, 1–14.

Barthes, R. (1977) The death of the author, in Heath, S. (ed.) *Image-music-text: Roland Barthes selected essays*. Fontana: London, 142–149.

Battaglia, D. (1991) The body in the gift: Memory and forgetting in Sabarl mortuary exchanges, *American Ethnologist* 19, 3–18.

Bauer, A., and Preucel, R. (2001) Archaeological pragmatics, *Norwegian Archaeological Review* 34, 85–96.

Baxandall, M. (1985) *Patterns of intention: On the historical explanation of pictures*. Yale University Press: New Haven.

Bender, B. (2002) Time and landscape, *Current Anthropology* 43, 103–112.

Benjamin, W. (1999a) Excavation and memory, in Jennings, M. W. (ed.) *Selected writings, vol. 2, 1927–1934*. Harvard University Press: Cambridge, MA, 575–577.

Benjamin, W. (1999b) *Illuminations*. Pimlico: London.

Bentley, R. A., Price, T. D., Gronenborn, D., Wahl, J., and Fullagar, P. D. (2002) Human migration in Early Neolithic Europe, *Current Anthropology* 43, 799–804.

Bentley, R. A., Krause, R., Price, T. D., and Kauffmann, B. (2003) Human mobility at the Early Neolithic settlement of Vaihingen, Germany evidence from strontium isotope analysis, *Archaeometry* 45 (3), 471–486.

Bergson, H. (1991[1908]) *Matter and memory.* Zone Books: New York.

Binford, L. R. (1972) *An archaeological perspective.* Seminar Press: New York.

Biró, K. (1991) The problem of continuity in the prehistoric civilization of raw material, *Antaeus* 19/20, 41–50.

Blake, E. (1998) Sardinia's nuraghi: Four millennia of becoming, *World Archaeology*, 30, 59–72.

Bloch, M. (1995a) People into places: Zafimaniry concepts of clarity, in Hirsch, E., and O'Hanlon, M. (eds.) *The anthropology of landscape: Perspectives on place and space.* Oxford University Press: Oxford, 63–77.

Bloch, M. (1995b) 'Questions not to ask of Malagasy carvings' in Hodder, I., Shanks, M., Alexandri, A., Buchli, V., Carmen, J., Last, J., and Lucas, G. (eds.) *Interpreting archaeology: Finding meaning in the past.* Cambridge University Press: Cambridge, 212–215.

Bloch, M. (1998) *How we think they think: Anthropological approaches to cognition, memory and literacy.* Westview Press: Boulder, CO.

Boast, R. (1998a) Patterns by design: changing perspectives of beaker variation, in Edmonds, M., and Richards, C. (eds.) *Understanding the Neolithic of north-western Europe.* Cruithne Press: Glasgow, 385–406.

Boast, R. (1998b) A small company of actors – A critique of style, *Journal of Material Culture* 2, 173–198.

Boast, R. (2002) Pots as categories: British beakers, in Woodward, A., and Hill, J. D. (eds.) *Prehistoric Britain: The ceramic basis.* Oxbow: Oxford, 96–105.

Bogucki, P. (1988) *Forest farmers and stockherders: Early agriculture and its consequences in north-central Europe.* Cambridge University Press: Cambridge.

Bohncke, S. (1983) The pollen analysis of deposits in a food vessel from the henge monument at North Mains, in Barclay, G. (ed.) Sites of the third millennium bc to the first millennium ad at North Mains, Strathallan, Perthshire, *Proceedings of the Society of Antiquaries of Scotland* 113, 122–281.

Boivin, N., and Owoc, M.-A. (2004) *Soils, stones and symbols: Cultural perceptions of the mineral world.* UCL Press: London.

Bolt, B. (2004) *Art beyond Representation: The performative power of the image.* IB Tauris: London.

Bourdieu, P. (1977) *Outline of a theory of practice.* Cambridge University Press: Cambridge.

Bradley, R. (1984) *The social foundations of prehistoric Britain.* Longman: Harlow.

Bradley, R. (1989) Death and entrances: A contextual analysis of megalithic art, *Current Anthropology* 30, 68–75.

Bradley, R. (1990) *The passage of arms*. Cambridge University Press: Cambridge.

Bradley, R. (1993) *Altering the Earth*. Society of Antiquaries of Scotland Monograph Series No. 8: Edinburgh.

Bradley, R. (1997a) 'To see is to have seen': Craft traditions in British field archaeology, in Molyneaux, B. L. (ed.) *The cultural life of images: Visual representation in archaeology*. Routledge: London, 62–71.

Bradley, R. (1997b) *Rock art and the prehistory of Atlantic Europe: Signing the land*. Routledge: London.

Bradley, R. (1998a) Architecture, imagination and the Neolithic world, in Mithen, S. (ed.) *Creativity in human evolution and prehistory*. Routledge: London, 227–240.

Bradley, R. (1998b) *The significance of monuments: On the shaping of human experience in Neolithic and Bronze Age Europe*. Routledge. London.

Bradley, R. (2000) *An archaeology of natural places*. Routledge: London.

Bradley, R. (2002) *The past in prehistoric societies*. Routledge: London.

Bradley, R. (2007) *The prehistory of Britain and Ireland*. Cambridge University Press: Cambridge.

Bradley, R., and Chapman, R. (1986) The nature and development of long-distance relations in Later Neolithic Britain and Ireland, in Renfrew, C., and Cherry, J. F. (eds.) *Peer polity interaction and socio-political change*. Cambridge University Press: Cambridge, 127–136.

Bradley, R., and Edmonds, M. (1993) *Interpreting the axe trade*. Cambridge University Press: Cambridge.

Bradley, R., and Williams, H. (1998) The past in the past: The re-use of ancient monuments, special edition of *World Archaeology* 30 (1).

Bradley, R., Jones, A., Nordenborg-Myhre, L., and Sackett, H. (2003) Sailing through stone: Carved ships and the rock face at Revheim, south-west Norway, *Norwegian Archaeological Review* 35, 109–118.

Brindley, A. (1999) Sequence and dating in the Grooved Ware tradition, in Cleal, R., and MacSween, A. (eds.) *Grooved Ware in Britain and Ireland*. Oxbow: Oxford, 133–144.

Brophy, K. (1999) The cursus monuments of Scotland, in Barclay, A. and Harding, J. (eds.) Pathways and ceremonies: the cursus monuments of Britain and Ireland. Oxbow: Oxford, 119–129.

Bueno Ramirez, P. (1992) Les plaques décoreés alentéjaines: Approaches de leur etudes et analyse, *L'Anthropologie* 92, 573–604.

Buchli, V., and Lucas, G. (2001) Between remembering and forgetting, in Buchli, V., and Lucas, G. (eds.) *Archaeologies of the Contemporary Past*. Routledge: London, 79–83.

Burl, H. A. W. (1984) Report on the excavation of a Neolithic mound at Boghead, Speymouth Forest, Fochabers, Moray 1972 and 1974, *Proceedings of the Society of Antiquaries of Scotland* 114, 35–73.

Burgess, C. (1980) *The age of Stonehenge*. Dent: London.

Burgess, C., and Schmidt, P. K. (1981) *The axes of Scotland and Northern England*. Prahistoriche Bronzefunde series: Abteilung IX, band 7. Beck'sche Verlagsbuchhandlung: Munich.

Busby, C. (1997) Permeable and partible persons: A comparative analysis of gender and the body in South India and Melanesia, *Journal of the Royal Anthropological Institute* 3, 261–278.

Butler, J. (1993) *Bodies that matter*. Routledge: London.

Butler, J. (1997) *Excitable speech: A politics of the performative*. Routledge: London.

Callander, J. G. (1916) Notice of a jet necklace found in a cist in a Bronze Age cemetery, discovered on Burgie Lodge Farm, Moray with notes on prehistoric jet ornaments, *Proceedings of the Society of Antiquaries of Scotland* 51, 201–240.

Callon, M. (1991) Techno-economic networks and irreversibility, in Law, J. (ed.) *A sociology of monsters: Essays on power, technology and domination*. Routledge: London, 132–161.

Campbell, A.T. (1989) *To Square with Genesis: causal statements and shamanic ideas in Wayapí*. University of Iowa Press: Iowa City, IO.

Cappelletto, F. (2003) Long-term memory of extreme events: From autobiography to history, *Journal Royal Anthropological Institute* (N.S.) 9, 241–260.

Carruthers, M. (1990) *The book of memory: A study of memory in Medieval culture*. Cambridge University Press: Cambridge.

Casey, E. (1987) *Remembering: A phenomenological study*. Indiana University Press: Bloomington, IN.

Childe, V. G. (1981[1950]) *Man makes himself*. Moonraker Press: Bradford-on-Avon.

Chapman, J. (2000a) *Fragmentation in archaeology*. Routledge: London.

Chapman, J. (2000b) Tension at funerals: Social practices and the subversion of community structure in Later Hungarian prehistory, in Dobres, M.-A., and Robb, J. (eds.) *Agency in archaeology*. Routledge: London, 169–195.

Clark, A. (1997) *Being there: Putting brain, body and world together again*. MIT Press: Cambridge, MA.

Clarke, D. L. (1970) *The Beaker pottery of Great Britain and Ireland*. Cambridge University Press: Cambridge.

Cleary, R. M. (1983) The ceramic assemblage, in O'Kelly, M., Cleary, R. M., and Lehane, D. (eds.) *Newgrange, Co. Meath, Ireland: The late Neolithic/beaker period settlement*. British Archaeological Reports: Oxford, 58–117.

Coles, J. (1969) Scottish early Bronze Age metalwork, *Proceedings of the Society of Antiquaries of Scotland* 101, 1–110.

Coles, J., and Simpson, D. D. A. (1965) The excavation of a Neolithic round barrow at Pitnacree, Perthshire, Scotland, *Proceedings of the Society of Antiquaries of Scotland* 31, 34–57.

Conan Doyle, A. (1981[1887]) *A study in scarlet*. Penguin: London.

Conan Doyle, A. (1981[1902]) *The hound of the Baskervilles*. Penguin: London.

Connerton, P. (1989) *How societies remember*. Cambridge University Press: Cambridge.

Cooney, G. (1996) Comments on Dronfield, *Cambridge Archaeological Journal* 6: (1), 59–60.

Cooney, G. (1999) *Landscapes of Neolithic Ireland*. Routledge: London.

Corrington, R. S. (1993) *An introduction to C. S. Peirce: Philosopher, semiotician, and ecstatic naturalist*. Rowan and Littlefield. Lanham, Maryland.

Coudart, A. (1998) *Architecture et sociétés néolithique: l'unité et la variance de la maison danubienne*. Éditions de la Maison des Sciences de L'Homme: Paris.

Cowie, T. (1988) *Magic metal: Early metalworkers in the North-East*. Anthropological Museum, University of Aberdeen: Aberdeen.

Cowie, T., and Ritchie, G. (1991) Bronze Age burials at Gairneybank, Kinross-shire, *Proceedings of the Society of Antiquaries of Scotland* 121, 95–109.

Cox, C., and Warner, D. (2004) *Audio culture: Readings in modern music*. Continuum: New York.

Crane, S. (2000) Introduction: of museums and memory, in Crane, S. A. (ed.) *Museums and memory*. Stanford University Press: Stanford, CA.

Craw, J. (1931) Further excavations of cairns at Poltalloch, Argyll, *Proceedings Society of Antiquaries of Scotland* 65, 269–280.

Cutler, C. (2004) Plunderphonia, in Cox, C., and Warner, D. (eds.) *Audio culture: Readings in modern music*. Continuum: New York, 138–156.

De Boeck, F. (1998) The rootedness of trees: Place as cultural and natural texture in rural southwest Congo, in Lovell, N. (ed.) *Locality and belonging*. Routledge: London, 25–52.

D'Errico, F. (1998) Palaeolithic origins of artificial memory systems: An evolutionary perspective, in Renfrew, C., and Scarre, C. (eds.) *Cognition and material culture: The archaeology of symbolic storage*. McDonald Institute Monographs: Cambridge, 19–50.

de Grooth, M. (1998) The flint mines at Rijckholt-Sint Geertruid and their socio-economic interpretation, in Edmonds, M., and Richards, C. (eds.) *Understanding the Neolithic of north-western Europe*. Cruithne Press: Glasgow, 328–350.

Derrida, J. (1982) Signature, event, context, in Derrida, J. (ed.) *The margins of philosophy*. Harvester Press: Brighton, 307–330.

Derrida, J. (2001[1978]) *Writing and difference*. Routledge: London.

Dewey, W. J., and Childs, S. T. (1996) Forging memory, in Roberts, M. N., and Roberts, A. F. (eds.) *Memory: Luba art and the making of history*. Prestel: Munich, 61–83.

Dickson, J. (1978) Bronze Age mead, *Antiquity* 52, 108–113.

Donald, M. (1991) *Origins of the modern mind: Three stages in the evolution of culture and cognition*. Harvard University Press: Cambridge, MA.

Donald, M. (1993) Précis of Origins of the Modern Mind, *Behavioural and Brain Sciences* 15, 183–206.

Donald, M. (1998) Hominid enculturation and cognitive evolution, in Renfrew, C., and Scarre, C (eds.) *Cognition and material culture: The archaeology of symbolic storage*. McDonald Institute Monographs: Cambridge, 7–17.

Douglas, M. (1992) The person in an enterprise culture, in Heap, S. H., and Ross, A. (eds.) *Understanding the enterprise culture: Themes in the work of Mary Douglas*. Edinburgh University Press: Edinburgh, 41–62.

Draaisma, D. (2000) *Metaphors of memory: A history of ideas about the mind* (translated by P. Vincent). Cambridge University Press. Cambridge.

Dronfield, J. (1995a) Subjective vision and the source of Irish megalithic art, *Antiquity* 69, 539–549.

Dronfield, J. (1995b) Migraine, light and hallucinogens: The neurocognitive basis of Irish megalithic art, *Oxford Journal of Archaeology* 14, 261–275.

Dronfield, J. (1996) Entering alternative realities: Cognition, art and architecture in Irish passage tombs, *Cambridge Archaeological Journal* 6 (1), 37–72.

Earle, T. (1991) *Chiefdoms: Power, economy and ideology*. Cambridge University Press: Cambridge.

Earle, T., and Ericson, J. E. (1977) *Exchange systems in Prehistory*. Academic Press: New York.

Eco, U. (1984) Horns, Hooves and Insteps: Some hypotheses on three types of abduction in Eco, U., and Sebeok, T. A. (eds.) *The sign of three: Dupin, Holmes, Peirce* Indiana University Press: Bloomington, IN, 198–220.

Eco, U. (2004) The poetics of the open work, in Cox, C., and Warner, D. (eds.) *Audio culture: Readings in modern music*. Continuum. New York, 167–175.

Eco, U. (2005) *The mysterious flame of Queen Loana*. Secker & Warburg: London.

Edwards, E. (1999) Photographs as objects of memory, Kwint, M., Breward, C., and Aynsley, J. (eds.) *Material memories: Design and evocation*. Berg: Oxford, 221–237.

Eogan, G. (1963) A Neolithic habitation site and megalithic tomb in Townleyhall townland, Co. Louth, *Journal of the Royal Society of Antiquaries of Ireland* 93, 37–81.

Eogan, G. (1986) *Knowth and the passage-tombs of Ireland*. Thames & Hudson: London.

Eogan, G. (1994) *The accomplished art: Gold and gold-working in Britain and Ireland during the Bronze Age*. Oxbow: Oxford.

Eogan, G. (1997) Overlays and underlays: Aspects of megalithic art succession at Brugh Na Boinne, Ireland, *Brigantium*, 1997, 10, 217–234.

Eogan, G. (1998) Knowth before Knowth, *Antiquity* 72, 162–172.

Eogan, G., and Roche, H. (1999) Grooved Ware from Brugh na Bóinne and its wider context, in Cleal, R., and MacSween, A. (eds.) *Grooved Ware in Britain and Ireland*. Oxbow: Oxford, 98–111.

Evans, C. (2000) Megalithic follies: Soane's 'Druidic remains' and the display of monuments, *Journal of Material Culture* 5, 347–366.

Eves, R. (1996) Remembrance of things passed: Memory, body and the politics of feasting in New Ireland, Papua New Guinea, *Oceania* 66, 266–277.

Fabian, J. (1983) *Time and the other*. Columbia University Press: New York.

Fentress, J., and Wickham, C. (1992) *Social memory*. Blackwell: Oxford.

Forty, A. (1999) Introduction, in Forty, A., and Kuchler, S. (eds.) *The art of forgetting*. Berg: Oxford, 1–19.

Fowler, C. (2003) Rates of (Ex)change, in Williams, H. (ed.) *Archaeologies of remembrance*. Kluwer Academic/Plenum: New York, 45–64.

Foster, R. J. (1991) Nurture and force-feeding: Mortuary feasting and the construction of collective individuals in a New Ireland society, *American ethnologist* 19, 431–448.

Gardin, J.-C. (1992) Semiotic trends in Archaeology, in Gardin, J.-C., and Peebles, C. S. (eds.) *Representations in archaeology*. Indiana University Press. Bloomington, IN, 87–104.

Gell, A. (1985) How to read a map: Remarks on the practical logic of navigation, *Man* NS 20, 271–286.

Gell, A. (1992) *The anthropology of time*. Berg: Oxford.

Gell, A. (1996) Vogels net: Traps as artworks and artworks as traps, in *Journal of Material Culture* 1, 15–38.

Gell, A. (1998) *Art and agency: An anthropological theory*. Clarendon: Oxford.

Gell, A. (1999) Strathernograms, or the semiotics of mixed metaphors, in Hirsch, E. (ed.) *The art of anthropology: Essays and diagrams*. Athlone: London, 29–75.

Geismar, H. (2004) The materiality of contemporary art in Vanuatu, *Journal of Material Culture* 9, 43–58.

Gibson, J. J. (1979) *The ecological approach to visual perception*. Lawrence Erlbaum: Hillsdale, NJ.

Gilchrist, R. (1999) *Gender and archaeology: Contesting the past*. Routledge: London.

Ginzburg, C. (1984) Clues: Morelli, Freud and Sherlock Holmes, in Eco, U., and Sebeok, T. A. (eds.) *The sign of three: Dupin, Holmes, Peirce*. Indiana University Press: Bloomington, 81–118.

Goody, J. (1977) *The logic of writing and the organisation of society*. Cambridge University Press: Cambridge.

Gosden, C. (1994) *Social being and time*. Blackwell. Oxford.

Gosden, C. (2004a) *Archaeology and colonialism: Culture contact from 5000 BC to the present*. Cambridge University Press: Cambridge.

Gosden, C. (2004b) Aesthetics, intelligence and emotions: Implications for archaeology, in DeMarrais, E., Gosden, C., and Renfrew, C. (eds.) *Rethinking materiality: The engagement of mind with the material world*. McDonald Institute Monographs: Cambridge, 33–40.

Gosden, C., and Marshall, Y. (1999) The cultural biography of objects, *World Archaeology* 31, 169–178.

Gottdiener, M. (1994) *Postmodern semiotics: Material culture and the forms of postmodern life*. Blackwell: Oxford.

Graves, P. (1989) Social space in the English medieval parish church, *Economy and Society* 18, 3, 297–322.

Gronenborn, D. (1990) Mesolithic-neolithic interactions: the lithic industries of the earliest Bandkeramik culture site at Freidberg-Bruchenbrücken, Wetteraukreis (West Germany), in Vermeersch, P. and van Peer, P. (eds.) *Contributions to the Mesolithic in Europe*. Leuven University Press: Leuven, 173–182.

Gronenborn, D. (1999) Variations on a basic theme: The transition to farming in southern central Europe, *Journal of World Prehistory* 13, 123–210.

Grøn, O., and Kuznetsov, O. (2004) Ethno-archaeology among the Evenkian forest hunters: Preliminary results and a different approach to reality!, in Larsson, L., Kindgren, H., Knusson, K., and Loeffler, D. (eds.) *Mesolithic on the Move*. Oxbow: Oxford, 216–221.

Hacking, I. (1995) *Rewriting the soul: Multiple personality and the science of memory*. Princeton University Press: Princeton, NJ.

Halbwachs, M. (1993 [1950]) *On collective memory*. Translated by L. A. Coser. University of Chicago Press: Chicago.

Harley, J. B. (1988) Maps, knowledge and power, in Cosgrove, D., and Daniels, S. (eds.) *The iconography of landscape*. Cambridge University Press: Cambridge, 277–312.

Harris, R. (1995) *Signs of writing*. Routledge: London.

Hauptmann Wahlgren, K. (1998) Encultured rocks: Encounter with a ritual world of the Bronze Age, *Current Swedish Archaeology* 6, 85–96.

Hamilakis, Y. (1999) Food technologies/technologies of the body: The social context of wine and oil production and consumption in Bronze Age Crete, *World Archaeology* 31, 38–54.

Harrison, R. (1974) Origins of the Bell beaker cultures, *Antiquity* 48, 99–109.

Helms, M. (2005) Tangible materiality and cosmological others in the development of sedentism, in DeMarrais, E., Gosden, C., and Renfrew, C. (eds.)

Rethinking materiality: The engagement of mind with the material world. McDonald Institute Monographs: Cambridge, 117–127.

Helskog, K. (1999) The shore connection: Cognitive landscape and communication with rock carvings in northernmost Europe, *Norwegian Archaeological Review* 32, 73–94.

Helskog, K. (2004) Landscapes in rock art: Rock carving and ritual in the old European North, in Chippindale, C., and Nash, G. (eds.) *The figured landscapes of rock-art: Looking at pictures in place.* Cambridge University Press: Cambridge, 265–288.

Hendon, J. (2000) Having and holding: storage, memory, knowledge and social relations, *American Anthropologist* 102 (1), 42–53.

Henshall, A.S. (1966) *The chambered tombs of Scotland, vol. 1.* Edinburgh University Press: Edinburgh.

Henshall, A. S. (1972) *The chambered tombs of Scotland, vol. 2.* Edinburgh University Press: Edinburgh.

Heyd, T. (2005) Rock art aesthetics: Trace on rock, mark of spirit, window on land, in Heyd, T., and Clegg, J. (eds.) *Aesthetics and rock art.* Ashgate: Aldershot, 37–50.

Higham, C. (2005) East Asian agriculture and its impact, in Scarre, C. (ed.) *The human past.* Thames & Hudson: London, 552–593.

Hingley, R. (1996) Ancestors and identity in the later prehistory of Atlantic Scotland, *World Archaeology* 28, 231–243.

Hobsbawm, E. (1983) Introduction: Inventing traditions, in Hobsbawm, E., and Ranger, T. (eds.) *The invention of tradition.* Cambridge University Press: Cambridge, 1–14.

Hodder, I. (1982) Theoretical archaeology: A reactionary view, in Hodder, I. (ed.) *Symbolic and structural archaeology.* Cambridge University Press: Cambridge.

Hodder, I. (1984) Burials, houses, women and men in the European Neolithic, in Miller, D., and Tilley, C. (eds.) *Ideology, power and prehistory.* Cambridge University Press: Cambridge, 51–68.

Hodder, I. (1986) *Reading the past, second edition.* Cambridge University Press: Cambridge.

Hodder, I. (1990) *The domestication of Europe.* Blackwell: Oxford.

Hodder, I. (1995) *Theory and practice in archaeology.* Routledge: London.

Hodder, I. (1998a) The Domus: Some problems reconsidered, in Edmonds, M., and Richards, C. (eds.) *Understanding the Neolithic of North-western Europe.* Cruithne Press: Glasgow, 84–101.

Hodder, I. (1998b) Creative thought: A long-term perspective, in Mithen, S. (ed.) *Creativity in human evolution and prehistory.* Routledge: London, 61–76.

Holtorf, C. (2002) Excavations at Monte de Igreja near Évora (Portugal): From the life-history of a monument to re-uses of ancient objects, *Journal of Iberian Archaeology*, 4, 177–201.

Hoskins, J. (1998) *Biographical objects*. Routledge: London.

Houston, S. D. (2004) The archaeology of communication technologies, *Annual Review of Anthropology* 33, 223–250.

Houston, S. D., and Stuart, D. (1998) The ancient Maya self: Personhood and portraiture in the Classic period, *RES* 33, 73–101.

Ingold, T. (1993) The temporality of the landscape, *World Archaeology* 25, 152–174.

Ingold, T. (2000a) Stop, look and listen! Vision, hearing and human movement, in Ingold, T. (ed.) *The perception of the environment: Essays in livelihood, dwelling and skill*. Routledge: London, 243–289.

Ingold, T. (2000b) To journey along a way of life: Maps, wayfinding and navigation, in Ingold, T. (ed.) *The perception of the environment: Essays in livelihood, dwelling and skill*. Routledge: London, 219–242.

Jeunesse, C. (1997) *Pratiques Funéraires au Néolithique ancien: sépultures et necropolis des societés danubiennes (5500–4900 av. J.C.)*, Éditions Errance: Paris.

Johnson, M. (1991) The imaginative basis of meaning and cognition, in Melion, W., and Küchler, S. (eds.) *Images of memory*. Smithsonian Institution Press: Washington, D.C., 74–87.

Jones, A. (1998) Where eagles dare: Landscape, animals and the Neolithic of Orkney *Journal of Material Culture* 3, 301–324.

Jones, A. (1999) The world on a plate: Ceramics, food technology and cosmology in Neolithic Orkney, *World Archaeology* 31 (1), 55–77.

Jones, A. (2000) Life after death: Monuments, material culture and social change in Neolithic Orkney, in Ritchie, A. (ed.) *Neolithic Orkney in its European context*. McDonald Institute Monographs: Cambridge, 127–138.

Jones, A. (2001a) Drawn from memory: The archaeology of aesthetics and the aesthetics of archaeology in Earlier Bronze Age Britain and the present, *World Archaeology* 33 (2), 334–356.

Jones, A. (2001b) Enduring images?: Image production and memory in Earlier Bronze Age Scotland, in Brück, J. (ed.) *Bronze Age landscapes: Tradition and transformation*. Oxbow: Oxford, 217–228.

Jones, A. (2002a) *Archaeological theory and scientific practice*. Cambridge University Press: Cambridge.

Jones, A. (2002b) A biography of colour: Colour, material histories and personhood in the Early Bronze Age of Britain and Ireland, in Jones, A., and MacGregor, G. (eds.) *Colouring the past: The significance of colour in archaeological research*. Berg: Oxford, 159–174.

Jones, A. (2004) Matter and memory: Colour, remembrance and the Neolithic/Bronze Age transition, in DeMarrais, E., Gosden, C., and Renfrew, C. (eds.) *Rethinking materiality: The engagement of mind with the material world*. McDonald Institute Monographs: Cambridge, 167–178.

Jones, A. (2005a) Lives in fragments?: Personhood and the European Neolithic, *Journal of Social Archaeology* 5 (2), 193–224.

Jones, A. (2005b) Natural histories and social identities in Neolithic Orkney, in Casella, E. C., and Fowler, C. (eds.) *The archaeology of plural and changing identities: Beyond identification*. Kluwer Academic/Plenum: New York, 233–253.

Jones, A. (2005c) Between a rock and a hard place: Rock art and mimesis in Neolithic and Bronze Age Scotland, in Cummings, V., and Pannett, A. (eds.) *Set in stone: New approaches to Neolithic monuments in Scotland*. Oxbow: Oxford, 107–117.

Jones, S. (1997) *The archaeology of ethnicity*. Routledge: London.

Joyce, R. (2003) Concrete memories: Fragments of the past in the Classic Maya present (500–1000 AD), in Van Dyke, R., and Alcock, S. (eds.) *Archaeologies of memory*. Blackwell: Oxford.

Kaczanowska, M., and Kozlowski, J. K. (2003) Origins of the Linear Pottery Complex and the Neolithic transition in Central Europe, in Ammerman, A. J., and Biagi, P. (eds.) *The widening harvest: The Neolithic transition in Europe: Looking back, looking forward*. Archaeological Institute of America: Boston, MA, 227–248.

Kendrick, J. (1995) Excavation of a neolithic enclosure and an Iron Age settlement at Douglasmuir, Angus, *Proceedings of the Society of Antiquaries of Scotland* 125, 29–67.

Kinnes, I. A. (1992) Balnagowan and after: The context of non-megalithic mortuary sites in Scotland, in Sharples, N., and Sheridan, A. (eds.) *Vessels for the ancestors*. Edinburgh University Press: Edinburgh, 83–103.

Kinnes, I. (1995) An innovation backed by great prestige: The instance of the spiral and twenty centuries of stony sleep, in Kinnes, I., and Varndell, G. (eds.) *'Unbaked urns of rudely shape': Essays on British and Irish pottery*. Oxbow Monograph 55. Oxbow books. Oxford, 49–53.

Kinnes, I. A. (1998) Longtemps Ignoreés: Passy-Rots, linear monuments in northern France, in Barclay, A., and Harding, J. (eds.) *Pathways and ceremonies: The cursus monuments of Britain and Ireland*. Oxbow: Oxford, 148–154.

Kwint, M. (1999) Introduction: The physical past, in Kwint, M., Breward, C., and Aynsley, J. (eds.) *Material memories: Design and evocation*. Berg: Oxford, 1–16.

Lakoff, G. (1987) *Women, fire, and dangerous things: What categories reveal about the mind*. Chicago University Press: Chicago, IL.

Lakoff, G., and Johnson, M. (1980). *Metaphors we live by*. Chicago University Press: Chicago, IL.

Lambek, M. (2003) Memory in a Maussian universe, in Radstone, S., and Hodgkin, K. (eds.) *Regimes of memory*. Routledge: London, 202–216.

Lambek, M., and Antze, P. (1996) Introduction: Forecasting memory, in Antze, P., and Lambek, M. (eds.) *Tense past: Cultural essays in trauma and memory*. Routledge. London, xi–xxxviii.

Langer, S. (1942) *Philosophy in a new key*. Harvard University Press: Cambridge, MA.

Latour, B. (1990) Drawing things together, in Lynch, M., and Woolgar, S. (eds.) *Representation in scientific practice*. MIT Press: Cambridge, MA, 19–69.

Latour, B. (1991) Technology is society made durable, in Law, J. (ed.) *A sociology of monsters: Essays on power, technology and domination*. Routledge: London, 103–131.

Latour, B. (1993) *We have never been modern*. Harvard University Press: Cambridge, MA.

Latour, B. (1999a) Factures/fracture: From the concept of network to the concept of attachment, *RES* 36, 20–31

Latour, B. (1999b) *Pandora's hope: Essays on the reality of science studies*. Harvard University Press: Cambridge, MA.

Lecornec, J. (1994) *Le Petit Mont, Arzon*. Documents Archéologiques de l'Ouest: Rennes.

Lenoir, T. (1998) Inscription practices and materialities of communication, in Lenoir, T. (ed.) *Inscribing science: Scientific texts and the materiality of communication*. Stanford University Press: Stanford, California, 1–19.

Le Roux, C.–T. (1984) A propos des fouilles de Gavrinis (Morbihan): Nouvelles données sur l'art mégalithique Armoricain, *Bulletin de la Societé Préhistorique Française* 81, 240–245.

Leslie, E. (2003) Absent-minded Professors: Etch-a-sketching academic forgetting, in Radstone, S., and Hodgkin, K. (eds.) *Regimes of memory*. Routledge: London, 172–185

Levi-Strauss, C. (1969) *The raw and the cooked*. Jonathan Cape: London.

Lewis-Williams, J. D. (2002) *The mind in the cave*. Thames & Hudson: London.

Lewis-Williams, J. D., and Dowson, T. A. (1990) Through the veil: San rock painting and the rock surface, *South African Archaeological Bulletin* 45, 5–16.

Lewis-Williams, J. D., and Dowson, T. A. (1993) On vision and power in the Neolithic: Evidence from the decorated monuments, *Current Anthropology* 34, 55–65.

Lewis-Williams, J. D., and Pearce, D. (2005) *Inside the Neolithic mind*. Thames & Hudson: London.

Liebhammer, N. (2000) Rendering realities, in Hodder, I. (ed.) *Towards a reflexive method in archaeology: The example at Catalhöyuk.* McDonald Institute monographs: Cambridge, 129–142.

Lillios, K. (2003) Creating memory in prehistory: The engraved slate plaques of Southwest Iberia, in Van Dyke, R. M., and Alcock, S. E. (eds.) *Archaeologies of Memory.* Blackwell: Oxford, 129–150.

Lillios, K. (2004) Lives of stone, lives of people: Re-viewing the engraved plaques of Late Neolithic and Copper Age Iberia, *European Journal of Archaeology* 7 (2), 125–158.

LiPuma, E. (1998) Modernity and forms of personhood in Melanesia, in Lambek, M., and Strathern, A. (eds.) *Bodies and persons: Comparative perspectives from African and Melanesia.* Cambridge University Press: Cambridge, 53–80.

Locke, J. (1997[1690]) *An essay concerning human understanding.* Penguin: London.

Lucas, G. (2004) *The archaeology of time.* Routledge: London.

Lüning, J., and P. Stehli (1989) Die Bandkeramik in Mitteleuropa: von der Natur-zur Kulturlandschaft, *Spektrum der Wissenschaft* 1989, 78–90.

Mack, J. (2003) *The museum of the mind.* British Museum Press: London.

MacGregor, G., and Shearer, I. (2002) Eweford, Dunbar, *Discovery and Excavation Scotland* NS 3, 35.

Marshack, A. (1991) *The roots of civilization.* Moyer Bell: New York.

Marshall, A. (1981) Environmental adaptation and structural design in axially pitched long houses from prehistoric Europe, *World Archaeology* 13, 10–23.

Marshall, Y. (1998) Transformations of Nuu-chah-nulth houses, in Joyce, R. A., and Gillespie, S. D. (eds.) *Beyond kinship: Social and material reproduction in house societies.* University of Pennsylvania Press: Philadelphia, 73–102.

Massey, D. (2005) *For space.* Sage: London.

Mauss, M. (1979[1950]) Les techniques du corps, in *Sociology and psychology: Essays of Marcel Mauss.* Translated by B. Brewster. Routledge & Kegan Paul: London, 97–123.

Megaw, B., and Hardy, E. (1938) British decorated axes and their diffusion during the earlier part of the Bronze Age, *Proceedings of the Prehistoric Society* 4, 272–307.

Melion, W., and Küchler, S. (1991) Introduction: Memory, cognition and image production, in Melion, W., and Küchler, S. (eds.) *Images of memory.* Smithsonian Institution Press: Washington, D.C., 1–47.

Merleau-Ponty, M. (1962) *Phenomenology of Perception.* Translated by C. Smith. Routledge: London.

Meskell, L. (2004) *Object worlds in ancient Egypt: Material biographies past and present.* Berg: Oxford.

Middleton, D., and Edwards, D. (1997) Introduction, in Middleton, D., and Edwards, D. (eds.) *Collective remembering*. Sage. London, 1–23.

Midgley, M. S. (2005) *The monumental cemeteries of prehistoric Europe*. Tempus: Stroud.

Miller, D. (1987) *Material culture and mass consumption*. Blackwell: Oxford.

Miller, D. (1994) Artefacts and the meaning of things, in Ingold, T. (ed.) *Companion encyclopedia of anthropology*. Routledge: London, 396–419.

Mines, D. P., and Weiss, B. (1993) Materialization of memory: The substance of remembering and forgetting: Introduction, *Anthropological Quarterly* 70, 161–163.

Mitchell, G. F. (1992) Notes on some non-local cobbles at the entrances to the passage graves at Newgrange and Knowth, Co. Meath, *Journal of the Royal Society of Antiquaries of Ireland* 122, 128–145.

Mitchell, W. J. T. (1996) *Picture theory: Essays on verbal and visual representation*. Chicago University Press: Chicago.

Mithen, S. (1996) *The prehistory of the mind*. Thames & Hudson: London.

Mizoguchi, K. (1993) Time in the reproduction of mortuary practices, *World Archaeology*, 25, 223–235.

Modderman, P. J. R. (1988) *The linear pottery culture: Diversity in uniformity*, Berichten van de Rijksdienst voor het Oudheidkunding Bodemonderzoete, Jaargang 38.

Monaghan, J. (1998) The person, destiny and the construction of difference in Mesoamerica, *RES* 33, 137–146.

Mordant, D. (1998) Émergence d'une architecture funéraire monumentale, in Guilaine, J. (ed.) *Sépultures d'Occident et geneses des mégalithismes (9000–3500 avant notre ère)*, Séminaire du Collège de France, Éditions Errance: Paris, 71–88.

Morphy, H. (1991) *Ancestral connections: Art and an aboriginal system of knowledge*. Chicago University Press: Chicago.

Morris, R. (1977) *The prehistoric rock art of Argyll*. Dolphin Press: Poole.

Munn, N. (1986) *The fame of Gawa: A symbolic study of value transformation in a Massim (Papua New Guinea) Society*. Cambridge University Press: Cambridge.

Murray, H., and Fraser, S. (2005) Ower-by the river: New evidence for the earliest Neolithic on Deeside, *Scottish Archaeological News* 47, 1–2.

Needham, S. (1988) Selective deposition in the British Early Bronze Age, *World Archaeology* 20, 229–248.

Needham, S. (1996) Chronology and periodisation in the British Bronze Age, *Acta Archaeologica* 67, 121–140.

Needham, S., and Kinnes, I. A. (1981) Tinned axes again, *Antiquity* 55, 133–134.

Nieszery, N. (1995) Linearbandkeramische Gräberfelder in Bayern, *Internationale Archäologie* 16. Marie Leidorf: Espelkamp.

Nordbladh, J. (1978) Images as messages in Society. Prologomena to the Study of Scandinavian Petroglyphs and Semiotics, in Kristiansen, K., and Paludan-Müller, C. (eds.) *New directions in Scandinavian Archaeology*. Studies in Prehistory and Early History I, National Museum Press: Copenhagen, 63–79.

Olivier, L. C. (2001) Duration, memory and the nature of the archaeological record, in Gustaffson A. and Karlsson H. (eds.) *Glyfer och arkeologiska rum – en vänbok till Jarl Nordbladh*. Gotarc: Gothenburg, 529–535.

Olsen, B. (1990) Roland Barthes: From sign to text, in Tilley, C. (ed.) *Reading material culture*. Blackwell: Oxford, 163–205.

Olsen, B. (2003) Material culture after text: Re-membering things, *Norwegian Archaeological Review* 36 (2), 87–104.

O'Kelly, C. (1982) Corpus of Newgrange art, in O'Kelly M. (ed.) *Newgrange: Archaeology, art and legend*. Thames & Hudson. London, 146–185.

O'Kelly, M. (1982) *Newgrange: Archaeology, art and legend*. Thames & Hudson: London.

O'Kelly, M., and O' Kelly, C. (1983) The tumulus of Dowth, County Meath, *Proceedings of the Royal Irish Academy* 83C, 135–190.

O'Sullivan, M. (1986) Approaches to passage tomb art, *Journal Royal Society of Antiquaries of Ireland*, 116, 68–83.

O'Sullivan, M. (1993) *Megalithic art in Ireland*. Country House: Dublin.

Ong, W. (1982) *Orality and literacy: Technologizing the word*. Routledge. London.

Peirce, C. S. (1958[1904]) *Values in a universe of chance: Selected writings of Charles S. Peirce (1839–1914)*. Doubleday Anchor: New York.

Pels, P. (1998) The spirit of matter: On fetish, rarity, fact, and fancy, in Spyer, P. (ed.) *Border fetishisms: Material objects in unstable spaces*. Routledge: London, 91–121.

Pétrequin, P., Pétrequin, A.-M., Jeudy, F., Jeunesse, C., Monnier, J.-L., Pelegrin, J., and Praud, I. (1998) From the raw material to the Neolithic stone axe: Production processes and social context, in Edmonds, M., and Richards, C. (eds.) *Understanding the Neolithic of north-western Europe*. Cruithne Press: Glasgow, 277–311.

Pietz, W. (1985) The problem of the fetish, I, *RES* 9, 5–17.

Pietz, W. (1987) The problem of the fetish, II, *RES* 13, 23–45.

Piggott, S. (1978) *Antiquity depicted: Aspects of archaeological illustration*. Thames & Hudson: London.

Pollard, J. (1992) The Sanctuary, Overton Hill, Wiltshire: A re-assessment, *Proceedings of the Prehistoric Society* 58, 213–220.

Pollard, J. (2004) The art of decay and the transformation of substance, in Renfrew, C., Gosden, C., and DeMarrais, E. (eds.) *Substance, memory and display: Archaeology and art*. McDonald Institute Monographs: Cambridge, 47–62.

Price, T. D., Bentley, A., Lüning, J., Gronenborn, D., and Wahl, J. (2001) Prehistoric human migration in the Linear Pottery Culture of Central Europe, *Antiquity* 75, 593–603.

Prown, J. D. (1996) Material/culture: Can the farmer and the cowman still be friends?, in Kingery, D. (ed.) *Learning from things: Method and theory of material culture studies*. Smithsonian Institution Press: Washington, D.C., 19–31.

Radley, A (1997) Artefacts, memory and a sense of the past, in Middleton, D., and Edwards, D. (eds.) *Collective remembering*. Sage: London, 46–60.

Ralston, I. (1982) A timber hall at Balbridie Farm, *Aberdeen University Review* 168, 238–249.

Rawson, J. (1998) Chinese burial patterns: Sources of information on thought and belief, in Renfrew, C., and Scarre, C. (eds.) *Cognition and material culture: The archaeology of symbolic storage*. McDonald Institute Monographs: Cambridge, 107–133.

RCAHMS (1999) *Kilmartin: An archaeological landscape*. HMSO: Edinburgh.

Renfrew, C. (1998) Mind and matter: Cognitive archaeology and external symbolic storage, in Renfrew, C., and Scarre, C. (eds.) *Cognition and material culture: The archaeology of symbolic storage*. McDonald Institute Monographs: Cambridge, 1–6.

Renfrew, C., and Cherry, J. F. (1986) *Peer polity interaction and socio-political change*. Cambridge University Press: Cambridge.

Richards, C. (1991) Skara Brae: Revisiting a Neolithic village in Orkney, in Hanson, W., and Slater, E. (eds.) *Scottish archaeology: New perceptions*. Aberdeen University Press: Aberdeen, 24–43.

Richards, C. (1992) Doorways into another world: The Orkney-Cromarty chambered tombs, in Sharples, N., and Sheridan, A. (eds.) *Vessels for the ancestors: Essays on the Neolithic of Britain and Ireland* Edinburgh University Press. Edinburgh, 62–76.

Richards, C. (1993) Monumental choreography: Architecture and spatial representation in Late Neolithic Orkney, in Tilley, C. (ed.) *Interpretative Archaeology*. Berg: Oxford, 143–178.

Richards, C. (1998) Centralising tendencies? A re-examination of social evolution in Late Neolithic Orkney, in Edmonds, M., and Richards, C. (eds.) *Understanding the Neolithic of north-western Europe*. Cruithne Press: Glasgow, 516–532.

Richards, C. (2005) *Dwelling among the monuments: The Neolithic village of Barnhouse, Maeshowe passage grave and surrounding monuments at Stenness, Orkney.* McDonald Institute Monographs: Cambridge.

Ritchie, A. (1973) Excavation of the Neolithic farmstead at Knap of Howar, Papa Westray, Orkney, *Proceedings of the Society of Antiquaries of Scotland* 113, 40–121.

Roberts, M. N. (1996) Luba memory theater, in Roberts, M. N., and Roberts, A. F. (eds.) *Memory: Luba art and the making of history.* Prestel: Munich, 117–147.

Robinson, D. (2004) The mirror of the Sun: Surface, mineral applications and interface in California rock art, in Boivin, N., and Owoc, M.-A. (eds.) *Soils, stones and symbols: Cultural perceptions of the mineral world.* UCL Press: London, 91–106.

Rose, S. (2003) *The making of memory: From molecules to mind.* Vintage: London.

Rowlands, M. (1993) The role of memory in the transmission of culture, *World Archaeology* 25, 141–151.

Rowlands, M. (2005) The materiality of sacred power, in DeMarrais, E., Gosden, C., and Renfrew, C. (eds.) *Rethinking materiality: The engagement of mind with the material world.* McDonald Institute Monographs: Cambridge, 197–203.

Rubin, D. (1988) Go for the skill, in Neisser, U., and Winograd, E. (eds.) *Remembering reconsidered: Ecological and traditional approaches to the study of memory.* Cambridge University Press: Cambridge, 374–382.

Ruestow, E. G. (1996) *The microscope in the Dutch Republic.* Cambridge University Press: Cambridge.

Saloman, F. (2001) How an Andean "writing without words" works, *Current Anthropology* 42, 1–27.

Scarre, C. (2002) Coast and cosmos: The Neolithic monuments of northern Brittany, in Scarre, C. (ed.) *Monuments and landscape in Atlantic Europe.* Routledge: London, 84–102.

Scarre, C. (2004) Choosing stones, remembering places: Geology and intention in the megalithic monuments of western Europe, in Boivin, N., and Owoc, M.-A. (eds.) *Soils, stones and symbols: Cultural perceptions of the mineral world.* UCL Press: London, 187–202.

Schiffer, M. (1999) *The material life of human beings: Artefacts, behaviour and communication.* Routledge: London.

Scott, J.G. (1989) The stone circle at Temple Wood, Kilmartin, Argyll, *Glasgow Archaeological Journal* 15, 53–124.

Seremetakis, N. (1994) *The senses still: Perception and memory as material culture in modernity.* University of Chicago Press: Chicago.

Shanks, M., and Tilley, C. (1987) *Re-constructing archaeology*. Cambridge University Press: Cambridge.

Shackleton, N., and Renfrew, C. (1970) Neolithic trade routes re-aligned by oxygen isotope analysis, *Nature* 228, 1062–1064.

Shapin, S., and Schaffer, S. (1985) *Leviathan and the air pump: Hobbes, Boyle, and the experimental life*. Princeton University Press: Princeton, NJ

Shee Twohig, E. S. (1981) *The megalithic art of Western Europe*. Clarendon: Oxford.

Shennan, S. (2002) *Genes, memes and human history*. Thames & Hudson: London.

Shepherd, I. (1985) Jet and amber, in Clarke, D. V., Cowie, T. G., and Foxon, A. (eds.) *Symbols of power at the time of Stonehenge*. Edinburgh: HMSO, 204–216.

Shepherd, I. (1986) *Powerful pots: Beakers in north-east prehistory*. Anthropological Museum, University of Aberdeen.

Shepherd, A. (1996) A Neolithic ring-mound at Midtown of Pitglassie, Auchterless, Aberdeenshire, *Proceedings of the Society of Antiquaries of Scotland* 126, 17–51.

Sheridan, A. (1986) Megaliths and megalomania: An account, and interpretation, of the development of passage tombs in Ireland, *Journal of Irish Archaeology* 3, 17–30.

Sherratt, A. (1990) The genesis of megaliths: Monumentality, ethnicity and social complexity in Neolithic north-west Europe, *World Archaeology* 22, 147–167.

Sherratt, A. (1997) *Economy and society in prehistoric Europe: Changing perspectives*. Princeton University Press: Princeton, NJ.

Siegel, J. T. (1983) Images and odours in Javanese practices surrounding death, *Indonesia* 36, 1–14.

Sommer, U. (2001) 'Hear the instructions of thy father, and forsake not the law of thy mother': Change and persistence in the European Neolithic, *Journal of Social Archaeology* 1 (2), 244–270.

Soudsky, B. (1973) Higher level archaeological entities – Models and reality, in Renfrew, C. (ed.) *The explanation of culture change*. Duckworth: London, 195–207.

Spyer, P. (1998) Introduction, in Spyer, P. (ed.) *Border fetishisms: Material objects in unstable spaces*. Routledge: London, 1–12.

Stafford, B. (1996) *Good looking: Essays on the virtue of images*. MIT Press: Cambridge, MA.

Stallybrass, P. (1998) Marx's coat, in Spyer, P. (ed.) *Border fetishisms: Material objects in unstable spaces*. Routledge: London, 183–207.

Stevanovic, M (1997) The Age of Clay: the social dynamics of house destruction, *Journal of Anthropological Archaeology* 16, 334–395.

Stewart, M. (2004) Remembering without commemoration: The mnemonics and politics of Holocaust memories among European Roma, *Journal of the Royal Anthropological Institute* (NS) 10, 561–582.

Strathern, M. (1988) *The gender of the gift*. University of California Press: Berkeley, CA.

Strathern, M. (1996) For the motion: 'The concept of society is theoretically obsolete', in Ingold, T. (ed.) *Key debates in anthropology*. Routledge: London, 60–66.

Strathern, M. (1998) Social relations and the idea of externality, Renfrew, C., and Scarre. C. (eds.) *Cognition and material culture: The archaeology of symbolic storage*. McDonald Institute Monographs: Cambridge, 135–147.

Sutton, D. (2001) *Remembrance of repasts: An anthropology of food and memory*. Berg: Oxford.

Taverner, R. (1987) Bannockburn: The pit and post alignment excavated in 1984 and 1985, *Scottish Development Department Central Excavation Unit and Ancient Monuments Laboratory Annual Report* 1987, 71–76.

Taylor, J. (1970) Lanulae reconsidered, *Proceedings of the Prehistoric Society* 36, 38–51.

Taylor, J. (1980) *Bronze Age goldwork of the British Isles*. Cambridge University Press: Cambridge.

Thomas, J. (1991) Monuments from the inside: The case of the Irish megalithic tombs, *World Archaeology* 22 (2), 168–178.

Thomas, J. (1992) Monuments, movement and the context of megalithic art, in Sharples, N., and Sheridan, A. (eds.) *Vessels for the ancestors: Essays on the Neolithic of Britain and Ireland*. Edinburgh University Press: Edinburgh, 141–55.

Thomas, J. (1993) The politics of vision and the archaeologies of landscape, in Bender, B. (ed.) *Landscape: Politics and perspectives*. Berg: Oxford, 19–49.

Thomas, J. (1996a) *Time, culture and identity*. Routledge: London.

Thomas, J. (1996b) Neolithic houses in mainland Britain and Ireland– A sceptical view, in Darvill, T., and Thomas, J. (eds.) *Neolithic houses in Northwest Europe and beyond*. Oxbow: Oxford, 1–12.

Thomas, J. (1998) Some problems with the notion of external symbolic Storage, and the case of Neolithic material culture in Britain, in Renfrew, C., and Scarre, C. (eds.) *Cognition and material culture: The archaeology of symbolic storage*. McDonald Institute Monographs: Cambridge, 149–156.

Thomas, J. (2000) The identity of place in Neolithic Britain: Examples from southwest Scotland, in Ritchie, A. (ed.) *Neolithic Orkney in its European context*. McDonald Institute Monographs: Cambridge, 79–87.

Thomas, J. (2002) Archaeology's humanism and the materiality of the body, in Hamilakis, Y., Pluciennik, M., and Tarlow, S. (eds.) *Thinking through the body*. Kluwer Academic/Plenum: New York, 29–45.

Thomas, J. (2004a) *Archaeology and modernity*. Routledge: London.

Thomas, J. (2004b) Materiality and traditions of practice in neolithic south-west Scotland, in Cummings, V. and Fowler, C. (eds.) *The neolithic of the Irish Sea: materiality and traditions of practice*. Oxbow: Oxford, 174–184.

Thomas, J., and Tilley, C. (1993) The axe and the torso: Symbolic structures in the Neolithic of Brittany, in Tilley, C. (ed.) *Interpretative Archaeology*. Berg: Oxford, 225–324.

Thomas, N. (1990) *Entangled objects: Exchange, material culture and colonialism in the Pacific*. Harvard University Press: Harvard, MA.

Tilley, C. (1991) *Material culture and text: The art of ambiguity*. Routledge: London.

Tilley, C. (1994) *A phenomenology of landscape: Places, paths and monuments*. Berg: Oxford.

Tilley, C. (1996) *An ethnography of the Neolithic*. Cambridge University Press: Cambridge.

Tilley, C. (1999) *Metaphor and material culture*. Blackwell: Oxford.

Tilley, C. (2004) *The materiality of stone: Explorations of landscape phenomenology*. Berg: Oxford.

Tipping, R. (1994) 'Ritual' floral tributes in the Scottish Bronze Age – Palynological evidence, *Journal of archaeological science* 21, 133–39.

Tringham, R. (2000) The continuous house: A view from the deep past, in Joyce, R. A., and Gillespie, S. D. (eds.) *Beyond kinship: Social and material reproduction in house societies*. University of Pennsylvania Press: Philadelphia, 115–134.

Umberger, E. (1987) Antiques, revivals, and references to the past in Aztec art, *RES* 13, 63–105.

van de Velde, P. (1996) Dust and ashes – A comparison of two Neolithic cemeteries, *Analecta Praehistorica Leidensia* 25, 173–188.

van de Velde, P. (1997) Much ado about nothing: Bandkeramik funerary ritual, *Analecta Praehistorica Leidensia* 26, 83–90.

Van Dyke, R.M and Alcock, S.E. (2003) *Archaeologies of Memory*. Blackwell: Oxford.

Vansina, J. (1973) *Oral tradition*. Penguin: London.

Veit, U. (1993) Burials within settlements of the Linienbankeramik and Stichbandkeramik cultures of Central Europe: On the social construction of death in early-neolithic society, *Journal of European Archaeology* 1992 (1), 107–140.

Wagner, R. (2001) *An anthropology of the subject: Holographic worldview in New Guinea and its meaning for the world of anthropology*. University of California Press: Berkeley, CA.

Wainwright, G. J., and Longworth, I. (1971) *Durrington Walls excavations 1966–68*. London Society of Antiquaries Monograph 29: London.

Wallace, J. (2004) *Digging the dirt: The archaeological imagination.* Duckworth: London.

Watkins, T. (1982) The excavation of an early Bronze Age cemetery at Barns farm, Dalgety, Fife, *Proceedings of the Society of Antiquaries of Scotland* 112, 48–141.

Weiner, J. (1991) *The empty place: Poetry, space and being among the Foi of Papua New Guinea.* Indiana University Press: Bloomington, IN.

Weiner, J. F. (1995) *The lost drum.* University of Wisconsin Press: Madison, WI.

Whitehouse, H. (1996) Memorable religions: Transmission, codification and change in divergent Melanesian contexts, *Man* 27, 777–797.

Whittle, A. (1996) *Europe in the Neolithic: The creation of new worlds.* Cambridge University Press: Cambridge.

Whittle, A. (2000) 'Very like a whale': Menhirs, motifs and myths in the Mesolithic-Neolithic transition of northwest Europe, *Cambridge Archaeological Journal* 10, 243–259.

Whittle, A. (2003) *The archaeology of people: Dimensions of Neolithic life.* Routledge: London.

Whittington, G. (1993) Palynological investigations at two Bronze Age burial sites in Fife, *Proceedings of the Society of Antiquaries of Scotland* 123, 211–213.

Williams, H. (2003) *Archaeologies of remembrance: Death and memory in past societies.* Kluwer Academic/Plenum: New York.

Wobst, H. M. (1977) Stylistic behaviour and information exchange, in Cleland, C. E. (ed.) *Papers for the director: Research essays in honor of James B. Griffin.* University of Michigan, Museum of Anthropology, Anthropological Papers 61, 317–334.

Yates, F. (1966) *The art of memory.* Pimlico: London.

Young, J. E. (1996) *The texture of memory: Holocaust memorials and their meaning.* Yale University Press: New Haven.

Index